by the same author

★

THE FREEDOM OF THE PRESS IN IRELAND
1784-1841

MALIN HEAD
Lough Foyle
Derry
DERRY
ANTRIM
DONEGAL
ULSTER
Larne
TYRONE
Omagh
Lough Neagh
Belfast
FERMANAGH
Ennis-killen
Armagh
DOWN
Sligo
LEITRIM
ARMAGH
Killala
MAYO
SLIGO
MONAGHAN
Newry
Achill Island
Carrick on Shannon
CAVAN
LOUTH
Dundalk
ROSCOMMON
LONGFORD
Kells
Battle of the Boyne
Drogheda
CONNAUGHT
MEATH
Tara
WESTMEATH
Lough Corrib
GALWAY
Athlone
Maynooth
DUBLIN
Dublin
Galway
LEINSTER
Dun Laoghaire
Aran Islands
OFFALY
KILDARE
The Curragh
CLARE
LEIX
WICKLOW
Wicklow
R. SHANNON
CARLOW
Shannon Airport
TIPPERARY
Kilkenny
Foynes
Limerick
Cashel
KILKENNY
LIMERICK
WEXFORD
MUNSTER
Wexford
Waterford
KERRY
Killarney
WATERFORD
Valencia Is.
CORK
Youghal
Bantry Bay
Cork
Cobh
Mizen Head
Kinsale
Cape Clear

STATUTE MILES
0 5 10   20   30   40   50
BORDER, SIX COUNTIES
BORDER, PROVINCES

HELLIER

THE STORY OF
IRELAND

by

BRIAN INGLIS

FABER AND FABER

24 Russell Square

London

*First published in mcmlvi
by Faber and Faber Limited
24 Russell Square London W.C.1.
Printed in Great Britain
at the Bowering Press, Plymouth*

To

DESMOND AND PADDY

CONTENTS

♣

ILLUSTRATIONS

♣

PREFACE

♣

A history need not begin at the beginning; there are countries whose story can be more easily told from what is already known, and then relating the past to what is happening in the present. This method happened to be particularly suitable for *The Story of Ireland* (to earlier users of the title I must apologize: it is generic to the Faber series). Irish history emerges slowly out of legend; and though many of the legends are delightful they cannot strictly speaking qualify—any more than, say, the romance of the Knights of the Round Table—for inclusion here; though I hope a time will come when means will be found to enable them to take their place, often a very important one, in the pattern of the past.

But I have a personal reason for concentrating on more modern times. An Anglo-Irishman of the type which Shaw described as a produce of the 'Danish, Norman, Cromwellian and (of course) Scotch invasions' is at the serious disadvantage that he is in Ireland, but not of it. His environment is—or was, when I was growing up there—English. I used to read English authors; Irish literature had no more existence for me than for a child growing up in France. I do not remember having heard Irish spoken, before I left school; and I did not myself learn the language.

I feel the need to stress this, because although it is possible to gain a fair idea of early Irish history from translations and commentaries, it is obviously impossible to assess the importance of the Irish cultural background. My opinions on that subject must, therefore, be second-hand.

I have dealt arbitrarily with some of the quotations from

earlier writers, abbreviating them, and occasionally altering them slightly—for example, by translating archaisms into modern English—in order to bring out their meaning.

There was little consistency in spelling of proper names in Ireland up to the beginning of the nineteenth century; in general the variant which is in commonest use—e.g., 'Brian Boru'—has been adopted.

It is impossible to set out the full range of my indebtedness to institutions and individuals. I owe much to casual encounters with—to name one of many—the late M. J. MacManus, whose interest in all Irish problems, past and present, was infectious, and to Trinity College, Dublin, where I had the privilege of working with Professor T. W. Moody and Professor Joseph Johnston. I have had much good advice from Professor R. Dudley Edwards, of University College, Dublin; Leland Lyons, of T.C.D.; and Thomas Woods, of the Department of External Affairs. Mr Woods' astringent comments on one draft sent to him, illustrated so pertinently the difficulties confronting any writer on Irish history that I was almost tempted to use the draft uncorrected, with his criticisms as footnotes.

But my greatest debt is to Patrick Lynch and Desmond Williams, both of University College, Dublin. I have wasted much of their time by asking for, and always obtaining, comments on sections of the book while it was being written, and opinions of particular problems. But I owe them much more than simple gratitude for that; without their company on many a pleasant occasion, I would never have learned enough about contemporary Ireland to be tempted to make this tentative exploration of her past.

INTRODUCTION

♣

The reactions of a visitor arriving in Ireland for the
first time tend to fall into an established pattern. He
is immediately entranced with the look of the countryside; the green of the grasslands, the translucent blues,
greens and browns that pursue each other on a showery day
among the mountains of the West. He is attracted, too, by
Dublin's mellow Georgian beauty, and its welcome. If the
visitor is English, he may have been under the impression
that his countrymen are not liked in Ireland; the hospitality
he receives soon shows him that they are. He is also dis-
abused of other misconceptions that he has brought over with
him. The Irish, he has heard, are always 'agin the Government': he finds that in the first quarter century of Ireland's
independence, from 1921–1946, her electorate changed its
Government only once. He has heard of 'Irish temper', and
expects to encounter a fairly rough, tough community; instead he finds a people whose manners are better (and whose
crime rate is lower) than those of the English. He has heard
the Irish are happy-go-lucky, thriftless, and unbusinesslike;
he finds himself in a reasonably prosperous community,
whose stomachs are kept better filled (according to United
Nations statistics) than those of any other people in the world.

A visitor will probably have known that the Irish are good
company: but it will come as a surprise to him how stimulating is the conversation in the Dublin 'pub' circle or at a
dinner party. He may have been warned not to talk politics
with the Irish: he finds he can do so with interest and without
embarrassment, provided he is prepared to listen. Even

religion is far from being the tabooed subject that it has been made out. The obvious devotion of the great bulk of the Irish people to their faith may not please a visitor who has been brought up to mistrust the Church of Rome; but he can hardly fail to be impressed by the discovery that this piety is little tinged with bigotry. Protestants and Jews, although they comprise little more than 5 per cent of the population, have suffered little from constitutional disabilities or unofficial discrimination.

It may happen, and frequently does, that the visitor is so delighted with what he finds in Ireland that he decides to make his home there. Traditionally, it will not be long before he begins to think of himself as Irish: often he becomes more Irish than the Irish themselves. In the preface to *John Bull's Other Island*, which in spite of some typical Shavian miscalculations and prejudices still provides a useful and entertaining introduction to the study of Anglo-Irish relations, Bernard Shaw attributes this tendency to the Irish climate, 'which will stamp an immigrant more deeply in two years, apparently, than the English climate will in two hundred'. But this is less true to-day than when the preface was written, fifty years ago; not because of a change in the climate, but because the two countries have grown apart. Shaw's Englishman, Tom Broadbent, could have settled down in Ireland in 1906 with no difficulty; it was, after all, still part of the United Kingdom, and his sentimental attraction towards his adopted country would easily have tided him over early social shoals. A newcomer to-day is forced to come to terms with an Ireland that is becoming yearly less like the Ireland of the Union—of pre-1921 times—and much less like England. He quickly reaches a second stage, where curiosity begins to intrude upon the delight with which he has accepted his new surroundings. When he tries to probe a little deeper beneath the surface Irish life, he finds it full of surprising contradictions.

There is the common attitude, for example, to the Irish language. One of the first things a visitor notices on arrival is that signposts and street names are written in two languages, Irish and English; but few of the people he meets speak, or even understand, Irish. The practice of exhibiting Irish in this way is defended on the grounds that it is the national language and that it ought to be revived. Substantial sums of money are voted annually by the state for this purpose; schoolchildren are compelled to learn it, and it is obligatory for entrance to the civil service and to some of the professions. All this is accepted with little demur by the public; and politicians of all parties, so far from denouncing the revival campaign as a waste of the taxpayers' money, appear united in urging still more strenuous efforts. Yet only a tiny minority of Irishmen, the visitor soon discovers, really care for the language; and they are often laughed at as cranks. The general attitude towards it is not dissimilar to most Englishmen's attitude towards Latin; it is a school subject, to be forgotten as soon as schooldays are over.

To profess aims publicly while caring nothing about them in private is not an exclusively Irish characteristic; but it is more noticeable in them, because the aims are more aggressively publicised. Their attitude to the division of the country is another example. Most visitors are aware, though dimly, that Ireland is divided into two administrative entities: Southern Ireland, which comprises twenty-six counties, and is a republic; and Northern Ireland, with six counties, which forms part of the United Kingdom, though it has a parliament and a civil service of its own handling domestic matters. When a visitor to the Republic refers to it as 'Eire', he is told not only that he has pronounced the word incorrectly— it should rhyme, for practical purposes, not with 'fire' but with 'fairer'—but also that he has used it in an incorrect sense. Eire is the Irish for Ireland—*all* Ireland; and this carries the implication that the Southern Irish do not recognise Northern Ireland's right to be a separate statelet.

Outwardly the feeling of resentment about the Partition of the country is strong in the South. Since 1921 posters have been proclaiming the duty of Irishmen to win back the North, by force if necessary; innumerable street corner meetings have been flanked with banners crying 'Smash Partition'; an underground military force, the Irish Republican Army, has carried on a species of guerilla warfare in Britain as well as in Ireland, with the professed design of restoring the country's unity; and politicians have been even more fervent in their denunciations of the Border than they are in their praise of the language movement. In casual conversation a visitor, if he wishes, will be inundated with reasons why the Border is unnatural, and ought to be abolished; reasons superficially so convincing that he often becomes an anti-Partitionist himself —an attitude in which he may be confirmed if he visits the North. Belfast at first acquaintance is a less welcoming city than Dublin. In the North, too, he finds symptoms of a plague rarely openly encountered in the South: sectarian bigotry, manifesting itself in discrimination against the Catholic minority. The injunction 'To Hell with the Pope' is less often encountered on walls and hoardings than it used to be before the second world war, but bigotry's rancid flavour is still occasionally to be tasted. When the visitor finds that the Catholic minority in Northern Ireland is also substantial—a third of the population—and that they passionately desire to be re-united with their southern co-religionists, he returns to Dublin convinced that a grave wrong has been done—an attitude that will be reinforced if he reads the story of the political manoeuvres that brought about Partition in the first place.

But when the visitor turns up again in the South fired (in a phrase of Daniel O'Connell's) 'with all the fervour of a renegade' he may be disconcerted to find that Southerners are a little embarrassed by him. Since 1950 little private enthusiasm—as distinct from public sympathy—has been given to the anti-Partition cause. The anti-Partition League, to a far greater extent even than the language movement, has decayed into a nest for cranks. The Irish Republican Army, though some of its exploits may arouse sympathy, tends to be looked on with suspicion as an organisation which seeks to put the gloss of patriotism over the activities of irresponsible young thugs and hotheads; it remains illegal, condemned by Church and State. References to partition by politicians in their speeches have become a formula, with as little sincerity attached as the proposal of a vote of thanks to a chairman; and the ordinary public, though still prepared to argue that the Border represents a piece of English-imposed injustice, no longer care deeply about it on the level where feeling is likely to be translated into action.

The Irish, in fact, have their own equivalent of those Erewhonian institutions, the Musical Banks; ideals to which they pay the service of their lips, and about which they would be shocked to be accused of insincerity, but which have ceased to occupy any significant place in their everyday lives. It is as if they have become so used to believing something, that they can continue to believe it on a level divorced from contact with reality.

The discovery of this double-think is likely to make a visitor feel he has been deceived. The Irish will no longer seem so delightful to him. If by this time he has made up his mind to settle among them, he will in any case be becoming aware that his first impressions of the country were unrealistic. In the same way that, if he turns off Dublin's most stately streets and squares, he finds himself confronted with tenements more squalid than any he is likely to remember from England, he begins to discover that the façade of a gay, amusing, hospitable Ireland masks many serious, and some ugly problems.

In the cities there is chronic, heavy unemployment: in the country, dissatisfaction with the old way of life reveals itself in a drift from the land. The countryfolk may be well-fed, but their standard of living, judged by social amenities, is low. Farms are for the most part small, backward and, considering the fertility of the soil, unproductive. Fields are too rarely put under the plough; much of the grass is poor in quality and in the absence of good drainage, rushes thrive. The small whitewashed farmhouses of the West, which so attract a visitor on his arrival with their thatch and their turf stack, turn out on closer inspection to be uncomfortable, dark and dirty. Villages are widely scattered—few of them can boast social amenities outside the usual grocery-cum-pub. Cinemas and dance halls have appeared in the larger villages, but over the greater part of the country social life stagnates. Young people have little encouragement to stay; they move to the towns; then to Dublin; in time to England, partly pushed by the dreariness of the life they are leaving, partly pulled by the beckoning glow of city lights.

When the first flush of enjoyment is over, too, a visitor finds his new Irish companions less amusing than he first thought them. The conversation which impressed him turns out to be not the beaded bubbles arising out of a genuine cultural fermentation, but a cheap substitute—a way by which clever men preserve the illusion of intellectual activity without having to work. The wit, though stimulating, can be as meretricious as the worst of Oscar Wilde's. Of creative writing there is progressively less evidence; and that evidence tends to be depressing. What the visitor has believed to be a real liking for him, is revealed to be nothing more than Irish tact, a mannerism which consists in not only agreeing with what a visitor says, but of providing additional evidence to confirm him in his opinions, regardless what his hearers' view of those opinions may be. He finds that he gets no further than congenial acquaintanceship; he does not know his Irish companions much better after a year in their company than after the first evening. Or he may find that they do not care twopence for him, and perhaps make fun of him behind his back—thereby confirming him in his opinion that the Irish are two-faced. If he hits back by reasserting his Englishness, he provokes a sudden outburst of resentment against him and his country and its institutions, couched in such bitter and wounding terms that he can only believe that the holders have been nourishing a secret grudge against him, all along.

The next time he meets them, they resume as if nothing

had happened, which puzzles him all the more. But he does not forget; he begins to take more note of the things that show the Irish up in a less pleasant light. He reads reports of a debate in the Irish parliament on defence; he is reminded that although the Irish are in principle as vehemently anti-communist as any Western nation, they refused to join the North Atlantic Treaty Organisation because of what seems to him to be a quibble, thereby possibly imperilling the defence of the West (just as they did, he recalls, in the second world war, when Southern Ireland remained neutral, at a vast cost of men and material to the Allies in the Battle of the Atlantic). He begins to find the antics of the Censorship of Publications Board increasingly irritating, banning as it does most of the serious fiction being written in the English language. If he lives in the country, he may find clerical pressure being exercised locally, in restricting the hours of dances, say, or supplementing the work of the Censors in the town library. On a national scale, he hears accounts of how ambitious or opinionated prelates have attempted to influence legislation by private advice to the Government. If he wishes to send his children to school in Ireland, he is probably deterred by the discovery that what to him seems an absurdly dispro-portionate amount of time has to be devoted to a study of the Irish language. In fact in many primary schools, other sub-jects have to be taught through the medium of Irish, which strikes him as being grossly unfair on the children, few of whom use Irish in their homes—and foolish too, because such evidence as he can find reveals that the effort has been barren of results.

It annoys a visitor to hear politicians who he guesses have no Irish—and who would not, if they had, speak it in their homes—prate about the need to revive the language; and to hear them denouncing the Government of Northern Ireland, when he knows they do not care a rap about the country's unity. He may come to wonder whether he might not have misjudged the Northerners. If he visits them again, he will quickly realise that he had. Now that he is less cocksure of his anti-Partitionist opinions, he finds that they have good practical grounds—however weak they may be when arguing on the principle—for their belief that the Border does not in itself divide the Irish people; it merely reflects (though inaccurately) a division which already exists; and even if the Border was unfairly drawn in the first place so that it cuts off the Catholic and Nationalist minority from their fellow-countrymen against their will, it cannot now be wiped away by a stroke of the pen.

At this stage the disillusioned visitor takes one of three courses. He may pack up his suitcases and return to England: not a few expatriates have done the same. Or, he may drift into the company of like-minded people in Ireland; the Anglo-Irish, and those whom the Irish lump together under the derisive title of 'West Britons'. Such people can live in a social and sporting enclave, worshipping their equine diety, touching on the political, economic and cultural Ireland at so few points that it is easily possible for them to lead an existence very similar to (though considerably less costly than) a 'county' life in England—so much so that it never ceases to surprise them, when they rise for the national anthem at the end of a Hunt Ball, that the anthem played is not 'God Save the Queen'. In this way an Englishman—or an American—can still be pleasantly assimilated into a land where it is always afternoon (though usually a wet afternoon); but his roots lie shallow, and as like as not the second generation, his sons and daughters, will depart again.

A third possibility remains: that the visitor will examine his conscience, and come to see that he has not been deceived about the Irish; he has simply deceived himself. The Irish problem, he will realise, remains bewildering, and often insoluble; but at least its origins can be understood. An important clue is provided by the reaction he encountered earlier—the change in his companions' attitude when he ceased to accept them on their own terms, and tried to impose his Englishness on them. Clearly they may like the Englishman as an individual; but they do not like what he stands for: England. If he seeks to discover why, he is referred to history: to the 'Economic War' of the 1930s; the 'Black and Tans'; the 1916 executions; the Famine; the Penal Laws; Cromwell; even Strongbow. The recital makes him recall, with jocular irritation, a story which still circulates, in various versions, of some negotiations between Lloyd George and the Irish leader, de Valera; how when Lloyd George came out at the end of the first session, a friend asked him how things were going and was told that de Valera, having talked all the morning about the historical wrongs done to Ireland from earliest times, had progressed only as far as Cromwell. An Englishman may be prepared to concede for the sake of argument that Ireland has had grievances in the past against her English rulers; never having read any Irish history, and remembering little of his own country's in relation to Ireland, he is not in a position dogmatically to assert the contrary, even though he is usually convinced the wrongs must be imaginary, or at least grossly exaggerated. But for the life of him he cannot see what relevance these past wrongs have to relations between England and Ireland in the present day—any more than the American War of Independence has to relations between England and the United States. He can appreciate that men who actually fought against the English thirty-five years ago may understandably cherish some bitterness; but bitterness about an event several centuries ago, such as a massacre at Drogheda by Cromwell (who, after all, is far from being a national hero to the English)—the idea is absurd!

The English have short memories; it takes very few years for the brutal Hun to become the decent, solid German. But the Irish not only remember, they live with their history. Wolfe Tone, the founder of the first separatist society in the country, died more than a century and a half ago; but he is more alive in the public mind than most present-day cabinet ministers, and his influence is still debated hotly in periodicals, almost down to the *Peg's Paper* level. It might be argued that habeas corpus and trial by jury are in the same sense alive in the English mind; but these institutions have become merged with the constitutional background, and as a rule they become issues only when a Briton is wrongfully deprived of their protection. Deprived of the protection of their institutions for centuries, the Irish continue to exalt the patriots who fought for them:

> *refashioning in burnished gold*
> *the images of those who died.*

Many of those who now hold the chief positions in the country's administration took up arms forty years ago, for Ireland's right to set up her own institutions; some, like de Valera, lay under sentence of death; some had relatives or close friends who were murdered, or killed in action, or executed. The next generation grew up, for the most part, in the shadow of the war of independence, feeling with all the intensity of childhood a hatred for the enemy their fathers and uncles fought; for such children it was a matter of pride and pleasure, not a wearisome school chore, to be able to recite Ireland's past sorrows; and to them, such men as Cromwell and Castlereagh were ogres as imminent as any living figure.

In any case, there are issues which are alive to this day, having their origins in past Irish helplessness. The Border remains; it may be ceasing to be the dominant political issue, but its existence is a reminder of what is considered as only one example of the duplicity of British politicians. Irish industry has still to be laboriously and expensively rebuilt after its collapse under English rule. Catholics squeezing into overcrowded comfortless churches recall that the English took their churches from them, handing them over to an alien and, to them, heretical Church, and forbidding the erection of any Catholic place of worship; to this day Dublin has two Protestant, but no Catholic, cathedrals, though there are a score of Catholic churchgoers to every Protestant. There are other pinpricks of injustice perpetuated: the fine collection of pictures which Hugh Lane wished to leave to the City of Dublin are still in the Tate Gallery in London, because no witness had signed the codicil with which he bequeathed them to Dublin in his will, before embarking for an Atlantic crossing on the *Lusitania*—a small matter, perhaps, but one which leaves much resentment.

The Irish, therefore, cannot be understood unless their history is understood first; and it had better be said straight away that for an Englishman, however detached he may consider himself to be on the subject of his country's history, this is not an agreeable task. He finds it difficult enough to bring himself to admit that English policy in the past has been misconceived, except where events have proved the critics' case too conclusively to admit of doubt—for example, in the treatment of the American Colonists. But he finds it harder still to accept the possibility that British policy may not only have been wrong-headed: that it may have been— by his own standards—infamous, over a period of centuries. Yet it was an Englishman, Lord Shelburne, who, two centuries ago, said that the history of Ireland 'is the history of England in regard to Ireland; and it will be found to have always been to the shame of England.'

The word 'shame' does not imply that the English maltreated the Irish out of malice or churlishness. Many of the most misguided decisions were taken by English Governments in the conviction, or at least in the hope, that Ireland would benefit from them. But a cursory examination of their effects reveals that Ireland did not benefit; and a closer look at the motives behind them suggests that the great majority were primarily designed to benefit England. The assumption that Ireland would benefit was sometimes sincere, sometimes a clever rationalisation. Either way, it could be disastrous. Perhaps the most striking example was the English reaction to the Great Famine of 1845-8. The remedies that the Government of the day applied were designed chiefly to avoid upsetting trade and jeopardising Britain's economy. They had no relevance to Irish conditions. As a result, the Irish starved.

For long periods of her history Ireland has suffered under laws whose effect, had it always been possible to enforce them, would have been to stamp out all traces of her distinctive culture and faith, and to leave her economically prostrate. Most of the laws which regulated Irish commerce, for example, were enacted at the request of the English mercantile interest, whose main concern was that a possible rival should be crushed. When the Irish protested at such laws (as Jonathan Swift did in his pamphlets) they were rebuked for being factious: when they rebelled, they were suppressed as enemies of the state. In time this bred an attitude of mind inimical to trust, so that even when English Governments or viceroys genuinely sought to be of service to Ireland, their motives were suspect. The Irish had come to believe that the right to manage their own affairs, however badly, was preferable to having their affairs managed for them, however well. Once that stage had been reached the chance of Ireland joining Scotland and Wales as reasonably contented partners in a United Kingdom vanished.

The inability of English Governments to understand this feeling led to confusion, frustration and resentment. When they found that measures designed, as they thought, to improve conditions in Ireland, met with savage resistance, they felt that the Irish were biting the feeding hand; and for this reason, repressive measures were often made doubly harsh. For much of the time after the Union of 1800 English rule could be maintained only with the help of a garrison and a semi-alien ruling caste—the Anglo-Irish Ascendancy—over the uncooperative Irish; and this prompted a growing belief in England that the Irish were so irresponsible that they would be incapable of governing themselves. Before the end of the century this had become a settled conviction among Conservatives, who justified their opposition to Irish Home Rule on the grounds that it would leave the Irish a danger to themselves, as well as to their neighbours.

In Ireland, the failure of English Governments to understand the situation led to the growth of nationalism, and then of separatism. 'Nationalism' embraced a variety of people: the merchant whose only desire was the removal of English restrictions on commerce; the Catholic who wished to be allowed the free exercise of his religion; the doctrinaire republican who wished to sever all ties with the Crown; the politician who had visions of power at home which he could never hope to exercise at Westminster. These ingredients rarely blended into a common policy. The nationalist movement was always more or less divided, and its divisions meant that when rebellion broke out it was usually put down without much difficulty: in 1798, in 1848 and in 1867. Their failure, however, did not discredit the use of force. It helped to create a patriot myth—using the word 'myth' not in its colloquial derogatory sense, but Irish-fashion, to describe a body of emotion that has far more power over the destinies of a nation than the promptings of reason or self-interest. The myth culminated in the 1916 Rising, whose leaders not only did not expect success, but actually courted self-immolation:

> *O plain as plain can be*
> *There's nothing but our own red blood*
> *Can make a right Rose Tree;*

—the men of 1916 believed that by their sacrifice they would move their fellow-countrymen to the final effort for independence; and they were proved right.

Nationalism at the best of times is not a reasonable emotion. It tends to impute the worst of motives to the oppressor, and the best to the oppressed, regardless of circumstance. For centuries England was the oppressor; from any Irish history (except, of course, those written from the English viewpoint) the impression is quickly gained that the English must have been a race of sadistic, untrustworthy, black-hearted, mercenary villains. An Englishman has always to remember that this is how the Irish tend to feel. And not just the Irish alone: an Englishman, and an eminently sane one —Sydney Smith—admitted that 'the moment the name of

Ireland is mentioned the English seem to bid adieu to common feeling, common prudence, and common sense, and to act with the barbarity of tyrants, and the fatuity of idiots.'

Thackeray too—who normally regarded the Irish with affectionate derision—could say of the history of Ireland that it was a 'frightful document against ourselves—one of the most melancholy stories in the whole world of insolence, rapine, brutal endless persecution on the part of the English master. . . . There is no crime ever invented by the eastern or western barbarians, no torture of Roman persecutors or Spanish inquisitors, no tyranny of Nero or Alva but can be matched in the history of the English in Ireland.' The exaggeration is itself symptomatic of the effect on ordinary Englishmen who learn for the first time in detail about their country's record in Ireland; a record which brought Thackeray to the conclusion that 'we may learn humility at last by defeat, and common prudence and expediency, as well as by the consciousness of shameful wrong.'

This, in fact, is the real reason why the English should learn something about Irish history. The proper study of great nations is humility, and nowhere can the English study it better than in the story of their relations with their neighbour—particularly in recent centuries. The English have made a notable contribution to the development of ways to lift subject races up through the stages of colonialism to self-government; Ireland provides an excellent instance of what can happen when the process is retarded in a country where the force of nationalism is underestimated. Irish nationalism was variously attributed to faction, to ingratitude, to ingrained untrustworthiness, or to foreign gold. Noting that it was most vocal among the young and rootless, English Governments first tended to pooh-pooh it as adolescent irresponsibility; then, faced with evidence of its deeper hold, they applied coercion, arguing that no cencessions could be made until order was restored; then, when order was restored, they used the unaccustomed tranquility as a pretext for letting the sleeping terrier lie. Nationalism under such treatment grows frustrated, and dangerous. If recognised and understood early enough it can be given remedial treatment: it cannot with impunity be ignored.

There is also a more practical justification of the study of Irish history. The Irish have been second only to the Jews as the chronic exiles of this world: more people who think of themselves as Irish live out of Ireland than live in it. Their influence on other countries, particularly England and the United States, has been very great; but for the purposes of this book it is impossible to do more than give a few examples here.

It was Irish missionaries who brought classical learning and traditions back to Europe after the Barbarian invasions; the names of Columba, of Columbanus and John Scotus Eriugena are still familiar. 'The flight of the wild geese' brought a host of Irishmen to the Continent after 1690, many of whom won military renown there. Others went further afield: Ambrose O'Higgins became Viceroy of Peru, the most distinguished office in Spanish South America; his son Bernardo helped San Martin to liberate Chile, and became that country's first dictator. The influence of Irish immigrants in the United States has been enormous. The Ulster dissenters formed a sizable proportion of the population at the time of the War of Independence, and provided many of its most intransigent anti-British soldiery. They were followed after the Hungry Forties by hundreds of thousands more Irishmen. They retained their national identity to a greater degree than other immigrants, and their bitter racial memories must be considered at least in part responsible for the characters and careers of such figures as Senator McCarthy, Senator McCarran and Mayor O'Dwyer.

The influence of the Irish on the history of England is even more far-reaching; for example, in the impact of Anglo-Irish culture. (The clumsy term Anglo-Irish has to be used to make the distinction from *Irish* culture, which from the time of the Synod of Whitby till the present century, when it began to permeate abroad once again, following the Gaelic

revival, has had little perceptible influence outside Ireland.)
A look back over the English Theatre reveals eight names
which in any assessment of its achievements since the Restora-
tion would be in the front row, as it were, of the stalls;
Congreve, Farquhar, Goldsmith, Sheridan, Wilde, Shaw,
Synge and O'Casey. All of them were Anglo-Irish.

Or were they? It is advisable here to indulge in a digres-
sion, to consider a controversy which has aroused some
irritation and much amusement in Ireland. Congreve was of
English parentage; but he was brought up and educated in
Ireland, and may have had more of the Irishman in him than,
say, Farquhar, who was of Irish extraction, but was at school
in England. *The Playboy of the Western World* was the fruit of
Synge's stay in the Aran Islands; it is certainly very far from
being an English play. But it might conceivably have been
written by an Englishman who had allowed himself to be
emotion-washed into Irishness by his environment; whereas
Shaw's plays, though superficially they have little of Ireland in
them, were certainly a by-product of his aggressive Irishness.

It would be tempting to accept Shaw's view that the Irish
climate is responsible: using the word 'climate' in its loosest
sense might help to account for the remarkable predominance
of the Anglo-Irish in the English Theatre, on the assumption
that there is something in their environment particularly
conducive to word-spinning for the benefit of audiences.

In English prose literature, too, the influence of the Anglo-
Irish, though less extensive, has been profound, through the
genius of Swift and Burke. Laurence Sterne, like Congreve,
was of English stock; but his childhood was spent in Ireland,
and critics have pointed out that *Tristram Shandy* in conception and execution is the most Irish of novels before James
Joyce wrote *Ulysses*. Then there is Goldsmith, again, and
Shaw, and many others of less eminence. But at this point
it becomes necessary to admit, regretfully, that whatever
may be their importance in a history of English letters, they
are of little relevance to a history of Ireland. Take the case
of Maria Edgeworth. Her novels, of which *Castle Rackrent* is

to-day the least unfamiliar, provided the inspiration which induced Walter Scott to embark on his *Waverley Novels*, and they also influenced Turgenev; but they were written for English, rather than Irish consumption. The same applies to such writers as Lever, and Somerville and Ross. This is not to say, as some Irish critics have suggested, that *The Experiences of an Irish R.M.* gives a false picture; on the contrary, the stories in it are as well-observed and as entertaining a portrayal of the rather restricted Anglo-Irish society of which the authors were members as was, say, *The Diary of a Nobody* of London clerkdom. Characters like Flurry Knox are still by no means rare (though it must be admitted that 'Slipper's' are fewer. As Frank O'Connor has written somewhere, the characteristic Irish face like Goldsmith's, with 'the long upper lip of his like a shutter, by which Victorian caricaturists always identified the native Irishman—and which I remember having seen in my youth—has disappeared in the last thirty years almost as though it never existed'). But in spite of their promising novel *The Real Charlotte*, and their entertaining short stories, Somerville and Ross must be placed on the English side of the imaginary barrier that divides English from Irish history; along with Sheridan and Goldsmith, Oscar Wilde and George Moore. They have no place in this story. Burke, even, were it not for his influence behind the scenes in Britain in the events leading up to the revolution of 1782, and to the removal of penal legislation against the Catholics, would have to be ignored. The same applies to Bishop Berkeley. Although he lived and worked most of his life in Ireland, his philosophy might have been developed anywhere.

Some Irish writers have gone further, and argued that the Anglo-Irish in Ireland had a destructive influence, in that they fostered the illusion of a separate Irish culture while in fact infecting it with Englishness. Be that as it may, there existed and still exists a body of recognisably Irish writing, drama, poetry and prose in the English language, whose effect on Ireland, as well as on England, cannot be gainsaid.

The general influence of the Irish in England cannot be ignored, either; though it can only be surmised. They have emigrated to England in large numbers from the sixteenth century—from the time that employment prospects became obviously better in England than at home—to the present day. Charles I felt it necessary to enact laws to round them up and ship them home again; but the laws were either not enforced or not enforceable. The greatest influx came after the Union of 1800, when the destruction of Irish industry began to throw thousands of men out of work. They helped to depress still further the low standard of living among industrial workers, because they were able-bodied (more so than the English) and were prepared to work longer hours for less wages in more unpleasant jobs. Naturally they were welcomed by the English employer; Friedrich Engels was of the opinion that the great expansion of English industry following the industrial revolution would not have been possible without them. And naturally they were unpopular among the English workers whose standards they depressed. Nonetheless some of them were influential in the nascent Trade Union movement—notably John Doherty—and still more so in the Chartist movement, in which Feargus O'Connor and Bronterre O'Brien became the leading figures. In politics the Irish at Westminster helped to produce, or at least to precipitate, many of the great political changes of the nineteenth century. Daniel O'Connell used to boast that his vote in the Commons had been responsible for the safe passage of the Reform Bill of 1832; and he can be held responsible for it in a deeper sense, in that his Catholic Emancipation campaign in Ireland had provided the precedent for parliament to yield to the threat of force, where force was likely to be overwhelmingly backed by public opinion. It would have been far more difficult for the peers to give way in 1832, had Wellington and Peel not shown them how to do it in 1829.

Thereafter the Irish question was never far in the background at Westminster. Again and again, it made and unmade ministries: Government after Government fell on Irish policy. The importance of Ireland in English politics can be exaggerated, because ministries and ministers were under a constant temptation to exploit her troubles for their own ends. A minister might prefer to resign 'on principle' over a minor Irish issue about which nobody was likely to tax him with inconsistency or duplicity. Still, the existence of Irish M.P.s at Westminster, sometimes holding the balance of power, meant that Governments were constantly compelled to devote time and energy to their appeasement. The Irish party under Parnell was to bring about radical changes in the procedure of the House of Commons; and the Home Rule question came near to undermining parliamentary authority.

But perhaps the most important of Ireland's claims on English attention has been her geographical position, which has meant that England's enemies in Europe have always had a possible ally behind England's back.

'They say it is the fatal destiny of Ireland', Edmund Spenser wrote over three and a half centuries ago, 'that no purposes whatsoever which are meant for her good will prosper or take effect; which, whether it proceeds from the very genius of the soil, or influence of the stars, or that Almighty God has not yet appointed the time for her reformation, or that he reserves her in this unquiet state still for some secret scourge which shall by her come to England, it is hard to be known, but yet much to be feared.' Spenser's alarm was justified; time after time in the years to come it looked as if Ireland was indeed to be England's scourge—or even her hangman's noose. If Philip of Spain had grasped Ireland's strategic importance to him, or realised what an ally he might have had in Hugh O'Neill; if Charles I had given Strafford his head (instead of allowing it to be cut off) to make use of the Irish against Parliament; if the 'prentice boys had not shut the gates of Derry, thwarting James II's plans; if an incongruous easterly gale had not blown up to keep Grouchy's army from disembarking in Kerry in 1796; if the

Battle of the Atlantic had gone just that little bit harder, owing to Ireland's neutrality, against the Allies than it did in the early 1940s: these and many similar 'ifs' may appear to constitute unprofitable speculation, but together they reveal the extent of the influence that Ireland has wielded, or might have wielded, over the course of English history.

The same or similar problems still remain. The futures of the two islands are for better or worse closely bound together. Tens of thousands of Irish men and women still emigrate to England every year, bringing with them their national characteristics, which in time will permeate British life—their Catholicism, especially, if it merges with English Catholicism instead of—as at present—lying uneasily alongside it. There is still an Irish Republican Army in existence. It may be small in numbers, but so was the force that waged the war of independence from 1916 to 1921. So long as Northern Ireland remains cut off from the South—which it seems certain to be in the foreseeable future—the possibility cannot be ignored that this army will attempt some coup based on the assumption that the act of self-sacrifice of the 1916 leaders can be profitably repeated in, say, Derry. The flow of Irish culture may have diminished, but it has not dried up altogether; the most talked-about play put on in London during 1955, *Waiting for Godot*, was by an Irishman, Samuel Beckett; and the mark of its country of origin was nonetheless clearly stamped on it even if it was originally written in French, its author, like Joyce, having gone into voluntary exile in France. In defence and in economic problems, too, Ireland must continue to be of immediate concern to English Governments.

I have therefore tried to tell the story of Ireland with an eye always upon the present: to relate Irish history not so much for its own sake, as to explain how it has brought about the political, economic, social, and cultural conditions that exist there to-day. For this purpose I have found it convenient (in spite of the obvious minor inconveniences, including the need for some repetition) to divide the story up into three parts: on nationalism; on the land and the people; and on culture and religion.

The importance of nationalism in Irish history is easy to over-emphasise, for the same reason that the importance of kings and their wars and battles has been over-emphasised in English history—they make romantic telling. I have put it first of the three mainly because it provides the framework for the others; it can conveniently be used to provide the narrative. In the second part, on the land and the people, I have included eye-witness accounts of life in Ireland; unfortunately the first-hand material is rudimentary for mediaeval times. The linkage in the third part is not fortuitous. A Dominican writer has asserted in a recent book on rural Ireland that 'religion and culture have always been perfectly integrated into Irish life since our conversion to Christianity; a purely secularist culture, if that be possible, has never developed here.' This is no longer true, but it was largely true for early Irish history—possibly even in pre-Christian times. These three parts each bring the story up to 1921; the recent history of Ireland I have dealt with in a single section, 'Conclusions'.

Part One

NATIONALISM

♣ One ♣

To 1603

It is not worth attempting to assess exactly when the inhabitants of Ireland became recognisably *Irish*: all that can safely be said is that at the time the Roman Empire was collapsing, the inhabitants of Ireland had achieved a common Gaelic culture and language, and—at least in theory—a common 'Brehon' law, all contributing to the sense of 'oneness' characteristic of the race. But there was no political or administrative unity in Ireland, not even the realisation of a need for it. The institution of the 'High King', to whom all regional kings owed allegiance, was nominal; although the High Kings provided the centre around which a sense of nationalism could develop, the development was slow in spite of the fact that from the fifth to the eighth century it was not hindered by upheavals of the kind which shook the continent of Europe and Britain. Possibly the absence at the time of any serious threat from abroad actually discouraged the growth of a national consciousness; local kings were not deterred from fighting among themselves by the need to unite against a common enemy. Local rivalries continued to flare up into raids and counter-raids, and no unified military organisation came into existence that could be turned to meet invaders, should the need arise.

It arose at the end of the eighth century. The Norsemen landing on the Irish coast met with no coherent resistance; they were able to plunder almost at will and, when little more booty remained, to establish settlements from which they could trade with the Continent. Dublin, Waterford, Wexford, Cork, Limerick—these and other towns founded by the Norsemen survived the struggle between Gael and 'Gall' (foreigners) which continued for over two centuries. Even when the High King Brian Boru won his last decisive victory in 1014 at Clontarf—a present-day Dublin suburb— his army could not take the town of Dublin itself.

But by this time the distinction between Gael and Gall was blurred. The battle of Clontarf was not a straight fight between the Irish and the foreigner; it was fought by two opposing Irish factions, one of whom had enlisted Norse aid. This was not considered treacherous; the Norsemen had been sufficiently long in the country for their presence to be accepted. To some of his countrymen Brian Boru was a usurper, who had assumed the High Kingship by force. Nevertheless it was through Brian that the Irish nationalist tradition was transmitted. The legend of his personality and generalship imposed themselves upon his fellow country-men; he was in retrospect 'High King' in fact as well as in name. Patriotism, reaching backwards into history, was to find in him its first national hero.

At the time, however, Brian's influence seemed hardly to survive his death at Clontarf. His successors lost authority; the title of High King ceased to be a rallying-point and became at times little more than an excuse for ambitious disaffection. The latent nationalism that Brian reflected did not mature.

No doubt if the rulers of neighbouring England had not been occupied with their own affairs, their attention might have been drawn sooner to the rich openings Ireland offered. As it was, the occasion did not arise until a century after the Norman Conquest. Henry II of England cherished ambitions in connection with Ireland; he obtained the sanction of the Papacy to subdue the country, under the pretext of bringing it back into proper dependence upon the Church. When a defeated Irish king, Dermot MacMurrough, asked for per-mission to recruit help from among the Anglo-Norman barons, Henry gave his consent. Chief among the barons was Strongbow, Earl of Pembroke, who was promised the hand of Dermot's daughter and succession to the Kingdom of

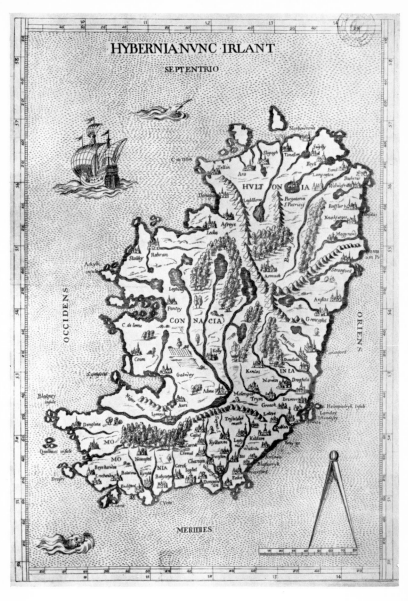

PLATE I. One of the earliest known maps of Ireland
(*circa* 1590)

Leinster, if it could be regained. A small force of Norman knights and archers was sent on to Ireland to establish a bridgehead; in 1170 they were followed up by Strongbow himself, who captured first Waterford and then Dublin; and on MacMurrough's death the following year Strongbow assumed the title King of Leinster.

MacMurrough's name has since been execrated in Ireland for selling his country to an alien foe. At the time his action attracted little notice. The Anglo-Normans were more foreign than the Norsemen they ejected from Dublin only in that they were more recent arrivals; an Irish family that had suffered under Norse rule might conceivably have welcomed Strongbow as a liberator. There was no common front against the newcomer. The combined strength of the Norsemen and the Irish would easily have sufficed to annihilate him if it had been combined; as it was, Strongbow was able to meet and defeat them separately. Nor did the invaders consider themselves as English, in any patriotic sense. They were tempted to come to terms with the Irish and enjoy the benefits of conquest without reference to Henry II; Henry had to forestall the move by arriving in person.

As far as Henry was concerned Ireland was to be a personal possession, of which he would be the feudal landlord. There was no formal colonisation. Strongbow and his followers owed fealty to Henry, not to the Crown; and when Henry handed over the lordship of the country to his son John, not at that time considered as a successor to the English throne, the link with England appeared to become weaker still. The Irish chiefs had little reason to suspect that by coming to terms with the invaders, they were putting their country under a heavy alien heel. If they thought about it at all, they probably congratulated themselves on getting rid of an intruder so easily. By recognising Henry as overlord—they may have argued—they could induce him to return home. As soon as he was back in England his authority in Ireland would vanish.

In this the Irish chiefs deluded themselves. Absence of

royal authority cut both ways; it meant that the Anglo-Norman barons in Ireland could proceed to further appropriations in defiance of agreements that Henry had made. Individual barons made themselves masters of fresh territory by straightforward conquest, and held it by force of arms; or they insinuated themselves, as Strongbow had, at the invitation of a dispossessed Irish chief who wanted to recover his property. Either way their greatly superior military skill and equipment gave them the advantage. Norman rule, therefore, continued to spread over the country piecemeal.

It remained to be found whether Irish and Anglo-Norman ways would fuse, or co-exist, or whether one system would absorb the other.

Fusion proved impossible. Between the Gaelic and the feudal structure there were divergences which could not be reconciled. The feudal system was based on primogeniture; freemen were bound to their lord and to his heirs. The Gaels attached themselves to a lord by their own free choice, and the contract terminated with his death. Of the two systems, feudalism was administratively the more efficient, with its centralisation, planning and direction; it took hold wherever the newcomers were present in sufficient numbers to form a predominantly Norman society. In and around Dublin, and extending out over the country in the course of the century and a half after Strongbow's arrival, Anglo-Norman institutions took root: a Justiciar, representing the overlord; a Parliament; a county system; sheriffs; and courts presided over by itinerant justices. On the fringes of the occupied territory, however, there was a tendency for feudalism to crumble. It was not only the Irish who were prepared to make promises in order to secure allies; Norman barons, squabbling among themselves, found it equally useful to make allies among the Irish, and sociability prompted the same course. Strongbow's marriage to MacMurrough's daughter may have been inspired simply by expediency; his followers took Irish wives for more homely reasons. Soon the line between Irish and Anglo-Norman became indistinct. This process was accelerated by the fact that the newcomers did not take a solid bite out of the territory. They tended to advance along lines of least resistance, leaving pockets of Irish-held territory among the mountains or forests, so that there was no clearly defined boundary between the two races.

The tendency of the Anglo-Normans to 'go native' began to arouse the alarm of the administration in Dublin. Before the end of the thirteenth century legislation was being directed against the 'degenerate English' for adopting Irish clothes and Irish hairstyles, and the description 'mere Irish' began to appear in statutes, reflecting the trend towards a society with three divisions: English, Old English and Irish. By acting as a cushion, the Old English helped to preserve the Irish from the extinction with which feudalism had threatened them; and although the Irish did not attain real unity, even under pressure, they remained as possibly formidable allies should some outside threat to English rule materialise.

The threat came after Bannockburn had destroyed English power in Scotland. Robert Bruce, anxious to find an outlet for the energies of his ambitious brother Edward, despatched him to harass the English in Ireland. The success of the invading force encouraged the Irish to resume operations on their own account; but the English were saved by disunity among their enemies. Some of the Irish preferred the English devils they knew; others who at first cast in their lot with Bruce were soon disgusted by the savagery of his followers, who were too lazy to distinguish between friend and foe, and who left the countryside so devastated that the inhabitants, if contemporary annalists can be believed, were reduced to cannibalism. Bruce's defeat and death in 1318 went unlamented.

By this time the pattern of Irish nationalism was becoming established. An intangible but recognisable 'Irishness' existed, drawing its inspiration from memories of past golden ages, some of its heroes legendary like Cuchullain; some around whom legends could grow, like St. Patrick and Brian Boru. This Irishness was strong enough to transmit itself to settlers where their settlements were not too concentrated. In time, it infiltrated sufficiently even into feudal society to keep the central administration alarmed. This infiltration, however, made it more difficult for the Irish to throw up another Brian, or to congregate round the standard of a Bruce; it filed down the jagged edges of Anglo-Norman penetration until the existence of the settlers ceased to be a source of nagging discomfort. The de Burgos, who at the beginning of the fourteenth century were the spearhead of the Anglo-Norman advance westward, were not long established in Connaught before they 'degenerated' into 'Burkes', speaking Irish, basing their title on Gaelic laws, and defying royal authority. Irish absorption began to be quicker than English settlement. To the administration in Dublin the Irish ceased, after the Bruce invasion period, to be a subject race whose lands would be swallowed and digested in due course; they became instead a threat from which the English needed protection.

This change is reflected in the Statutes of Kilkenny, passed in 1366. So serious had the position become to English eyes that Lionel, Duke of Clarence, a son of Edward III's, was sent to Ireland with almost unrestricted powers. He had a personal interest in checking the Irish revival; the de Burgh inheritance, which ought by feudal law to have passed to his wife, had by Gaelic law been seized by rival claimants. With him he brought sixty-four Irish lords—not a sign of strength, as they were merely representatives of the great class of absentee landlords who feature so prominently in the country's history. His task proved too much for him. The English, he found, were more anxious to keep what they had than to embark on further conquest or reconquest; the Old English were to his eyes hardly distinguishable from the Irish themselves. All he could do was try to halt the trend which, he assumed, had been responsible for their defection. The Statutes of Kilkenny were designed to prevent the drift from English rule, custom, and language; they forbade the English to intermarry with the Irish, to speak Irish or to adopt Irish ways, under pain of torture or forfeiture of their titles. The statutes were to remain in force for two centuries, and although they could never be effectively enforced they helped to preserve a consciousness of the existence of two separate races.

By the time that Richard II came to the English throne the distinction had even arisen between English land—'The Pale', as it was known—and the rest of the country. Only within the Pale were feudal institutions fairly secure. Richard himself was soon made aware of the situation, when he arrived in Ireland. A letter to his uncle the regent in England notes the threefold division of 'the wild Irish, our enemies; English rebels; and obedient English'; and though he had hopes that the English rebels and even the wild Irish might be won over to allegiance by the promise of justice, he intended that the full extent of the Pale should be firmly demarcated, and where necessary replanted with new settlers. His precaution proved necessary. Irish kings and chieftains, great and small, arrived to take advantage of his offer to confirm in their possessions all who would submit to the royal authority. But the royal authority existed only for as long as the king and his army were there to enforce it. Had it not been for the firmness with which the English core maintained itself within the dwindling Pale, the Irish might have flowed back over the whole country, whenever civil strife or preoccupation with continental affairs distracted English attention.

On the other hand, the eagerness with which the Irish chiefs flocked in to take advantage of Richard's terms showed that they were still without any real sense of nationalism. There is nothing to show that they came with tongue in cheek. And although the great families—the Geraldines and Butlers, who were beginning to dominate the scene outside the Pale—were alarmingly Irish to English eyes, they retained English connections and sympathies, taking sides with the Yorkists against the Lancastrians. The weakness of the Crown during the wars of the Roses enabled these Irish families to extend their power; Richard of York, for example, during his term as Lieutenant in Ireland from 1447, was more concerned to see them as allies than as a potential threat to English dominion. Had they been moved by any nationalist leanings they would have exploited the situation to their own advantage; but in fact they remained loyal to the Yorkists, even to the extent of supporting enthusiastically, nearly half a century later, the cause of the Pretender Lambert Simnel, under the impression that he was Richard's grandson.

Although Irish nationalism scarcely existed as a political force, the weakness of the English monarchy helped to create a desire for administrative independence. Irish parliaments had long claimed exclusive jurisdiction over Irish affairs; and when early in the fifteenth century English parliaments sought to legislate for Ireland, an Irish parliament repudiated their statutes. The 'Home Rule' trend was confirmed in 1460 by the accident of Richard of York's popularity; when the Lancastrians drove him out of England, and had him attainted, he was able to retain his authority as viceroy in Ireland, though only on the tacit assumption that Ireland's allegiance was to the individual whom the Irish believed to be the true king—not to England's usurping rulers, and certainly not to England's legislature.

In other words, even that part of the country which remained English was claiming Home Rule; and the Yorkists, when they re-established themselves in power in England, were not happy at the prospect. In particular they feared the influence of the earls of Desmond, who had emerged as the most powerful family in the country. Earl James commanded over his widespread lands the allegiance of English, Old English and Irish subjects alike. He was confident enough of his position to defy the law by recognising Irish chiefs and Irish laws, and his heir, Earl Thomas, actually brought Irish chiefs to Dublin for the 1464 parliament. The Yorkist Government decided it must act against its former ally. Earl Thomas was attainted for breaking the anti-Irish laws, and beheaded.

His execution amounted to a declaration of war, for which

44

the Government was ill-prepared; the Yorkists were never again sufficiently sure of themselves to take so decisive an action in Ireland, which was left for the next few years to pursue its own ways. Political control fell into the hands of the Earl of Kildare, who had been attainted at the same time as Desmond, but pardoned; although George Duke of Clarence remained nominally Lieutenant of Ireland, Kildare became his Deputy, and in reality the country's ruling prince. Home Rule was virtually in operation, with Kildare building up his own territories by alliances and marriages with the old Irish and using his powers as Deputy still further to strengthen his position. At the time of his death in 1477 the family fortunes were so well established that his son Gerald— 'Garret More' to the Irish—automatically succeeded him in office. Although Edward IV sent over a new Deputy, the Irish parliament reinstated Garret More, and Edward had to withdraw his nominee.

Ireland had become almost an independent country. Garret More was a Home Ruler rather than a separatist; he had no ideological notions about Irish independence, and so long as he was left alone he had no ambition to sever the connection with the Crown. He must have recognised the risk that an English king would seek to send him the way Earl Thomas went in 1466; but this recollection prompted him to look around for a more amenable king, rather than to throw off allegiance to the Crown. He chose to back Lambert Simnel, who was crowned as King Edward VI of England and Ireland in Dublin in 1487; and the pretender's ignominious failure, by helping to consolidate the Tudors on the throne of England, was to prove fatal to Irish prospects.

Henry VII was not sure enough of himself to retaliate immediately; he waited until 1494 before despatching Sir Edward Poynings to Ireland with a small efficient army and some English officials. Their task proved easier than they could have expected. Under the weight of the Kildares' exactions in taxes, billeting, requisitioning, and occasionally straightforward plunder, their subjects, too, tended to grow restive, and to wonder whether they might not be better off under an alien but perhaps more just administration. Poynings' plans were carried through without mishap; Kildare was attainted and sent to the Tower; and the administration, at least within the Pale, was brought back into English ways. The promise that the Earl's extortions would be stopped was enough to restore the confidence of settlers who would otherwise have resented the newcomers. Home Rule was given a decisive check; no Irish parliament, it was enacted by 'Poynings Law,' should initiate legislation without first securing the consent of king and council in England.

All these moves would have been valueless had Henry not been astute enough to realise how their gains could be preserved. He could not afford to keep Poynings and the army in Ireland indefinitely; the only man who could have the same influence was the attainted Kildare. 'Since all Ireland cannot rule this man,' Henry is said to have remarked, 'this man must rule all Ireland.' The royal decision had a crafty ring about it, and crafty it proved, from Henry's viewpoint; Kildare did what was required of him when he was restored as Deputy. Where he suffered reverses it cost the Crown nothing; where he won victories it was possible to claim them as Crown victories. The Irish were not fully aware what was happening, because Garret More was carrying on the Irish traditions of his father and of the earls of Desmond; under him Irish culture blossomed. But as time was to show, Garret More had in fact turned back from the path that they had followed; it only required an ambitious English king to reveal the Kildare family's weakness.

Henry VIII provided the demonstration. In 1520 he felt strong enough to dismiss Kildare's son Garret Oge, who had carried on in his father's ways, and to resume direct rule in Ireland though a Lieutenant. The experiment proved a failure; the cost of direct rule was too high. Henry therefore experimented with indirect rule, with frequent changes of Deputy in order to prevent any one individual or family from growing too powerful. He only succeeded in weakening the authority of the office, as well as of the persons who held it; eventually not even Garret Oge himself could hold down the job, and after an unhappy period of restoration returned finally to the Tower. A rumour that he had been executed sparked off rebellion, compelling Henry to revert to force. He sent over a soldier, Sir William Skeffington, to repeat the Poynings treatment. By 1540 Garret Oge was dead, his son executed and the family power broken. The Tudors were to appoint no more Irishmen to the post of viceroy; the Home Rule system was finally abandoned.

It is doubtful if its passing was much lamented by the Irish. Apart from the greater anglicism of the administration, little change was at first apparent. Henry wanted to try conciliatory methods—they were cheaper—and in spite of the failure of his experiments he did not lose hope. In one respect, in fact, his policy became still more conciliatory. Any Irish chieftain who wished to make his peace with the Crown was encouraged to give up his lands, on the tacit understanding that they would be given back to him again, with the royal blessing. This 'surrender and regrant' idea worked, as it had done under Richard II; Irish and Old English flocked in to avail themselves of the offer, and for a time Henry achieved a measure of personal popularity such as no Englishman had won since Richard of York. Evidently the Home Rule years had imparted little nationalist feeling; alien strength could still win admiration, especially when it brought forth sweetness.

The momentary harmony helped to disguise the fact that 'surrender and regrant' must inevitably promote future strife; the chiefs were surrendering what in Irish law was theirs only for life, whereas Henry's regrant was based on primogeniture. It was still impossible to fuse the two systems; they would continue to provide a source of discontent until one or the other became dominant throughout the whole island.

The Reformation further emphasized the difference between English and Irish. Protestantism never made any headway in Ireland among the mass of the people, so that their religion began to cut them off still more effectively from the English. This did not mean that English policies in Ireland were necessarily dictated by the religious situation in England; it was in Queen Mary's reign that the first serious effort was made to extend the policy of 'plantation', which had so often been recommended as a means of getting rid of Irish pockets within the Pale, to a region outside it. In 1556 the decision was taken to 'plant' the district now covered by the counties of Leix and Offaly, whose chiefs had been in rebellion; it was distributed among settlers equipped to defend themselves against the Irish. Irish Catholics probably seemed as untrustworthy to Mary as English Protestants.

Mary's death left her successor Elizabeth with a problem that was to last throughout her reign. The Irish, alarmed by the plantation plan, were everywhere on the edge of war, if not actually in arms; their cause might, and soon did, attract the attention of her continental enemy Spain—especially when Irish leaders began to elevate their campaigns to the status of crusades. For this the rebels could claim constitutional justification. The Bull *Laudabiliter*, on which Henry II's title to Ireland had been based, could no longer be held to apply when England's king was a heretic. Those Irish Catholic families who had remained loyal to the Crown were provided with an excuse, if they wished, to renounce their allegiance. But it proved difficult to convince Philip of Spain that a war of liberation in Ireland would help his cause. The jingle,

> *He that England would win*
> *Let him in Ireland begin,*

an Irish emissary assured him, was a traditional Irish prophecy; but neither Philip nor the Pope realised their opportunity until, as events turned out, it was too late. Although rebellions large and small broke out, there was little cohesion between the Irish leaders. The most serious, the Munster rising of 1579 ,was aided by a small expeditionary force from the Continent. The rebels failed to make contact with it, and all that the rising achieved was the provision of more land to be distributed among English settlers. Inadequately though the plantation policy was carried out, it helped to spread English influence through the heart of the country; 'surrender and regrant' spread it further, because the regrant was given only where the chiefs abandoned Irish titles and primogeniture; and terror helped to enforce it— Walter Raleigh, in particular, excelling in butchery.

By the time of the Spanish Armada the Queen's writ ran far and wide in Ireland. Of the crews of the Spanish galleons which were driven ashore on the Irish coast, only a few found shelter. The great majority were slaughtered—some, admittedly, for plunder, but most in obedience to royal command. One of the Armada captains, Don Francisco de Cuellar, left a harrowing account of his experiences in which the impression is conveyed that most of the natives were savages preoccupied with rapine: 'the chief inclination of these people is to be robbers and to plunder each other . . . and the English from the garrisons getting to know who has taken most cattle, then come down upon them, and carry away the plunder.' Only in the North were the Spaniards well treated; only there was the Queen's power still negligible. And it was in the North the Irish were to make their last stand.

In Ulster they found a leader of outstanding ability in Hugh O'Neill. He had been brought up in England, at Court; and his education had taught him the virtue of patience and dissimulation in dealing with the English. For years he was content to bide his time, building up an army, establishing friendly relations with his Irish neighbours and converting them from dangerous rivals into useful allies. From the course of events in Munster he could see that his own position was secure only when he was strong enough to defy the English; the question was whether the English would realise what was in his mind and strike before he was ready. He was helped by Elizabeth's parsimony. She hated to finance any campaign that was not made absolutely necessary by overt rebel acts. No move was made against him even when he assumed the old Irish title of 'The O'Neill', which amounted to defiance of her authority. Not until 1597 was a full-scale attack launched on Ulster. It failed; and in a second assault the following year the English suffered the worst defeat their arms had ever received in Ireland, at the Battle of the Yellow Ford.

His victory made O'Neill the undisputed champion of the Irish. All over the country risings followed; the Munster plantations were swept away in a few weeks; the Spanish promised help; and it looked as if O'Neill had only to avoid a rash engagement for the English to be overwhelmed. For a time his strategy appeared to work satisfactorily; the Earl of Essex, arriving to redeem a tarnished reputation by putting down the rebals, succeeded only in finally damaging it psat redemption. Yet Essex's failure in a sense only showed how firmly English rule was established; it could survive even an incompetent leader. Under his successor Mountjoy, a man in the Poynings/Skeffington tradition, the Fabian tables were turned on O'Neill, who found his allies melting away, or being defeated piecemeal. Mountjoy systematically wore the Irish down, the final act being played out at Kinsale in 1601. The Spanish had sent over a small army; and this time, the rebels were able to make contact with it, but too late. They were out-generalled and routed by Mountjoy's men; and the Spaniards were glad to return home as the price of surrender. Soon afterwards O'Neill himself submitted. Although James I magnanimously confirmed him in his possessions, insecurity fretted him, and in 1607 he and other Ulster chiefs sailed for the Continent. That this 'flight of the earls' was not condemned as a betrayal by the old Irish they left behind—that on the contrary, O'Neill was praised for leaving when he could no longer breathe freely in the alien atmosphere that his conquerors brought with them—indicates the extent to which the old Ireland had disintegrated.

Unlike Garret More before, and Patrick Sarsfield after him, O'Neill could not be accused of lending himself to further English designs. His long wait before he came out decisively against the English might be criticised as unscrupulous, but not as a betrayal of his countrymen. O'Neill, therefore, helped to create a new separatist ideal that was to survive the destruction of the old Ireland for which he had fought, and to become the moving spirit two centuries later of the United Irishmen; a spirit different from that which inspired the Home Rule movement of the earls of Desmond and Kildare. Although O'Neill was driven into his separatist ways by circumstances, rather than by nationalist ideals, and although his defeat finally destroyed the old Ireland beyond hope of revival, he was to be one of the decisive influences in the moulding of nationalist tradition in later years.

✤ *Two* ✤
1603 - 1690

Three hundred years in Ireland had taught the English that it was not enough to defeat the Irish in time of war; their influence seeped back again in time of peace. The obvious solution was to anglicise the whole country, leaving no reservoir of Gaeldom from which seepage could begin. The plantation policy must be more systematically applied, and English administrative and judicial institutions extended to embrace every part of Ireland.

The opportunity for fresh plantation was provided by the flight of the earls, whose lands were automatically forfeit to the crown. Most of Ulster was therefore available for distribution; it was dealt out to 'undertakers' from England and the Scots lowlands, pledged to permit only British settlers on their estates, and to those Irish supporters of the Crown who were awaiting reward for past services, military or civil. Where traces of the old Gaelic social order were found they were expunged. The anglicising process, however, remained superficial. The administration was not efficient enough to ensure that the settlers really settled, or that undertakers performed what they undertook. The natives remained on planted lands, sometimes as tenants winked at by authority, sometimes as outlaws whom authority was powerless to remove.

Yet although the native Irish remained, they were in no position to maintain their old social and legal institutions. During James's reign the Gaelic structure disappeared. English law, administration and justice were imposed; the first all-Ireland parliament of 1613 finally abolished the old

Irish—Brehon—laws, and finally established primogeniture. The swiftness of the change was disturbing even to those Old English who had no particular affection for Irish ways. Fearful for their own property, they mistrusted Plantation; and they had less in common with the new settlers, many of whom were simple adventurers, than with the Irish—particularly as the predominantly Catholic 'Old English' shared with the Irish a common fear of militant English puritanism. On the accession of James I they had been hopeful of toleration; but although James was prepared to relax the laws against the practice of the Catholic faith, he was unwilling to risk giving offence to his Protestant subjects in England. The Gunpowder Plot scare brought James finally down on the Protestant side of the fence; the Oath of Supremacy remained, preventing Catholics from holding office; and the recusancy acts, even if they were not strictly enforced, continued to promote sympathy between the Irish and the Old English.

To Charles I, this tendency appeared beneficial. One of the conditions of his marriage to a French princess had been that he would try to prevent the enforcement of anti-Catholic laws; and his inclination was to propitiate the Irish and Old English by remitting their recusancy fines, confirming them in their estates, and similar measures—these 'graces' being offered in exchange for grants sufficient to enable him to pay for the upkeep of the Irish army. But again, public opinion in England was too strong for him; neither the graces nor the grant were forthcoming. For a time Ireland had to be left to its own devices, under the control of political adventurers like Richard Boyle, Earl of Cork, who had arrived almost penniless in Ireland and with the help of ability eked out by fraud had made himself the wealthiest man in the country.

But the more Charles's relations with parliament deteriorated, the more he was inclined to see in Ireland a possible way out of his difficulties. In 1833 he sent Sir Thomas Wentworth to Dublin as Lord Deputy, with instructions to fashion

Ireland into an instrument useful to the royal cause. In his seven years of office Wentworth showed how much an able administrator could do in Ireland. He shook the Government into efficiency, secured a fatter revenue, and raised and trained a formidable army—the army which, by rousing the fears of the parliamentarians, was later to damn him at his impeachment.

The comparative prosperity of the country under Wentworth was incidental to his policy. Had it suited Charles to have Ireland impoverished, Wentworth would have performed the task with the same determination. He had no hesitation in stamping out anything which might make the Irish feel too independent, and in the end his policy alienated friends, neutrals, and enemies alike. His efforts to reform the Established Church, for example, with a view to using it for the propagation of the royal cause, antagonised all sects. Anglicans disliked being treated as an administrative convenience; Catholics foresaw the rise of a new state religion to which eventually they would be asked to conform; and the dissenting settlers in Ulster were goaded into hatred of the administration. The fundamental weakness of the policy was that it could succeed only so long as a Wentworth was there to enforce it; and even Wentworth could do little when the political situation in England deteriorated to such an extent that Charles could no longer give him unqualified support. The Irish were left in the position of a turbulent class of schoolboys, long cowed by the threat of the birch, who become aware that their headmaster is being deprived of his authority; and the Scots rebellion encouraged them to take that authority into their own hands.

But whereas in Scotland the issues were reasonably clear, in Ireland they were confused. By this time the population had four main strands; in addition to the Irish, the Old English and the English, the influence of the Scots-Irish in Ulster had to be considered. These strands, too, were intertwined. Of the New English, some leant towards the king, others favoured the Parliamentary cause. Of the Old English, some were prompted by loyalty to maintain their allegiance to Charles, others were tempted by the Crown's growing weakness to throw in their lot with the parliamentarians, in the hope of securing concessions from them; and the Irish were becoming increasingly anxious to break the English connection altogether. Plans for risings for and against the Crown proceeded side by side; indeed, the conspirators themselves were often not clear exactly what their conspiracies were designed to attain.

When rebellion broke out in 1641, it took the form of an uprising of the Catholic gentry and peasants in Ulster, who were seizing the opportunity to take back the land which had been ejected by plantation and were little concerned with constitutional niceties. Amid the confusion, two loyalties were constant. One was the devotion of the commander of the royal forces, James Butler, Earl of Ormonde, to Charles's cause; the other was the devotion of the civil authority, upheld by the Lords Justices in Dublin, to the cause of parliament. At first, both felt bound to co-operate in the suppression of the rebels, as the rising took place before the final breach between king and parliament. But within a few months it became impossible for Ormonde and the Lords Justices to trust each other; Charles was urging Ormonde to come to terms with the rebels in Ireland in the hope of securing them as allies. The Old English were anxious to accommodate him out of conservatism, as well as loyalty; the Irish wavered whether to take advantage of his weakness to secure better terms from him, or to repudiate him altogether.

In the Confederation of Kilkenny, set up in 1642 to provide Catholic Ireland with a central government, the Old English at first were dominant. Of the two experienced commanders who arrived from the Continent to assist the rebels, the more cautious Thomas Preston was favoured at the expense of the abler Owen Roe O'Neill, a nephew of Hugh, who had separatist leanings; and of the home leaders the ablest, Rory O'More, was snubbed for the same reason.

But the hopes of the Old English were destroyed by the vacillations of Charles. In one sense only was he consistent: he worked exclusively for his own restoration to power in England. This meant blowing hot or cold on the Irish rebel terms according to the state of his fortunes, and to the state of his relations with parliament; it meant, too, that what he was prepared to promise the rebels in private he might think it wise to deny in public. It proved impossible to tie him to specific terms, or to trust him to keep them.

The attitude of the Confederates was hardly more consistent, depending as it did on the state of the balance of power in the Confederation Council between Irish and Old English. Ormonde, as the go-between, was like a man trying to knot two eels together; it was March 1646 before he finally secured an agreement that was acceptable both to Charles and to the Old English majority on the Council. By that time it was too late; in a few days, Charles was to surrender to the Scots. In any case, the terms were unacceptable to the Irish. They had acquired a formidable ally in Rinuccini, the papal nuncio, who became so convinced that the Catholic cause was being betrayed by the royalism and conservatism of the Old English, that their decision to conclude a treaty with Charles through Ormonde had to be kept secret from him. When the secret came out, Rinuccini and the Irish felt they had been betrayed. The Irish, too, were greatly heartened in June by Owen Roe O'Neill's resounding defeat at Benburb of the Scots parliamentary forces under General Monroe. Strategically Owen Roe's victory turned out to be of little importance, but it decisively altered the balance of power at Kilkenny. Rinuccini was able to repudiate the peace and to imprison the councillors who had agreed to it. The Protestant Ormonde in disgust delivered Dublin up to parliament rather than let it fall into what he considered alien control.

Ormonde's departure left the Confederates free at last to concentrate on their real enemy, the parliamentary forces. But the divisions at Kilkenny remained; and they were in-

creased by growing hostility even among the Irish to Rinuccini's high-handed ways. Within a few months the split
between the Rinuccini group, to which Owen Roe remained
faithful, and the Old English, who still had hopes of the
Ormonde peace, had led almost to a state of war between
the two wings. In exile, later, the wings were to beat at each
other with malevolent recriminations. Rinuccini's followers
accused the Old English of betraying the rebel cause in order
to preserve their political and social superiority over the
Irish; and the Old English replied that so far from being
swayed by self-interest, they had been prepared to risk their
great possessions by joining the confederates, whereas few of
the Irish had much to lose but their lives. Each side blamed
on the other the division which, unhealed, had left the
country an easy prey to Cromwell.

Before Cromwell's arrival the Confederate ranks had to
outward appearances closed. Ormonde, returning to Ireland,
persuaded the Confederates to make their peace with him;
Rinuccini angrily left the country. But the internal divisions
remained; between Owen Roe and Ormonde lay greater
enmity than between Owen Roe and the parliamentary forces.
The quarrel left the way open in August 1649 for Cromwell,
convinced not only of the need to put down royalists and
rebels, but also of his mission to act as the instrument of
divine vengeance for the Protestant dead. His first action
was to storm Drogheda, and to cause almost the entire
populace to be slaughtered: 'a righteous judgment of God
upon these barbarous wretches', he told parliament, adding
that it would tend to prevent the effusion of blood in future.
The shock compelled the Irish, the Old English and the
royalists to try to compose their differences; Ormonde came
to terms even with Owen Roe. But Owen Roe was a dying
man, and there was no other general on the Irish side that
could have commanded the same respect: Ormonde proved
incapable of halting Cromwell's progress, and in October
Wexford's inhabitants met the same fate as those of Drogheda.
Within a few months, the rebels were sufficiently cowed for

Cromwell to return to England, confident that his deputy Ireton could empty the remaining pockets of resistance.

The rebellion had been a melancholy episode for Ireland, more expressive of divisions than of national purpose. Yet it has been argued that 'once national patriotism had taken possession of an old European people, generous and otherworldly, but proud, tenacious and inexorable, it became a consuming passion which could never afterwards be extinguished.' Later patriots harked back for inspiration to Owen Roe and Rory O'More, whose deeds were kept alive in many a stirring ballad. Even more decisive than the rebellion itself was the memory of the manner in which it was stamped out. Cromwell's claim that it would tend 'to prevent the effusion of blood' for the future was theoretically well-founded; but in the long run it helped to create the bitterness that was to lead to far more blood being spilt. Cromwell's name branded itself onto the national consciousness; to this day, it comes first to mind wherever Ireland's wrongs are recited.

The settlement that followed differed from that of James I; the dispossession was far more widespread, and more thorough. The great bulk of Irish proprietors lost their possessions as Catholics or as royalists; they were instructed to depart to holdings beyond the Shannon, in Connaught, and their land was distributed among Cromwell's followers, the process being carried out with callous efficiency. According to Sir William Petty, who surveyed the country for the purpose, over half the total acreage of Ireland was replanted, including almost all the fertile land. For the first time Protestants became the dominant land-owning class.

Cromwell abolished the Irish parliament and gave the Irish representation instead in an all-British legislature. But on his death, the settlers called a convention in Dublin which reasserted Ireland's right to her own parliament—so short a time had it taken them to identify their own with what they took to be their country's interest. They also understood their own interest sufficiently to be quick to recognise the

Restoration—an action which in a sense made Charles II's task more difficult; relieved to find them co-operative, he was unwilling to antagonise them by too drastic a revision of the Cromwellian settlement, particularly as this might rouse Protestant fears in England. On the other hand, he could not ignore entirely the claims of the dispossessed royalists, many of them Catholic, who had remained true to him in exile. His policy was a compromise. The land settlement tended to favour the Cromwelliam settlers because they were in possession, and the risk of disturbing them was greater than the risk of offending the dissatisfied royalists. In religion *de jure* strictness (to reassure English Protestants) was in practice tempered at least until the witch hunt after popish plotters began towards the end of his reign. For most of the reign the administration was left to Ormonde; and though in the circumstances nobody in Ireland could feel secure, the insecurity was not alarming enough to provoke resistance.

Charles cared nothing for Ireland. He would have been prepared to accept any policy there which avoided trouble. James II's interest in the country lay no deeper; but the lack of it was masked, as it had been with Charles I, by the realization that Ireland was potentially useful to him, as a source of Catholic strength. The Old English had been dispossessed, but not destroyed. As soon as the administration, the courts and the army were re-opened on James's instructions to Catholics, they flocked back into positions of authority, and by the revolution of 1688 they had re-established themselves in power to an extent that alarmed the Cromwellian settlers, many of whom fled to England.

The recovery of the Old English was not wholly to James' advantage. When he arrived in Ireland after the revolution of 1688 it was pleasant for him to find an army awaiting him, ready for use against the usurper William. But the 'Patriot Parliament' which assembled to greet him, Catholic and loyal though it was, was also an embarrassment. One of its first decisions, naturally enough, was to dispossess absentee Protestant landlords. This was carried against James's will;

he realised what the effect would be on public opinion in England, where the absentees' grievance would be fully exploited by the Williamites. And when the patriots suggested that Poynings' Law should be abolished, James felt that he had to put his foot down.

Not only were James's interests very different from those of the Irish; the antagonism between Old English and Irish had not been removed. The military campaign lacked the incisive edge needed to cut off Protestant resistance before the Williamite forces should be ready to come to its support. The Protestant apprentice boys of Derry were able to shut the gates in the faces of James's army, and to hold out long enough for William to prepare the expeditionary force which in 1690 defeated James, and his mixed Irish and French army, at the Battle of the Boyne.

James fled to France; the Irish fought on less with any real hope of victory than to secure an equitable treaty. William was anxious to accommodate them; fighting in Ireland as far as he was concerned meant only that he was kept 'as it were out of knowledge of the world'. But the English parliament's authority could not be overridden, and its ear was held by Protestants, eager to seize the opportunity of making the Protestant position in Ireland secure. In the end only Patrick Sarsfield's determined resistance enabled the Irish to avoid the humiliation of unconditional surrender; the Treaty of Limerick permitted the remnants of the Irish and Old English to go into exile on the Continent.

The 'flight of the earls' had signalled the disappearance of the old Gaelic social order: the flight of 'the Wild Geese', as Sarsfield's fellow exiles came to be known, finally destroyed the prospect of an Old English social order. The weakness of the Old English had lain in loyalty to the British crown—or, rather, to its Stuart wearers. Neither Charles I nor James II could have been trusted to carry out any pledges they made had they succeeded; that they failed brought ruin upon their Irish followers. With the Wild Geese, almost the entire remaining Old Irish and Old English catholic aristocracy took wing to fight as mercenaries on the Continent. Their departure left the mass of the Catholic population leaderless and without resources. The way was open for the English to impose English policies in deference to English requirements, confident that any opposition there might be in Ireland would be powerless to make its protest heard, let alone felt, for many years to come.

❧ Three ❧
1690 - 1800

Under William III, and later under Anne, the English government's interest in Ireland was limited to a determination that she should be prevented from giving service to the Stuart pretenders, and that she should be kept commercially and politically dependent on England.

With the first of these aims the Irish Protestants wholeheartedly concurred. The provision in the treaty of Limerick whereby Catholics were guaranteed their former rights—such as they were—had to be abandoned by William in the face of Protestant hostility. In its place a series of Acts, collectively to be known as the Penal Laws, deprived Catholics of the right to sit in Parliament and to vote at elections; barred them from formal education; restricted their right of entry into commerce or the professions; and limited their property rights. It was not thought possible to prevent them from practising their religion; priests were permitted to continue their ministrations. But the severity of the Penal Laws was sufficient to set more wild geese on their way to join Sarsfield; and those who remained sometimes found it expedient to change their faith, at least outwardly. By the beginning of the Hanoverian dynasty the bulk of the Catholic population had been reduced to the level of Egyptian fellaheen. A few Catholics struggled on in trade, and in the professions; only a handful of the Catholic aristocracy, protected by their social standing, remained as landowners. That the old Irish culture did not entirely disappear was partly due to the miserable condition of the peasantry; it survived in oral tradition, as primitive lore so often survives. But for a century Catholic nationalism as a political force hardly existed.

With the second aim of the English government—an Ireland commercially and politically dependent—Irish Protestants had no sympathy at all. On Wentworth's precepts, the English were prepared to allow the Irish to keep England provided with goods which were not much manufactured in England, such as linen; but nothing was allowed which might cut across an English commercial interest.

At the same time, the English government took care to safeguard its political authority. Elections were held as rarely as possible; the parliament summoned at the coronation of George II in 1727 was still there when he died in 1760. Parliament was in any case drawn from so small an electorate that no very skilful management was required to ensure that it would be kept obedient; Poynings' Law, which deprived it of real power, was reinforced in 1719 by the Declaratory Act, reaffirming the right of the British parliament to legislate for Ireland; and Irish administrative posts, as well as nearly all the positions of authority in the church and the judiciary, were filled with Englishmen, or reliable 'Anglo-Irish'—as the descendants of the Stuart settlers came to be called.

These measures had their intended effect; they kept Ireland dependent. Inevitably, they also created an opposition—not among the Catholics, too poor or too cowed to be influential, but in the Protestant middle class, irritated by its subjection to laws in whose making it had no say. An overt expression of this annoyance appeared as early as 1698: Molyneux's denunciation of English selfishness in *The case of Ireland's being bound by acts of parliament in England, stated*. A quarter of a century later the opposition secured its first substantial victory in the battle of 'Wood's Ha'pence'. Wood had been given a contract to mint coins for Ireland. It transpired that the substantial profits were to be split between himself and a mistress of George I's; and the deal was denounced by Jonathan Swift, Dean of St. Patrick's Cathedral in Dublin, in the *Drapier's Letters*. So menacing was the public indignation that the project had to be abandoned. The government was

unable to persuade even a Protestant Grand Jury to assent to
the prosecution of the *Drapier's* printer. In these letters and
in other scarcely less celebrated diatribes, Swift gave the new
nationalism trenchant expression. There was little that was
specifically 'Irish' about it; the opposition he represented
had no social contact with the Irish, and tended to ignore or
despise their traditions.

Swift himself disclaimed any sense of patriotism; what he
did, he said was 'owing to perfect rage and resentment, and
the mortifying sight of slavery, folly, and baseness about me,
among which I am forced to live.' Mortified by his failure to
obtain preferment in England, and harassed by personal problems, he was ready to give vent to his indignation wherever
opportunity offered, and Ireland gave him opportunities by
the score. But his motives did not matter; they led him to
patriotism, whether he liked it or not. In his *Drapier's Letters*
he could leave the narrower question of Woods Ha'pence to
write, 'I find that cordials must be frequently applied to
weak constitutions, political as well as natural. A people
long used to hardships lose by degrees the very notions of
liberty . . . hence proceeds poverty and lowness of spirit, to
which a kingdom may be subject as well as a particular
person.' In much the same way, what was to some extent a
struggle by resentful have-nots— the Irish commercial classes
—against the English haves, developed into patriotism by
association of ideas: the slogan (adapted from a phrase of
Swift's) 'burn everything English except their coal' gave a
national twist to a commercial argument.

The development from a have-not opposition into a genuine
patriot movement was slow, mainly because the Irish government handled dangerous-looking opposition not by repressive
measures—they would have won the sufferer sympathy, and
might in any case have been baulked by antagonistic juries—
but by the distribution of titles, 'places', and pensions.

In theory Ireland was ruled by an elected parliament and
an executive appointed by the Crown; in practice, both
parliament and executive were in fact managed by 'Under-

takers', magnates whose functions were described by one of the most respected of viceroys, Lord Chesterfield. Lord Lieutenants, Chesterfield said, had to rule by a faction, to which they were only the first slaves. The faction would guarantee to manage parliament, to see that supplies were voted, and to maintain public order. In return, it demanded control of patronage, and deprived the Lord Lieutenant of all political power. The Undertakers' argument that the administration could be carried on only by this means was borne out in the middle of the century, when an energetic Lord Lieutenant tried to curb their influence; a vigorous 'patriot' party promptly made its appearance under Henry Boyle, the Speaker of the Irish Commons, and the Earl of Kildare. The malcontents were bought off with places—the Speaker became an earl, and the earl, a duke—but the Undertaker system had received a wound which was to prove fatal. The idea of a patriot party had been revived, and it was to be carried on by an able propagandist, Charles Lucas, and an ambitious politician, Henry Flood. Lucas died, and Flood allowed himself to be persuaded that he could work more effectively for the cause in office without damaging his name as a patriot—not the last time this error was to be made by Irishmen; but Henry Grattan and the Earl of Charlemont took over the direction of the patriot party. Before they too could be tempted by patronage or disillusionment, they found themselves thrust up on the surge of events that unexpectedly provided Ireland with the promise of nationhood.

The opportunity arose as a result of the American War of Independence. Troops had to be sent from Ireland across the Atlantic; in their place, for the preservation of order and as a precaution against a possible French invasion, the Protestant middle classes were encouraged to form a force of Volunteers. When they saw themselves, thousands strong, in uniform, the Volunteers realised that they could be masters in their own house. At first they were mainly concerned to secure commercial parity with England; the English Government, shaken by its defeat in America and by threats from the

Continent, prudently gave way, and agreed to a measure of free trade with Ireland. But by this time the word 'patriot' had begun to mean more than simply a hungry have-not. Hussey Burgh's outburst in the Irish Parliament, 'England has sown her laws like dragon's teeth, and they have sprung up armed men,' reflected a new determination to secure political, as well as economic justice. The patriot movement grew in self-confidence; with the Duke of Leinster and the Earl of Charlemont as its military leaders, the Volunteer force was eminently respectable, and in some ways even conservative; but Grattan as its parliamentary spokesman kept it resolutely revolutionary in its determination to obtain a new constitution. The temper of the Volunteers at their Dungannon convention in 1782 left no doubt that they contemplated the use of force if necessary; but Lord North's fall from office, by bringing in a whig government well-disposed to Grattan, helped to keep the revolution bloodless. The Declaratory Act was repealed: the right of the English Privy Council to alter Irish Bills was abolished; only the royal veto remained between the Irish administration and formal legislative independence. 'Ireland', Grattan could say, 'is now a nation.'

Three years later Grattan must have regretted that he had said anything so foolish. He had decided to remain outside the new Government, thinking aloofness would make his position stronger. It left him powerless. The Irish legislature was independent only in name. It was controlled by the executive through patronage; and the executive, appointed by the English Government, was hardly less bound by English interests than its predecessors. The patriot ranks disintegrated. Some took office, or became 'placemen': the remainder were divided by an unedifying squabble between Grattan, who was trying to live down his revolutionary past, and Flood, who was trying to prove that his past flirtation with the Government did not mean that he was any less of a patriot. The executive used the excuse given by a factious press and outbreaks of violence among Dublin craftsmen, to enforce repressive measures and to disband the Volunteers. The patriots were forced to recognise that the constitution of 1782, on which they had based such high hopes, was a fraud.

The executive—'the Castle', as it was coming to be known from its seat of government in Dublin—owed its security mainly to the number of nomination boroughs returning members to the Dublin parliament. About two-thirds of the seats were in effect privately owned, usually by some local magnate, who in his turn was bought by the Government with preferment. Outside this Junta the Castle had little support; but the Junta held all the important executive and judicial posts, and with the help of a secret service fund was able to buy agents to keep it informed of all that went on in the hostile community around it. It contained a few men, too, who made up in firmness what they lacked in imagination: John FitzGibbon, later to be Earl of Clare, John Beresford— between them they stage-managed the Junta—and Lord Clonmell, the Chief Justice, whose court acted as an extra arm of the executive. Against the firmness of these men Grattan, Flood and the rest of the opposition were powerless; and by 1788 the political situation was little different from pre-revolutionary times.

In that year, however, George III became insane, and the prospect of a regency, under the Prince of Wales as regent, altered the political balance in Ireland. The prince was known to have Whig sympathies; the English Whigs were friendly with Grattan; and Irish placemen who were dependent on continued government favour—including the majority of members of the Irish Commons—prepared to trim. They would have deserted the Government for Grattan or anybody else, the moment the signal was given. But the king recovered; titles and pensions were distributed to waverers; and Grattan's prospects receded once again. He continued painstakingly to pursue his correct constitutional ways; dissident patriots found themselves increasingly attracted by the less orthodox methods being employed on the Continent. The ideas of the French revolutionaries spread rapidly in

Ireland, and when the Society of United Irishmen was founded in 1790 by Wolfe Tone, it was to France that its members looked for their example.

The Society drew its members from the same class that had formed the Volunteers, except that the aristocrats held aloof, and the dissenting Protestant element played an even larger part. Dissenters from Scotland had been prominent among the settlers in the Ulster plantations; but their refusal to conform had brought them, side by side with Catholics, under the Penal Laws. Although the laws were less harsh against Protestant dissent than against Popery, they were galling enough to put Dissenters firmly on the have-not side. They were to provide the staunchest members of the Society of United Irishmen, and it was by them that its mouthpiece, the Belfast *Northern Star*, was published.

The breach between Grattan and the United Irishmen was one of the decisive events in the country's history. The split it created between constitutional and revolutionary separatism lingers to this day. Grattan wished merely to revise the 1782 constitution; Tone hoped to bring it into discredit, because in his eyes the 1782 constitution had 'only enabled Irishmen to sell at a much higher price their honour, their integrity, and the interests of their country'. At first, although they differed in their choice of weapons, Tone and Grattan shared the same target—parliamentary reform. Grattan wished to persuade, the United Irishmen to frighten, the Government into agreeing to a more democratic franchise, so that the rest of their aims—religious, commercial and political—could be effected later. Had the French revolution's course been different—had Louis been able to govern with a stable ministry—the course of events in Ireland would have been different too. The United Irishmen might have become an even more powerful and homogeneous body than the Volunteers. But the trend of the revolution towards Jacobinism disrupted the Society. It was little more 'revolutionary', in the new sense of the word, than the Volunteers had been; anxious to obtain what members thought were their rights, but not at all anxious to be denounced as Jacobins. They could not condone the execution of Louis, or the Terror. The radical wing of the society, on the other hand, though it might have qualms about justifying the revolution's excesses, was inclined to regard them as unfortunate blemishes on what was essentially a just cause.

The Junta not unnaturally looked upon the French revolution with indisguised horror: and it took little time for them to determine to wage preventive war against potential Irish Marats and Robespierres in the Society. In spite of the efforts of Chief Justice Clonmell it was not always possible to secure their conviction: the owners of the *Northern Star* were acquitted by a friendly jury; so was Dr. Drennan, one of the leaders of the Society in Dublin. But another of its leaders, Hamilton Rowan, was sentenced for seditious libel; and Wolfe Tone allowed himself to be embroiled in a conspiracy for which, if he had not discreetly taken himself into exile, he would have had to face a treason charge.

Tone was later to assert that the Society had really been republican from the start. In fact, it was not until after he had left Ireland that it became avowdly separatist, less through his teaching than through anger at the Government's repressive policies. Deciding that their best hope of over-turning the Junta was to secure foreign help, the Society began to look to France for assistance; at the same time Tone, who had returned from America, was badgering the Direc-tory in Paris to send an expeditionary force to Ireland. The prospects were favourable; Carnot was impressed; and a force under General Hoche was despatched. It arrived off Ireland at Christmas 1796, but without Hoche, whose ship had lost contact. In any case so violent and prolonged a gale blew that Grouchy vetoed disembarkation, and a depressed Tone was carried back with the fleet to France.

John Beresford believed that only providence and English weather had stood between Ireland and French domination; had an army been able to land, he said, no force capable of opposing it was available. Whether or not this was true, it was a useful excuse for the Junta to resort to still more oppressive measures; its militia roamed the countryside employing arson, torture and murder in the cause of security. Meanwhile the United Irishmen were laying their plans for rebellion. They were joined by two men who rapidly rose to leadership within the Society, Arthur O'Connor and Lord Edward Fitzgerald; after canvassing for help in France, they returned to put the movement in readiness at home. But before help could reach them from France, the Government had struck. By 1798 its spies and informers riddled the Society, whose leaders were easily rounded up. Lord Edward was mortally wounded trying to escape arrest; a few of the rest were hanged and the remainder imprisoned.

Nevertheless bloodshed was not averted. The methods employed by the militia merely succeeded in provoking the rebellion they were intended to quell. The peasantry of the south-eastern counties, inflamed by their treatment, rose against their oppressors. Without military leaders and with only makeshift arms they were soon crushed; the rest of the country, except for an ineffective rising in Ulster, remained quiet, and the rebellion was easily suppressed. French aid arrived too late. After one swift victory a small expeditionary force, led by Humbert, was rounded up and compelled to surrender. Tone, captured on a French frigate, committed suicide in prison; the surviving leaders of the United Irishmen exchanged their Dublin prison for captivity in exile.

Although the '98 rising was a fiasco, the work of the United Irishmen was to have important results. The memory of Wolfe Tone, the first republican, came to be revered; it was to him that the separatist movements of the next century owed their inspiration. The United Irishmen, too, had created a new ideal of a society in which members of all religions would have equal rights. Although Tone was repelled by the Catholic peasantry's boorishness and irritated by the Catholic bishops' timidity, he strove to bring them to a realisation of their own importance; and the fact that it was the Catholic peasantry who in the end rebelled helped to link their cause with that of the patriots, and to provide later generations with the argument that armed rebellion was justified against tyranny.

Long before the rebellion, William Pitt had come to the conclusion that the only way in which England could protect her flank from the threat of invasion was to deprive Ireland of even her show of independence. He had decided to restore her to the position she had once occupied for a few years during the Protectorate; she was to be incorporated, as Scotland had been, into the Union.

The project of Union was brought up in 1799. It met vigorous opposition in Ireland not only from the patriot party (which was no longer in a position to exert much influence) but from the placemen and borough-owners whose livelihood was threatened, and from commercial interests who foresaw that such protection as they had been able to secure might be withdrawn. Grattan and his followers found themselves on the same side as staunch government men like John Foster, the Speaker of the Irish Commons, and the proposal was defeated. Cornwallis, the Lord Lieutenant, and Castlereagh, the Chief Secretary, went to work to undermine this resistance. Borough-owners were bought out, placemen compensated (the cost was added to the Irish National Debt); more than a score of new peerages were created; the Catholics, who might have provided dangerous allies to the anti-Union movement, were assuaged with a promise of a measure of emancipation; and in 1800 the Union was carried.

Unrepresentative though the Irish parliament had been, its loss came to be mourned partly because it was a symbol of Irish claims to independence, and partly because the country happened to enjoy a period of unprecedented prosperity towards its close. Under 'Grattan's Parliament' too—the name is a tribute to him as architect, rather than to his influence within its counsels—Dublin really became a capital city. From in and around this period date many of the noble buildings and the Georgian streets and squares that are the city's architectural pride; their existence continued to testify to her former greatness, and the period came to be recalled with a nostalgia that was none the less potent for being misplaced.

♣ Four ♣

1800 - 1845

Before Ireland had shaken down into its new political quarters, one further attempt was made to shake her out of them again: Robert Emmet's rising in 1803. In the event this turned out to be little more than a street riot, owing to the rebels' mishaps and miscalculations. But it might have been more serious than the peasant uprising of 1798; the authorities were unprepared, not because they had no advance warning from their spies but because so much inaccurate information had come from them so often that the Castle had grown sceptical. Emmet was hanged, his speech from the dock lifting him to join Tone and Lord Edward in the highest circle of patriot martyrs, all the more influential because his death appeared so inevitable in retrospect.

But this was later. At the time, the prevalent feeling was that Emmet had done a rash disservice to the national cause. Owing to the comparatively conciliatory policy employed by the Lord Lieutenant, Hardwicke, the scars of '98 had begun to heal; nowhere in the country was there much enthusiasm for a rising. Grattan condemned it: so, a few years later, did Daniel O'Connell, to whom the lesson both of '98 and of 1803 was that the liberation of Ireland must be accomplished without the shedding of blood.

For twenty years after Emmet's death, Ireland remained politically prostrate. So long as Napoleon ruled the English could not afford to relax their security vigilance; a brief interlude of Whig rule by 'All the Talents' in 1806, in spite of earlier Whig promises of conciliation, proved even less sympathetic than its predecessor. An attempt at a more liberal administration was reversed in 1812 by Robert Peel, when he was appointed Chief Secretary; he preferred what he termed 'honest despotism' and there was never any lack of informers to keep the Castle plied with alarming rumours to justify his repressive policies.

When nationalism reappeared, it was on the shoulders of another movement: the Catholic Emancipation campaign.

The worst of the Penal Laws had been abolished by 1772; and in 1793 Pitt, who had come to the conclusion that the Catholics could best be kept out of political mischief by a conciliatory policy, had compelled the reluctant Junta to give the vote to Catholics owning a freehold property worth 40s. His tactics were successful. The Catholic leaders shunned the Society of United Irishmen, and the hierarchy, which had no sympathy with the Jacobin leanings of the United Irishmen, lent its support to the Government in the rebellion years. Pitt's promise of full Emancipation—to enable Catholics to sit in parliament as well as to vote at elections—was not carried out; the king's conscience proved an insuperable obstacle. If the Catholic aversion from the United Ireland movement had verified Pitt's prediction that conciliation would make them conservative, the failure to give them full Emancipation verified it again in reverse; frustration made them more radical. Divisions of opinion between the moderates, who were prepared to compromise on some vexatious issues, and the intransigents, who were not, prevented the movement for Emancipation from gathering velocity for some years; but in the course of these internal dissensions the intransigents' leader, the barrister Daniel O'Connell, gained experience and authority which was to prove invaluable to the cause when its unity was at last achieved.

In some ways Emancipation was to be decisive in the story of Irish nationalism. It showed how much could be done by a campaign starting without money or influence behind it, in a popular cause. O'Connell had proved capable not only of rousing the peasantry but also, which might have been more difficult, of disciplining it. After a century and a half, too, Catholics had been made once again politically conscious. Emancipation itself meant little, especially as it was bought by the sacrifice of the electors who had won it. As the 40s. freeholders could no longer be trusted to vote as their landlords ordered, a higher property qualification for voters was imposed. But the fact that Emancipation had been fought for and won meant a break with the predominantly Protestant, Anglo-Irish nationalism of the past century. This process was unintentionally assisted by O'Connell's demagoguery, which tended to set Protestants—and many of the more conservative of his co-religionists—against him. In this period the description 'Protestant Ascendancy' took on a new meaning. Originally used about the Junta in pre-Union days, it came to embrace almost the whole Protestant population, who joined with the 'Castle Catholics' in support of the Union and the administration. The growth of Catholic nationalism also helped to increase the division of opinion between the predominantly Protestant districts of the North and the rest of the country. At the same time, Ulster industry was surviving the Union better than industry elsewhere, and as it began to depend on the British market, its beneficiaries lost what sympathy they had with separatism. The Ulster Dissenters, relieved of their disabilities, shed the resentment that had made them Tone's closest supporters. Characteristically, when a new opposition newspaper appeared in the Twenties in Belfast, it was called the *Northern Whig*, looking to the English reformers, not to O'Connell, for its inspiration. It was not long before the Protestant Ulsterman began to think of himself as in some way distinct from Southerners, and to pursue his own way unmindful of their controversies.

Hardly less important was the effect of the Emancipation campaign upon the future of Anglo-Irish relations. For a quarter of a century Catholic Emancipation had been one of the corrosive issues at Westminster, from the time it tumbled Pitt out of office until it forced Wellington and Peel to deny their consciences and repudiate their political promises, in order to carry it against their own Tory followers. That they gave way to the threat of an Irish insurrection was itself ominous for the future—as the Clare election had been, at which O'Connell's victory had proved that the Irish land-lord could no longer be relied upon to control his tenants' votes in his interests. Much would depend on whether O'Connell would choose to make his next move at West-minster or among his own green fields. His choice showed that Emancipation had not satisfied him; it had merely stimulated his appetite. Hardly was Emancipation in the statute book when he opened his campaign for repeal of the Union.

Events were later to show that his instinct was not basically unsound: that the demand for separatism, virtually extinguished since 1803, could be revived. But it was a process which would take time. The mass of the Catholic peasantry, on whom O'Connell so largely relied, were occu-pied with a more pressing issue—their war against the pay-ment of tithes to the Established Church. In any case, before the repeal movement was fully under way, O'Connell was side-tracked by his new interests at Westminster. His ex-perience of the Reform Bill (one Reading was passed by a single vote) had suggested to him that he might be able to play off party against party in the Commons; and to the dismay of some of his followers he suddenly abandoned Repeal of the Union in favour of an alliance with the Whigs. Had it not been for the intense dislike which a few influential Whigs felt for him, he would have been given office in the administration.

O'Connell, in fact, was not a dogmatic separatist. He had been one of the most fervent demonstrators in favour of the Crown during the royal visit in 1821; and at any time, he would have been satisfied with the Union provided that it could be made to work for the good of his fellow country-men. For a while, during the early years of the Melbourne administration of 1835-41, he sincerely devoted himself to the attempt to remedy Ireland's ills by constitutional parlia-mentary methods; while in Dublin the ablest of Irish Under

Secretaries, Thomas Drummond, was employing a firm but conciliatory policy designed to increase the country's prosperity. The results were reflected in a diminution of unrest, so that up to 1838 it could reasonably have been argued that a constitutional policy, if conscientiously adopted, could bring the benefits O'Connell had promised.

But the policy had fatal drawbacks. It was dependent not only on the Commons, where Whig party discipline might be expected to secure majorities, but on the Lords; and the Lords, though they might feel constrained to be careful about throwing out measures popular in England, thought nothing about throwing out Irish Bills. Melbourne's Irish projects were either rejected outright, or so mutilated that they were barely recognisable. O'Connell's reputation at home, too, was weakened by the twists and turns made necessary by the party game. He might know in his own mind that—say—a defiant speech threatening 'Repeal' was merely designed to scare the Whigs into accepting his terms. But his Irish followers might interpret it as an expression of unequivocal separatism. They would be disillusioned when the next day, his terms accepted, he was treating the Whigs as brothers. It happened more than once that his followers were tried, sentenced and jailed for printing speeches he had made attacking a Government with which he had since been reconciled, and with whose leaders he was again on dining terms. Inevitably all but the most loyal of his colleagues fell away disillusioned. By 1839 his influence was so diminished that an attempt to revive the Repeal campaign met at first with blank apathy.

Nor was the influence of Irish questions on English politics —in spite of the personality of O'Connell—as great as it appeared. On the occasions that Governments were changed, or fell, on Irish issues, they were usually the excuse rather than the fundamental cause. For example, if an individual minister wished to resign owing to growing differences of opinion with his colleagues which he was not anxious to disclose to the electorate, he could always seek out some

Irish issue about which his constituents would not care one way or the other—as Edward Stanley did, when he wanted to switch from the Whig to the Tory side. Similarly, should an opposition wish to defeat a Government without incurring the odium of opposing some popular measure, it, too, sought some Irish pretext for the decisive vote. With the exception of Emancipation—also an issue in England—issues in which the Irish were really interested did not make or unmake Governments. Where Irish Bills were put forward and defeated, the Government could put the blame on the Lords, and O'Connell was helpless.

The fact was that English politicians were not interested in Irish affairs. Their feelings about Ireland ranged from the positive dislike of the majority of Tories to the negative conciliatoriness of Melbourne, who was prepared to grant the Irish anything which kept them contented, provided that it did not cause him any trouble in England. Melbourne had been Chief Secretary for a year in Ireland in the 1820's, and had won a reputation for being hardworking, co-operative and just; but his correspondence reveals that his only positive policy was to let sleeping dogs lie, and to soothe them back to sleep the moment they awoke. Although he employed the policy with remarkable skill in his alliance with O'Connell, it could not succeed indefinitely; and its failure helped to disillusion not only O'Connell but later generations of Irishmen over the fruits of Westminster, tilting the balance in Ireland further towards unconstitutional methods.

The Repeal movement eventually revived under, but not because of, O'Connell's leadership. In 1842 three young men, Thomas Davis, John Blake Dillon and Charles Gavan Duffy, established a weekly, the Nation, whose influence in Ireland was never surpassed by any newspaper before or since. O'Connell's newspapers had rarely been able to reach a circulation of four figures: the Nation reached five—twice as many copies per issue as any Irish paper had reached before —within a few weeks of publication. A newspaper naturally could have little direct sway on the largely illiterate peasants, but they came in behind O'Connell; the *Nation* rallied 'Young Ireland,' all the liberal and nationalist elements behind Repeal. O'Connell was able to revive the methods of the Emancipation campaign, and with even more striking effect. His meetings in the country attracted hundreds of thousands of people, in strict order and sobriety (partly owing to the astonishing success of a temperance campaign that had just been completed in Ireland by Father Mathew). Nothing comparable to these meetings has been known in any country. O'Connell's reputation rose not only in Ireland, but on the Continent, where the historian Macaulay found to his annoyance that everybody he met, regardless of station, had only one question about British politics—'what will be done with O'Connell?'

Outwardly O'Connell was in a stronger position than he had been in 1829. But by this time he was in his sixties. Although he was determined to secure Repeal, the horror of bloodshed that he had felt throughout his life (it had been reinforced by his killing of a man who had challenged him to a duel) remained. Repeal—he insisted—was not worth a drop of Irish blood. Even at the greatest of his monster meetings at Tara, the one-time capital of the High Kings, he reiterated his antipathy to rebellion. He imagined that the simple threat of overwhelming force would be enough to move Peel and Wellington, once again in power, as it had fourteen years before. But Peel, who had learned much in the interval, called O'Connell's bluff. The Government proscribed a monster meeting billed to take place on the site of Brian Boru's victory at Clontarf, calling out the military to underwrite the ban. O'Connell, wavering, cancelled the meeting; the Government followed up its advantage promptly by arresting him and some of his Repeal colleagues, including Gavan Duffy. Neither this nor their condemnation and prison sentences was sufficient to spark off the once explosive material. It has been damped out by the Clontarf fiasco. Repeal, in its O'Connellite version, was finished.

O'Connell was only a few months in prison, as the

sentences were quashed on a technicality by the English Law Lords. But he came out a changed man, suffering, it must be assumed, from the disease of which he died three years later. Growing increasingly jealous of the popularity of the Young Irelanders, he quarrelled with them, only to find that authority had melted from him. In the Repeal Association he tended to leave affairs in the control of his son John; John's narrow sectarianism helped to widen the rift with the Young Irelanders, many of whom were Protestants, and his general incompetence further weakened the movement. For a time it seemed as if an alternative to straight Repeal might be found which had a better prospect of success: federalism. A federal government for Ireland was attractive to some Protestants and conservatives who baulked at separatism and wished to retain the English connection. But the movement threw up no leader, and achieved no real strength. Its failure left Young Ireland as the strongest political force facing the Government.

But just as he was most needed, its inspiration, Thomas Davis, died. Davis was a man in the Tone mould, with a breadth of vision and nobility of character that Tone could not match. Tone had thought of the peasants as potential allies; Davis saw them, more idealistically, as the descendants—and in time, he hoped, the reincarnation—of the old Ireland. His aim was not simply political, but cultural, in the widest sense. His was the guiding spirit of Young Ireland; his views continued to dominate the *Nation*, even after his death, through the prose of Gavan Duffy, a man raised above himself by Davis's friendship, and through the poetry of James Clarence Mangan. As a recent Irish historian has put it Davis 'once for all, established in Irish nationalist thought the principle of *Irish* nationality, including and uniting every race and every class and every creed. Since his day Irish nationalist thought has never wavered from that central principle, the building up of an Irish nation here which shall include Gael and Norman and English, Catholic and Protestant.'

Whether Davis would have been able to take over political

leadership successfully must remain an open question. Without him, Young Ireland was left rudderless. And in the month he died the first news came of a disaster which was to make even his loss seem insignificant: the potato blight, heralding the Great Famine of the next three years.

♣ Five ♣

1845 - 1921

The Irish had suffered in many a famine before, but never one on this scale. Far from assisting the Repealers the Famine increased their difficulties. A hungry peasant may make a dangerous rebel; a starving peasant thinks only of his next meal. In any case the Repealers were divided by the continuing quarrels between the dying O'Connell, backed by his sons, and the Young Irelanders. The final breach came in 1846; after efforts to heal it had been unsuccessful the Young Irelanders formed the Irish Confederation, still with repeal as its chief aim, but shedding the strict O'Connellite constitutionalism.

The nominal leader of Young Ireland by this time was Smith O'Brien. Like Davis, O'Brien was a Protestant. He was also a landowner, and a former M.P.; his acquisition had been considered of great value to the Repeal movement, of which he had been put in charge while O'Connell was in jail. Although his sympathies were with Young Ireland, in his attitude to physical force and to property rights he differed little from O'Connell; his was a restraining rather than a stimulating leadership. A far more forceful personality in Young Ireland by 1947 was John Mitchel, one of the few Ulster Protestants in the movement. Mitchel quickly grew dissatisfied with progress made by evolutionary means; he began to advocate revolution in their place. To supplement the campaign in Parliament he urged systematic opposition to the law in Ireland, under the guidance of a strong national party which would be ready to take over as soon as paralysis began to afflict the administration. The tone of his contributions to the *Nation* grew too violent for the majority of Young Ireland, and particularly for Smith O'Brien; Mitchel therefore left the Confederation to found a newspaper of his own, the *United Irishman*, from which he poured forth a cascade of corrosive articles the like of which had not been seen since the Drapier's day.

He attracted, too, the pen of another writer, James Fintan Lalor, who gave a new twist to the separatist movement. Lalor despised Repeal, because he considered political gains by themselves immaterial; the first objective, he insisted, should be to secure the land of Ireland for the people of Ireland. Mitchel was attracted to Lalor's ideas because they pointed a way by which the peasantry could be given a direct interest in the coming rebellion. Smith O'Brien naturally was not impressed.

This disharmony between the two Young Ireland wings, with its embarrassing echoes of the Young Ireland/O'Connell quarrels, was not of long duration; the success of the revolution in France swung even Smith O'Brien in favour of force. Young Ireland, however, was utterly unprepared for a rebellion, whereas the Government—forewarned by Mitchel's stridency—was ready to deal with it. Mitchel was arrested and sentenced to transportation; before the others were able to complete their preparations, sufficient arrests had been made virtually to behead the movement, and the rising was on an even more insignificant scale than Emmet's. What little hopes it had were destroyed by the gentlemanly methods —more appropriate to a football match than to an insurrection—insisted upon by the Young Ireland leaders, particularly Smith O'Brien. So feeble was their showing that the Government found it possible to be lenient. Although Smith O'Brien and others were sentenced to death, they were reprieved, and the sentences commuted to transportation for life.

The rebellion was to have an influence disproportionate to its immediate results. The fact that they had taken up arms endowed the Young Irelanders with virtue in the eyes of later nationalists; their courage was remembered, their incompetence forgotten. And they left a body of written work whose influence, unlike that of most patriotic journalism, was lasting. Articles and verse from the *Nation*, essays by Davis, Mitchel's *Jail Journal* and Lalor's letters continued to be read; and the moral drawn from them was not that rebellion was foredoomed to failure, but that it must be tried and tried again until it achieved success.

The rising created a bad impression in England. The Irish were felt to have displayed the meanest ingratitude for the help the English had given to them during the Famine; and the resentment was reflected in an Act unimportant in itself but significant in its illustration of the weakness inherent in the Union of the two countries. Many of the Boards which administered the Poor Law in Ireland had become bankrupt during the Famine, and a law was passed compelling those Irish Poor Law districts which had remained solvent to make up the deficit. If Britain and Ireland were really a single administrative unit, the Irish argued, the British Poor Law authorities, too, should have contributed their share. In spite of the constant emphasis on the political unity of the two countries, the impression remained in Britain as well as in Ireland that the two countries were in fact still separate; that expenses incurred in Ireland ought to be borne by the Irish alone, unless the English chose to exercise charity.

Irish separatism as a political force, however, was for a time discouraged by the collapse of the '48. In its place there was a reversion to O'Connell's methods of the '20's, based on the presumption that Irish agitation should rely on strong but law-abiding associations in Ireland. The first problem was the status of the tenants. Landowners were trying to clear the land of unprofitable tenantry, and the tenantry had no redress. A tenants' protective league was therefore formed on the model of O'Connell's associations; Gavan Duffy who, alone of the Young Irelanders, had managed to escape conviction (he had the good fortune to secure a succession of juries that were unable to agree) became its most influential figure.

The Tenant League pledged its support to those Irish
M.P.'s who, in their turn, were willing to pledge themselves
to keep aloof from office or other party ties at Westminster
until justice for the tenants was secured. But the relations
between the League and its parliamentary representatives
were not happy. As a former rebel Gavan Duffy was suspect
in the eyes of the conservatives in the movement, who had
for their mentor the formidable Cardinal Cullen, the Catholic
Primate, a man on the Rinuccini model. A group of Irish
M.P.'s led by John Sadleir and William Keogh traded on
Cullen's credulity to secure his support, which they repaid
with such slavish adulation that they won the title of 'the
Pope's Brass Band'. To such men the Tenant League was
useful only as a step to preferment. League M.P.s were returned in sufficient numbers at the General Election of 1852
to help the Whigs eject a Tory ministry from office; they
should also have been numerous enough to obtain concessions from the new Government. But the Government
realised that Sadleir and Keogh might be tempted by the
offer of ministerial posts. The posts were offered, and
accepted; the defection broke up the Tenant League. Gavan
Duffy left the country in despair, to carve out for himself
(as did many of the United Irishmen and Young Irelanders) a
distinguished career in exile; he was to become Prime
Minister of Victoria. Keogh became a judge; presiding over
the trials of later patriots, he was to be a living reminder to
Irish nationalists of the dangers of allowing their leaders to
play the English party game. Sadleir was soon afterwards
unmasked as a swindler, and committed suicide; a dead
reminder to them how easily the profession of piety can
provide a cloak for fraud.

The collapse of the Tenant League for a time discredited
parliamentary methods no less effectively than the collapse
of '48 had discredited force; and once again the English
Government was able to take advantage of the period of
bewilderment and frustration that followed.

When Pitt had carried through the Union of the two

countries, recognising that Ireland would be financially very much the weaker partner he had allowed her to retain different rates of taxation; his intention was that the two economies should be merged when Ireland's finances improved sufficiently to enable her to share the burden. Ireland's economic position, however, had continued to deteriorate relative to England's after the Union until the Famine made it clear that Pitt's expectations would never be realised. What Pitt had hoped would be made possible by Ireland's strength was accomplished by taking advantage of her weakness; her finances were 'assimilated' with England's, saddling her with what a Royal Commission was later to pronounce an unjustifiably high proportion of the revenue.

The political lull could not be lasting. During and after the Famine hundreds of thousands of Irishmen had sought escape from starvation by boarding emigrant ships for America. Their sufferings from the Famine itself and the horrors of the Atlantic crossing made an indelible impression on the minds of the survivors; the difficulties which faced them in America, where by flooding the labour market they made themselves feared and hated, helped to keep alive their sense of injustice and of nationality. Among them were many men who had been attracted by the ideas of Young Ireland. For them, few prospects could be more alluring than that of another rebellion in Ireland. If it succeeded, they might be restored to their rights. From these men sprang a new rebel movement, which quickly spread to Ireland and to England: Fenianism.

Its core was the Irish Republican Brotherhood, a secret oath-bound organisation stemming from the Wolfe Tone tradition. Its outstanding figure, John O'Leary, named Thomas Davis as well as Tone as his guide; and some of the Fenians combined the conspiratorial technique of the United Irishmen with the wider belief in an Irish Ireland that Davis had preached. Although there were fewer Protestants in the movement, it came from much the same class as Young Ireland; its leaders were men of culture, intellectual, mainly town-bred. They rejected constitutionalism on the one hand as a waste of effort; on the other, they had little sympathy with the tenant right movement, which they thought a side-issue.

But the Fenians suffered from the ailments traditional to national movements. When preparations for a rising—including the organisation of Fenian cells in the army in Ireland—were almost complete, a split occurred in the Brotherhood in America, which prevented the shipment of arms. Informers gave away secrets in Ireland; the Government was able to arrest the leaders before their final arrangements were made; and the rebellion which broke out in 1867 was no more effectual than that of 1848.

For the first time, however, the Irish war of independence was carried to England. In an attempt to rescue some Fenian prisoners, a wall of Clerkenwell jail was blown up, the explosion killing and injuring many people. Another attempt to rescue Fenian prisoners, in Manchester, led to the accidental shooting of a police officer, for which three Fenians were hanged. These men at once became known and remained known as the 'Manchester Martyrs'; the fact that their sentence was justified in English law only helped to propagate the belief in Ireland that English law must be thrust aside. From this and other incidents the English received two lessons: that the problem of Irish separatism could no longer be regarded as confined to Ireland; and that reprisals, even when carried out within the law, could arouse separatist feeling in Ireland more effectively than the teachings and actions of the separatists themselves. This point struck men of as different a cast of mind as William Ewart Gladstone and the Communist, Friedrich Engels. To Gladstone 'the influence of Fenianism was this—that when the Habeas Corpus Act was suspended, when all the consequent proceedings occurred, when the tranquility of the great city of Manchester was disturbed, when the metropolis itself was shocked and horrified by an inhuman outrage, when a sense of insecurity went abroad far and wide—then it was when these phenomena came home to the popular mind, and produced that attitude of attention and preparedness on the part of the whole population of this country which qualified them to embrace in a manner foreign to their habits in other times, the vast import of the Irish controversy.' To Engels, the Manchester executions marked the definite deed of separation between England and Ireland. From that date it was no longer a question of whether separatism would survive, but in what form, and how long it would take before its pressure became too overwhelming. The Irish Republican Brotherhood remained in existence, and was to continue to influence policy with gradually growing assurance until independence was won.

The Fenians' immediate successors, however, were constitutionalist 'Home Rulers', led by a barrister, Isaac Butt. Butt came of Protestant Ascendancy stock and in his youth had been the most effective advocate of the Union, succeeding so well that Young Irelanders and, later, Fenians preferred to entrust their defence to him in their trials for treason rather than to a repealer. In defending them Butt became convinced that some measure of administrative independence was necessary to prevent such uprisings—to remove the causes that drove these men, whom he came to like and admire, to conspiracy and violence. The movement's design was not to overthrow the English connection, but 'to obtain for our country the right and privilege of managing our own affairs by a parliament assembled in Ireland . . . to secure for the parliament under a federal arrangement the right of legislating for and regulating all matters relating to the internal affairs of Ireland. To leave to the imperial parliament the power of dealing with all questions affecting the Imperial Crown and Government, the relations of the United Empire with foreign states, and all matters appertaining to the defence and stability of the Empire at large'. It was on such a basis that the British Commonwealth was eventually to be founded: at the time, Westminster found the idea a joke. Although Butt secured a considerable following among Irish M.P.s, his

scheme was ridiculed in England as undesirable or impracticable or both—its opponents using the identical arguments
Butt had himself used against O'Connell. English politicians
found it easy to demonstrate that on the practical question
of Home Rule—how much self-government Ireland was to
be allowed, and what form it should take—the proposals
were imprecise; and Butt lacked the qualities to be able to
convince a hostile audience that these complications, serious
though they appeared, were trifles compared to the problems
that would arise if concessions were refused.

The qualities that Butt lacked were supplied in the character of one of his young lieutenants, Charles Stewart Parnell.
Parnell was an Anglo-Irish country gentleman, in whom
latent nationalism had been aroused by the fate of the
'Manchester Martyrs'. He threw himself into the Home
Rule movement, welcomed at first (as Smith O'Brien had
been) for his Ascendancy background, but soon feared as
more revolutionary than its nominal leader, Butt. The temper
of the times in Ireland was in any case working against Butt's
conservatism. In the late 1870s a combination of poor harvests
and falling prices for agricultural produce provoked a fresh
outbreak of hostility between landlord and tenant. A new
Land League sprang up under Michael Davitt, whose family
had been evicted after the Famine and who had himself
suffered imprisonment as a Fenian. Davitt was a disciple of
Mitchel and Lalor rather than of Young Ireland. He realized,
as nobody had realized before, that the chances of success
for nationalism depended largely upon co-operation between
the different nationalist elements, revolutionary and constitutional; if the constitutionalists could be induced to become
sufficiently revolutionary, he thought, it might be possible
to forge an alliance between them and what was left of
Fenianism. The use of obstruction at Westminster was an
indication that the constitutionalists were moving in this
direction. So was the rise of Parnell. Parnell for his part felt
about Davitt much as Smith O'Brien had felt about Lalor;
but Parnell was prepared to make an ally of the Land League

both to control it and to use it to further his parliamentary aims. Davitt for his part was impressed with Parnell, 'an Englishman of the strongest type', he thought, 'moulded for an Irish purpose'; and he felt that constitutional agitation of the Parnell type would be vigorous enough to secure the co-operation even of the former Fenians, for all their mistrust of such methods. In this belief Davitt was correct. Under Parnell all the strands of separatist feeling were more firmly plaited than at any other time in the country's history.

Parnell's aim was to secure concessions from Britain by any means in his power short of actual revolution. Land League violence he would tacitly condone, though rarely countenance, so long as it was of the sporadic, seemingly disorganised nature that would serve him for an illustration of the impossibility of keeping Ireland in subjection. He carefully avoided the trap that had snared earlier Irish parliamentarians; by embarking with his fellow Irish M.P.s on a policy of systematic obstruction in debates in the Commons he was able not only to bring the English parliamentary system to the verge of breakdown, but also to reassure his fellow countrymen that their representatives were doing their patriot duty, and not merely playing the parliamentary game. Therein lay the essential difference between the old and the new Home Rule policies. Butt disapproved of obstruction, because he wanted to gain his point by the power of reasoned argument: when reasoned argument was obviously going to fail, Parnell preferred instead to make himself so much of a nuisance that the English Parliament would be glad to see his back. Only by giving up some cherished traditions of free debate were the Commons able to get through their business.

Parnell's first real test came in 1881. Gladstone, who had come into office the previous year, decided to answer the growing provocations of the Land Leaguers in Ireland and the Parnellites at Westminster with coercion; Parnell and several of the league's leaders were prosecuted. When the prosecution broke down, the Government decided to suspend *habeas corpus* in Ireland, in order to make it possible to im-

prison them without trial. The Parnellites fought the measure
bitterly in the Commons, so bitterly that at one time every
member of the party was suspended. It was passed; but their
angry tenacity had its effect on Gladstone. He decided that
there would have to be concession as well as coercion if
Ireland was to be pacified; and to that end he introduced a
Land Bill, giving a measure of protection to tenants. It did
not give everything that Davitt sought, but it conceded the
vital principle that the landlord's rights were no longer to
be considered absolute. From it stemmed all the later concessions on the land that were to transform Irish land ownership, in a few years, from alien and absentee landlordism to
peasant proprietorship.

In 1882 Parnell, Davitt and the other league leaders who
had been imprisoned were released; the way seemed clear
for their co-operation with Gladstone and the Liberals. But
the ghost of the violence born of the Fenian and the land war
years could not easily be stilled; hardly was the conciliatory
policy under way than it was wrecked by assassination. At
the time when the Irish leaders were in jail, and coercion
was at its most virulent, a gang of desperate men had banded
themselves together in a plot with murder as its aim. The
change of government policy did not change their resolution.
On the day Davitt was released, when Home Rule seemed
within measurable distance, the 'Invincibles' struck down
Lord Frederick Cavendish, the Liberal Chief Secretary, and
an Under Secretary, while they were walking in Phoenix
Park. Not all the expostulations of Parnell and Davitt could
clear them of suspicion. The effect in England was immediate: to press forward to Home Rule, in the circumstances, was impossible.

The Government's immediate reaction was another, more
drastic Coercion Act. Its result was to consolidate Irish
opinion behind Parnell, so that in the general election of
1885 the Irish nationalists won every seat in three provinces
and a small majority even in the Unionist stronghold of
Ulster. Parnell returned to Westminster with the balance of

power between Liberals and Conservatives there at his command.

By this time Gladstone had been converted to the Butt view of Home Rule, that it was necessary to give Ireland a measure of independence rather than continue to provoke revolutionary activity by repression. The Conservatives, who had themselves toyed with the idea of giving Ireland some self-government for the same reason, promptly changed their minds, and came out strongly in favour of the maintenance of the Union. More serious to Gladstone was the defection of Joseph Chamberlain, a Liberal supporter of Home Rule who deserted the cause in the hope of discrediting Gladstone and replacing him as leader of the party. Chamberlain took enough Liberals with him to defeat the Bill; and at a fresh General Election the Conservatives and Chamberlain's Liberal-Unionists were returned with a majority large enough to kill, for the time being, the prospects of Home Rule.

Still more damaging to these prospects, in the long run, was the line taken during the election campaign by Lord Randolph Churchill. Churchill had decided some time before that if Gladstone went for Home Rule 'the Orange card would be the one to play.' In his speeches he asserted that parliament could not leave the Protestants of Ireland in the lurch. It was a short step to the suggestion that Ulster, where Protestantism was entrenched, should if necessary 'resort to the supreme arbitrament of force; Ulster will fight, Ulster will be right.' The Ulster Protestants did not need much convincing. They had not been assimilated into Irish national-ism: in the towns, employers and workers wondered whether the commercial ties that bound them to Britain might be severed by Home Rule; and in the Ulster countryside the tenant farmers, long protected by local usage from extor-tionate landlords, had scarcely been caught up in the land campaigns of the South, and were consequently not indoctrin-ated with nationalist ideas. As Protestants the majority of the Ulstermen feared, or were capable of being made to fear, that Home Rule would turn out to be 'Rome Rule'—

domination and perhaps oppression of Protestant Ulster by the Catholic South. The Conservatives in Britain realised for their part that the Orange card was a trump. Eagerly they fanned smouldering religious differences into sectarian strife.

Under the Unionist Government—it was in this period that the Conservative party acquired the label 'Unionist' that clung to it long after Home Rule had ceased to be an issue—it became clear that Parnell's position was less strong than it appeared. He wished to bide his time, in the hope that Gladstone would return later with a decisive majority; but Davitt went ahead with another 'no rent' campaign, which in Parnell's view was only likely to give the Unionists the justification they required in the eyes of English public opinion for their opposition to Home Rule. Further justification appeared to be provided by letters published in *The Times* disclosing that Parnell had connived at the Phoenix Park assassination; although they were later proved to be forgeries some of the mud stuck. Finally, in 1890, Parnell was involved as co-respondent in a divorce suit, the husband possibly proceeding at Chamberlain's instigation. The case itself might not have irreparably damaged Parnell's position. At first the Irish parliamentary party stood by him, unanimously re-electing him its chairman. Gladstone, however, threatened to throw over the Home Rule cause unless Parnell renounced its leadership. The news split the party, a majority siding against Parnell. Although the minority stayed with him their loyalty only served further to weaken the Home Rule movement; the bitterness of the cruel feud between the two sections lasted long after Parnell's death in 1891 removed its cause.

Gladstone was not discouraged: when he returned to office in 1892 he managed to push a second Home Rule Bill through the Commons, but it foundered in the Lords. He would have been willing to risk a showdown with the Lords; but he was old and deaf and his eyesight was fast going; his colleagues, were adverse; the Irish party was split; and he decided instead to retire from public life. In any case, he would certainly have found the British electorate cool, even hostile, had he chosen to go to the country on the Home Rule issue. Without Parnell, too, the separatist strands had begun once again to unravel. Although Home Rule remained outwardly the aim, the movement lacked leadership, and the younger generation were turning away from it.

Returning to power in 1895 with an overwhelming majority, the Conservatives decided to take advantage of the comparative torpor of Irish nationalism to institute a new policy of 'killing Home Rule by kindness'. This was in effect a return to the policy of Peel, under which coercion was accompanied by administrative concessions designed to make the Irish more contented with their lot. Land Acts hurried on the transference of property from owner to tenant; Government Commissions made inquiries; Boards sprouted; grants and subsidies were given more lavishly than ever before in the country's history. It was, however, possible for the Irish to argue that the money was no more than a fraction of their just due. Shortly before his resignation Gladstone had ordered an investigation into the financial relations between the two countries; and the Commission's report revealed that Ireland had been systematically and heavily overtaxed (relative to her capacity to pay) since the Union. One of the stock arguments in favour of the Union had always been that poverty-stricken Ireland was the beneficiary by the link with her wealthier neighbour; here was proof that Lazarus had actually been subsidising Dives. In any case, kindness might kill Home Rule, but it came too late to destroy separatism; the comparative quiet of the closing years of the century were illusory.

The most important of separatist forces was the Irish Republican Brotherhood. It had lent its support to Parnell, and was willing to aid, and if possible direct, any movement that might stimulate the growth of a separatist outlook. At the same time, it was ready to set up a provisional government whenever it should be required. The Brotherhood's central figure was Tom Clarke, a Fenian who had spent

fifteen years in jail before his release in 1898. It was a sig-
nificent year to choose; his reappearance revived memories
not only of the Fenians but of the United Irishmen a century
before. Clarke's newsagent's shop became the still centre of
the republican cause; from it, the I.R.B. began to permeate into other organisations through which it could
exercise its influence without betraying its presence. In this,
it was following Mitchel's precept, that a separatist campaign
could be fought simultaneously on a number of fronts—
obstruction at Westminster, lawbreaking in Ireland, and
preparation for a direct blow at English rule the moment
that England found herself in difficulties—for example, in the
event of a war.

One of the organisations suited to its needs was the Gaelic
League, founded by Douglas Hyde in 1893. Hyde, another
Ascendancy product, never became a nationalist in the narrow
political sense; but out of his great love of the Irish language
developed a belief that Ireland would lose her nationality if
she allowed her ancient culture to die—no matter what
politicians or revolutionaries might do to secure her political
independence. Earlier language revival efforts had failed,
largely because they had suffered from academic anaemia.
Hyde's wider vision inspired a full-blooded movement; the
League stimulated a remarkable revival of interest in Ireland's past, her history, poetry, song and legend. From it
sprang a revival of the sense of Irishness that had tended to be
lacking in past separatist movements, in spite of Thomas
Davis's efforts. The Gaelic revival provided the common
ground for men as diverse as the poet W. B. Yeats; the
author-painter-poet George Russell ('A.E.'); and Padraic
Pearse, later to be the leader of the 1916 rising. According
to Pearse 'the Irish revolution really began when the seven
proto-Gaelic Leaguers met. . . . The germ of all future Irish
history was in that back room.'

Even before the foundation of the Gaelic League, the
Gaelic Athletic Association had been set up for the preservation and cultivation of national pastimes. As most of its

original members were former Fenians, the Association acquired and spread a separatist outlook among many men who would have had no interest in political nationalism.

On the political level the I.R.B. found another instrument in the Sinn Fein movement, founded early in the new century by Arthur Griffith. The roots of Sinn Fein, Griffith maintained, were in the United Irishmen, Young Ireland, and the Fenians; but Griffith himself grew temperamentally more in sympathy with the policy of Grattan and the Volunteers—he was no doctrinaire republican. A forceful journalist, he used his *United Irishman* to bring together into an awareness of a common purpose all the diverse nationalist bodies. This suited the I.R.B., even though they might not be wholly in sympathy with Sinn Fein policy. Into Sinn Fein, the literary societies and the clubs, the I.R.B. sent its members; they in turn selected and won over suitable recruits; and a small but well-organised revolutionary body was gradually built up.

Other nationalist forces were stirring, too, though of less direct interest to the I.R.B. Enthusiasm for home industry was being stimulated by another journalist, D. P. Moran, whose pungent articles in the *Leader* tried to goad the timid or somnolent Irish industrialists into activity. In the towns, too, the Labour movement began to assume importance. The first Irish Trades Union Congress was held in 1894; and in the new century the unions gathered strength under a redoubtable demagogue, James Larkin, and a shrewd socialist, James Connolly. Connolly diverted Irish Labour from the internationalist approach common to such movements at the time, in the direction of a vigorous nationalism. Examining the history of revolutionary movements in Ireland, he detected the germs of socialist thought in some of the writings and speeches of the United Irishmen, and of Mitchel, Lalor and Davitt. These he brought into relation with the socialist teachings of William Thompson of Roscarbery, County Cork, a forerunner of Marx, who as early as the 1820's had been arguing that 'as long as a class of mere capitalists

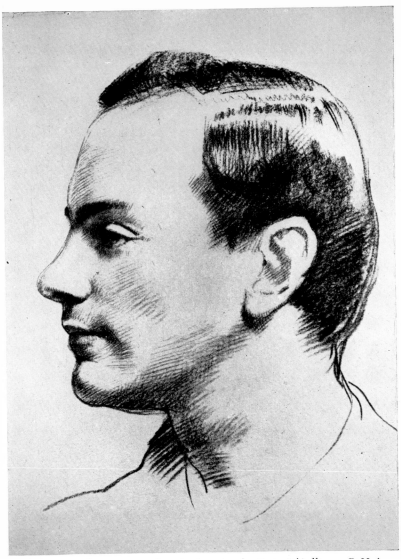

PLATE 2. Padraic Pearse: from a drawing by Sean O'Sullivan, R.H.A.

PLATE 3. Linen making in Belfast: the dye room (Northern Ireland Government Office)

exists society must remain in a diseased state. Whatever plunder is saved from the hand of political power will be levied in another way under the name of profit by capitalists who, while capitalists, must always be law makers.' Connolly's wide reading, lit by an incisive mind, made him a notable teacher to the infant Irish Labour movement, the more so because he grasped the need to modify the current international Socialist line to suit Irish conditions and particularly Irish nationalism. His ambition was to link nationalism to a Labour movement throughout the country; a point of view that did not commend itself to Griffith, whose reading of Irish history failed to shake his faith in capitalism. Nor did it please the I.R.B., who were unwilling to allow their pure separatism to be tainted with an alien socialist ideology. Connolly, therefore, went his own way, building up his own nationalist and socialist forces in Dublin.

All these movements—the Republican, Sinn Fein, Labour —won their main following in the towns. Just before the end of the century a new Land League of smallholders and landless men threatened to repeat the Davitt treatment, but another Land Act in 1903, acceding to their most pressing demands, lowered the political temperature again. From that time until the closing years of the Great War few farmers concerned themselves with nationalism in any of its forms.

By their attitude, they provided the authorities with a useful lesson: the policy of killing Home Rule by kindness could provide gratifying results where it was conscientiously applied. Tenants who were buying themselves (on very favourable terms) into the ownership of their land, and who were able to avail themselves of numerous state-provided facilities for rebuilding and re-equipping their farms, were unlikely to be attracted by nationalist conspiracies that might lead to a reversal of government policy, and a fresh bout of coercion. The Unionists were fortunate in that they had in their party a man of breadth of vision, Sir Horace Plunkett, whose co-operative movement was transparently not simply a device to keep the people politically contented; it represented a genuine effort to solve the land's most pressing problem, chronic under-development of its natural resources. The nationalists mistrusted Plunkettism, as well they might. Every benefit that Irish farmers received helped to make them more conservative, less inclined to hazard their gains on the throw of a national uprising.

At the same time, the authorities were given an opportunity to re-learn the old lesson that the converse was also true; that a policy of repression helped to create the spirit it was designed to destroy. In Dublin the young trade union movement encountered the implacable hostility of an industrialist, William Martin Murphy, who succeeded in convincing his fellow employers that concession to Labour would be the thin end of the wedge, rather than the stitch in time. They banded together to fight and defeat the Dublin workers in the great industrial dispute of 1913. The conflict was to leave even more bitter memories among Irish workers than the General Strike of 1926 was to leave in England. Its result, as 'A.E.' had warned the employers in a celebrated open letter, was to undermine the social order by encouraging workers to turn in despair to Connolly, in the conviction that only force could win them social justice.

All the strands of nationalism, in fact, loosely knotted as they were, could never have provided the rope by which the Irish people were to climb to political independence, if the policy of killing Home Rule by kindness had been more consistently adopted; for the speed and manner of their climb were determined less by the I.R.B. than by the policy, or lack of policy, of the Government.

This was fully demonstrated by the course of events at Westminster in the early years of the new century. Sinn Fein was a political by-product of Conservative rule—a separatist reaction to the unbending Unionism of the Government. But when the Liberals returned to office—and especially when, finding themselves once more dependent on the Irish votes for their majority, the Liberals re-opened the Home Rule issue—nationalist support flowed away from Sinn Fein back to the Irish parliamentary party, which for the first time since Parnell appeared to have a chance to secure independence by legislation. The divisions within the party were healing under the leadership of John Redmond; although in its constitutionalism the party savoured of the ways of Butt rather than of Parnell, this might even have helped to ease the passage of Home Rule through parliament, had the circumstances been more propitious.

But by this time Ulster had ceased to become a simple political problem. Egged on by Conservatives, the Ulster Protestants had decided to fight rather than to accept Home Rule; a few contemplated asking for German help—'If Protestant Georgie won't help us,' a poster ran, 'Protestant Willie will.' Throughout 1913 a Protestant Volunteer force was recruited, soon to be armed with rifles and ammunition smuggled in from the Continent. In England the Conservatives openly encouraged the Volunteers for personal as well as party ends. The party's leader, Bonar Law, was the son of an Ulster Presbyterian minister; Ulster was almost the only subject on which he had inflexible opinions. He really believed that a parliament in Dublin would mean the destruction of the Protestant North; and he was ready to sanction any intrigue, however hazardous, to prevent the granting of Home Rule. In this he was backed by Sir Edward Carson, the dominant personality of his day in Ireland—far more imposing than the nationalist leader Redmond—who set about converting Ulster into a powerful military camp. They were even prepared to use the party's majority in the House of Lords to reject the annual Army Bill, thereby putting military discipline into suspense and making army control over Ulster impossible.

The step proved unnecessary. The head of military operations at the War Office at the time was Sir Henry Wilson, a born intriguer who was not above passing on to Bonar Law and Carson confidential military information that might be useful against Home Rule. When early in 1914 some precautionary steps were to be taken to safeguard military supplies from possible Volunteer raids, some of the officers who would be responsible for their defence were prepared to resign, and Sir Henry supported their action when it was reported to the Government. The Secretary of State for War was even persuaded to give a definite undertaking that the army would not be used against the Home Rule Bill's opponents. Although this undertaking was quickly repudiated by the Government, the 'Curragh Mutiny' had had its effect; it had made clear that the army could not be relied upon to enforce Home Rule, if the Bill should be passed. It also, incidentally, caused grave concern in England; the suspicion that army officers had been encouraged to flout parliamentary decisions was not calculated to reassure parliament of its authority.

The combined strength of the Liberal and Irish parties might be sufficient to steer Home Rule through the Commons, and in time through the Lords, but a Bill was not enough, unless the way could be found to remove the threat of civil war. Asquith, the Liberal Prime Minister, toyed with various expedients before coming to the conclusion that the only feasible solution was to allow some of the counties of Ulster to be excluded from Home Rule. Before any final decision could be reached the Great War broke out; and although Home Rule was placed on the Statute Book a few weeks later, it was accompanied by another Bill suspending its operation indefinitely.

The reaction in Ulster, however, had already proved a decisive influence on the separatist movement in the rest of Ireland. The Ulster Volunteers, taking their tip from 1780, proclaimed that they had come into existence to protect the country from the threat of invasion. On the suggestion of Eoin MacNeill, a university professor and Gaelic enthusiast, a National Volunteer force was recruited in the South; and as the authorities were not prepared to put down the Ulstermen, they could not very well suppress the National Volunteers, either. This was exactly what the I.R.B. had hoped for. It quickly insinuated its men into the National Volunteer ranks, taking over their leadership, imposing discipline and

striving to fit the thousands of young men who had joined
with little or no nationalist sentiment into a single-minded
patriot force. The Irish parliamentary party found itself faced
with a formidable rival. Redmond decided that as he could
not prevent the volunteer movement from growing he had
better control it; and in 1914 he compelled the Volunteers
to 'strengthen' their executive by admitting his nominees,
which they felt bound to do in order to preserve the unity
of the nationalist cause.

As events turned out, the decision soon led to an irreparable
break. Redmond and the Irish party, accepting the postpone-
ment of Home Rule as an inevitable consequence of the outbreak of war, called upon the Volunteers to fight on the side
of the Allies to prove Ireland's right to full nationhood. To
the I.R.B., to Sinn Fein and to Labour this was a betrayal of
Mitchel's axiom that England's difficulty must be considered
Ireland's opportunity. The Volunteer movement split. The
minority, small in numbers but determined and well-
disciplined, stayed with Eoin MacNeill; alongside the Labour
Citizen Army they were to provide the soldiers of the 1916
rising.

Plans for the rising had been prepared by the supreme
council of the I.R.B. as soon as war appeared likely. The
difficulty remained, however, that even among the hard core
of separatists left after the Redmond Volunteers' breakaway
there were still serious divisions of opinion. Griffith in his
paper *Sinn Fein* denounced the action of the parliamentary
party, but he remained temperamentally out of sympathy
with MacNeill's Volunteers; MacNeill held different views
from the I.R.B. on the type of insurrection to be adopted;
and the I.R.B. had reason to fear that Connolly might bring
out his Citizen Army in a premature rising, which would
interfere with its own plans. In the end the I.R.B. settled the
Connolly difficulty by kidnapping him and holding him until
he agreed to co-operate; but a similar settlement could not
be reached with MacNeill, because MacNeill's objectives for
a rising differed fundamentally from those of the members

of the I.R.B. supreme council. MacNeill desired a full-scale military operation, for which help and supplies would have to be obtained from Germany; he was prepared to postpone the rising until it had a good prospect of success. The I.R.B., was determined to carry through its plans even if they were obviously doomed to failure, on the assumption that a blood sacrifice would attract, or shame, waverers into the cause of the Republic. Padraic Pearse, in particular, had more than once expressed his conviction that such a sacrifice might be necessary. In his panegyric at the grave of the Fenian, O'Donovan Rossa, in 1915 he said 'Life springs from death; and from the graves of patriot men and women spring living nations'; and on other occasions he had indicated that more graves might have to be dug before the nation could live.

By this time, Pearse was the virtual leader of the militant wing of the separatist movement. The son of an English father and an Irish mother, he had been attracted by the Gaelic movement at an early age; and with the desire to inculcate the idea of a Gaelic and independent Ireland he took up teaching; his school, St. Enda's, was notably progressive for the time. His writings reveal a keen, sensitive mind—as had also his helper at St. Enda's, Thomas Mac-Donagh. Although Pearse was still in his early thirties, his influence on the revolutionary council was such that he was made President of the shadow Republican Government; and it is probably to him, more than any other individual, that the project of a planned offensive insurrection (as distinct from emergency operations—say, to forestall Government action to disarm the Volunteers) owed its acceptance.

The date decided upon for the rising was Easter 1916. So well did the conspirators keep their secret that not even their fellow-members of the Brotherhood who were opposed to the idea heard of it, until too late for them to prevent it. Pearse used the news of the imminent arrival of a German ship, laden with arms, as an excuse to win over MacNeill, on the grounds that the opportunity would be too good to be missed; but when the ship was intercepted by the British, and the news followed that Sir Roger Casement, who had arrived in a submarine from Germany to assist in the rising, had been captured, MacNeill, as Chief of Staff of the Volunteers, countermanded the plans which had been laid for a rising on Easter Sunday. By this time the militants had their minds made up; they issued fresh orders for a 'route march' on Easter Monday. That morning about 1,500 men, rather more than half of them Volunteers and the rest from the Citizen Army, obeyed the usual summons to parade, to find that they were being called upon not for the usual 'manoeuvres' but for rebellion. They occupied the General Post Office in the centre of Dublin; and from its steps, Pearse proclaimed the birth of the Irish Republic as a sovereign independent state.

The rebels held out for less than a week. Hostilities were mainly in Dublin, around the few rebel strongpoints; only in a few country districts were the local constabulary called out to deal with insurgents. The Irish people were at first puzzled and annoyed; the rising received little public sympathy and less support, and had the authorities contented themselves with rounding up and interning the rebels, 1916 would have joined 1803, 1848 and 1867, as an example of the senselessness of insurrection. But the Ascendancy had been badly frightened. The authorities felt humiliated and resentful; they retaliated by executing Pearse, Connolly, Clarke and the other rebel leaders—not all together, in hot blood, but in ones and twos, over a period of days. The reaction was immediate and lasting. Bernard Shaw characteristically pointed out in a letter to the English press that it was 'impossible to slaughter a man in this position without making him a martyr and a hero, even though the day before the rising he may only have been a minor poet'. Even Redmond, though disgusted at the rising, begged for clemency; and among the nationalists who had consistently opposed the use of armed force, and who had regarded the rising as a stupid and dangerous mistake, the executions produced a revulsion of feeling that found its expression in Yeats's 1916 poems.

Constitutionalist nationalism of the traditional parliamentary type appeared anaemic when set beside the uncompromising republicanism of the insurgents. Within a few months, the whole weight of the nationalist movement had become separatist. Griffith had not been connected with the rising, but his prestige was such that this was not counted against him; and his Sinn Fein, though it had appeared moribund, provided the organisation required—it was as a Sinn Fein candidate that Count Plunkett, father of one of the executed rebel leaders, went forward at a by-election in 1917, revealing by his victory the way the nationalist tide was flowing. Soon afterward Eamonn de Valera, who had been sentenced to death in 1916 but reprieved, decisively won another by-election, caused by the death in action on the Western front of Will Redmond, one of the most popular of the Irish parliamentary party. The party's influence collapsed, never to recover. Constitutional nationalism in fact became almost synonymous with treachery; although 'A.E.' in moving verses sought to show that Redmond and Pearse had both died for their country, men who had fought on England's side on the western front came to be regarded as little better than mercenaries.

The English Government's reaction to the revival of Sinn Fein only helped to consolidate Sinn Fein's position. In the first place, the character of the Prime Minister, Lloyd George, inspired trust neither in the Home Rulers nor, later, in Sinn Fein. Time was to show that their suspicions were well-founded. To Redmond he offered 26-county Home Rule, leading him to think that the separation of the remaining six counties would only be temporary, and that they would be brought in as soon as the war ended. To the Ulster leaders he promised that whether the six counties wished it or not, they would never be allowed to go in with the other twenty-six. On the basis of this piece of deception he was able to secure an agreement with both parties—but not with his own cabinet. Resignations followed; Lloyd George, rather than forfeit office, abandoned his own scheme, helping to

POBLACHT NA H EIREANN.

THE PROVISIONAL GOVERNMENT
OF THE
IRISH REPUBLIC
TO THE PEOPLE OF IRELAND.

IRISHMEN AND IRISHWOMEN: In the name of God and of the dead generations from which she receives her old tradition of nationhood, Ireland, through us, summons her children to her flag and strikes for her freedom.

Having organised and trained her manhood through her secret revolutionary organisation, the Irish Republican Brotherhood, and through her open military organisations, the Irish Volunteers and the Irish Citizen Army, having patiently perfected her discipline, having resolutely waited for the right moment to reveal itself, she now seizes that moment, and, supported by her exiled children in America and by gallant allies in Europe, but relying in the first on her own strength, she strikes in full confidence of victory.

We declare the right of the people of Ireland to the ownership of Ireland, and to the unfettered control of Irish destinies, to be sovereign and indefeasible. The long usurpation of that right by a foreign people and government has not extinguished the right, nor can it ever be extinguished except by the destruction of the Irish people. In every generation the Irish people have asserted their right to national freedom and sovereignty; six times during the past three hundred years they have asserted it in arms. Standing on that fundamental right and again asserting it in arms in the face of the world, we hereby proclaim the Irish Republic as a Sovereign Independent State, and we pledge our lives and the lives of our comrades-in-arms to the cause of its freedom, of its welfare, and of its exaltation among the nations.

The Irish Republic is entitled to, and hereby claims, the allegiance of every Irishman and Irishwoman. The Republic guarantees religious and civil liberty, equal rights and equal opportunities to all its citizens, and declares its resolve to pursue the happiness and prosperity of the whole nation and of all its parts, cherishing all the children of the nation equally, and oblivious of the differences carefully fostered by an alien government, which have divided a minority from the majority in the past.

Until our arms have brought the opportune moment for the establishment of a permanent National Government, representative of the whole people of Ireland and elected by the suffrages of all her men and women, the Provisional Government, hereby constituted, will administer the civil and military affairs of the Republic in trust for the people.

We place the cause of the Irish Republic under the protection of the Most High God, Whose blessing we invoke upon our arms, and we pray that no one who serves that cause will dishonour it by cowardice, inhumanity, or rapine. In this supreme hour the Irish nation must, by its valour and discipline and by the readiness of its children to sacrifice themselves for the common good, prove itself worthy of the august destiny to which it is called.

Signed on Behalf of the Provisional Government,

THOMAS J. CLARKE,

SEAN Mac DIARMADA,   THOMAS MacDONAGH,
P. H. PEARSE,   EAMONN CEANNT,
JAMES CONNOLLY.   JOSEPH PLUNKETT.

remove what little confidence was left in Ireland in English good faith.

Secondly, in the spring of 1918 Lloyd George proposed to apply conscription to Ireland. He could hardly have chosen a better way to convince the non-political Irish—the farmers, particularly—of the value of the national independence movement. Thirdly, the Government decided to arrest every known Sinn Fein leader, following a German invasion scare. The move put control into the hands of one of the few leaders to escape arrest—Michael Collins, a military organizer of genius. In this period he received, and imparted to subordinates, the training that was to have remarkable results in the guerilla warfare of the next two years.

If Lloyd George hoped that the arrests would make it impossible for Sinn Fein properly to contest the 1918 General Election, he was disappointed. Sinn Fein went to the country on an outright republican programme; and it won 73 out of the 105 Irish seats. The result justified Sinn Fein's project of withdrawing the elected Irish members from Westminster, and setting them up as a Constituent Assembly in Dublin: and it revealed to England—and to the world in general—that the sympathies of the Irish people really were decisively separatist.

The Constituent Assembly—'Dail Eireann'—met in January 1919. Only 28 members attended: the Ulster Unionists stayed away, and half the Sinn Fein members were in prison, including de Valera, who as the only surviving 1916 leader had been elected President of Sinn Fein. But the mere fact that the assembly met, and functioned, helped to establish the idea that an independent Ireland was a practical possibility.

The authorities were in a difficulty. They could no longer make concessions, because such was the strength of the separatist movement by this time that no concession that it was politically possible to offer would have been considered. On the other hand, they did not care to adopt a violently repressive policy, out of respect for public opinion in England and in America. An attempt to find a compromise between repression and concession failed. As Sinn Fein's confidence grew, the authorities found themselves compelled to take more repressive measures; and eventually the decision was made to recruit in England an additional security force, half-way between police and military, soon to be known in Ireland from the colours of their makeshift uniforms as the Black and Tans. It was believed in Ireland, and still is, that this force was recruited largely from English jails; and although this account of its origins has been denied, the conduct of its members in Ireland left an indelible impression. By this time the war of reprisals and counter-reprisals was in full swing; and 'the Tans', new to the country, were not in a position to know where to strike. They would often raid the houses of Unionist families—sometimes of men who actually had sons serving in the British forces; they became even more unpopular, if possible, with the Unionists than with Sinn Fein—which was naturally not sorry to see public opinion veer sharply against the British. To this day 'the Tans' are remembered with a hatred and a bitterness more intense than any engendered in Ireland since the time of Cromwell.

From 1919-21, guerilla warfare was waged through the country, and gradually the grip of the nationalist forces strengthened. Sinn Fein obtained control of much of the machinery of government, and, following a precedent set by militant peasant organisations in the eighteenth century, set up law courts which even the Unionists had to use—and their justice was praised even in the Unionist press. Lloyd George began to realise that the attempt to hold Ireland by force in the hope that the republicans would lose support had failed: that in England, public opinion was becoming disillusioned and disgusted with an Irish policy whose unappetizing consequences were being daily denounced in the liberal press; and that American feeling was growing increasingly hostile. He decided to give way. In June 1921 he invited de Valera, as the recognised leader of the Irish national movement, to come to England to discuss terms of peace.

By recognising de Valera's right to act as spokesman, Lloyd George had in effect conceded Ireland's claim to nationhood. There remained to be decided what degree of independence she should be permitted; and, also, what should be done about Ulster. Neither of these problems could be solved without breaking past promises. The Irish leaders were irrevocably pledged not to accept anything short of a republic, and not to allow the country to be divided. Lloyd George was equally irrevocably pledged not to grant Ireland complete independence and not to compel Ulster to unite with the South. In the end it was Lloyd George, partly owing to his greater craft, partly because he was able to threaten immediate and total war if the negotiations fell through, who won the diplomatic battle. The Irish plenipotentiaries sent over by de Valera were induced to accept a treaty giving Ireland Dominion status, and confirming temporarily the separation from the rest of Ireland of six counties of Ulster, until such time as a Boundary Commission had made a report on the subject. The terms provided that the Irish Free State, as it came to be called, would be a co-equal member of the Commonwealth, with the rights of an independent country in such matters as membership of the League of Nations, though her ambassadors would be accredited by the Crown, and a Governor General would be appointed to represent the King. Members of the Irish parliament, too, would be required to swear an Oath of Allegiance to the Crown. The members of the Irish delegation were persuaded to accept, though in some cases with marked reluctance. In December 1921 the Treaty was signed; it was ratified in both countries; and the Irish Free State came into being.

Part Two

LAND AND PEOPLE

♣ *One* ♣
To 1782

'To tell the truth, though Ireland's pastures are naturally fertile, I would prefer to see fewer cows kept and men better off—rather than have such a huge increase of cattle, and no increase of good conditions. I would like some law made that whoever keeps ten beasts must also keep a plough going; for otherwise everybody will fall to grazing, and none to tillage. For if you look at the countries that live by keeping cattle, you will find they are all barbarous, uncivil, and much given to war.'

The poet Edmund Spenser, who spent most of his working life in Ireland, put these opinions into the mouth of one of the two characters whose dialogue provides his *View of the present state of Ireland*, written at the close of the sixteenth century. 'This keeping of cows', Spenser added, 'is of itself a very idle life, and a fit nursery for a thief.' The view had no doubt been expressed before, and it has certainly been echoed many times since; but with little effect. The *leit-motif* of Gaelic society, it has been said, was 'from time immemorial the lowing of cattle'; a bull is the central figure in the most celebrated epic of Irish mythology; and to-day, cattle still form the staple of the country's economy.

Dependence on cattle was encouraged by the combination of a suitable soil and a moist temperate climate, which gave Ireland the benefit of a crop that grows vigorously without sowing, tending, or (if livestock graze on it) reaping: grass. Although tracts of the central Irish plain were bogland, and much of the rest, at the time Spenser wrote, covered by forest, there were always large areas of grassland where a family could, by the mere possession of a few head of cattle, eke out a living. If the head of the family wished to better himself he would need, as Spenser suggested, to take a plough round his land; but that meant having to buy or borrow a horse, and it meant work—ploughing, harrowing, sowing; and reaping the crop. Besides—and this was something Spenser failed to appreciate—tillage farming could be a risky occupation.

He mistook cause for effect; the keeping of cows reflected, rather than caused, a state of war. If marauders appeared, a cattle-farmer could withdraw his herds into the forests until the danger passed, whereas growing crops could not be either withdrawn or concealed, and a year's labour might be destroyed in a few hours. With the Irish constantly fighting among themselves, or against invaders, mixed farming had been impracticable, so that the Irish had never been able to put their country's potential to good use: a failure which puzzled other observers besides Spenser in this period. Sir John Davies, for example, who was Attorney General for Ireland, was impressed by 'the good temperature of the air, the fruitfulness of the soil, the pleasant and commodious seats for habitation; the safe and large ports and havens lying open for traffic into all the west parts of the world; the long inlets of many navigable rivers and so many great lakes and fresh ponds with the land, as the like are not to be seen in any part of Europe; the rich fishings and wild-fowl of all kinds; and lastly the bodies and minds of the people endued with extraordinary abilities of nature'. Why, he asked, had these advantages not brought prosperity? In his view, the reason was that the English had made a conquest but had failed to impose their civilisation on the conquered. For three and a half centuries after the initial conquest, 'English law was not communicated to the Irish, nor its benefit and protection allowed to them, though they earnestly desired and sought it. For as long as they were out of the protection of the law, every Englishman might oppress, spoil and kill them without control. How was it possible that they should

PLATE 4. Shipbuilding in Belfast: part of Harland and Wolff's works (Northern Ireland Government Office)

PLATE 5. Celtic cross and round tower (Monasterboice Irish Tourist Board)

be other than outlaws and enemies to the crown of England?
If the King would not admit them to the condition of subjects, how could they learn to acknowledge and obey him as
their sovereign? When they might not converse or commerce
with any civil men, nor enter into any town or city without
peril of their lives, whither should they fly but into the woods
and mountains, and there live in a wild and barbarous
manner?'

Other observers confirm these impressions. Fynes Moryson, who came to Ireland as Mountjoy's secretary, laid the
blame for the country's poverty on its continued unrest: 'the
rebels not only being idle themselves, but in natural malice
destroying the labour of others, the inhabitants make little
effort to till the ground or plant trees, being content to live
for the day, in continual fear of mischief.' As a result, the
Irish lived in abject poverty. 'I trust no man expects among
these gallants any beds, much less feather beds and sheets;'
Moryson wrote; 'like the nomads, removing their dwellings
according to the suitability of pastures for their cows, they
sleep under the canopy of heaven, or in a poor house of clay,
or in a cabin made of the boughs of trees and covered with
turf, for such are the dwellings of the very lords among them.
They make a fire in the middle of the room and round about
it, they sleep upon the ground, without straw or anything
else under them, lying in a circle about the fire, with their
feet towards it. And their bodies being naked, they cover
their heads and upper parts with their mantles, which they
first make very wet, deliberately steeping them in water, for
they find that as soon as their bodies have warmed the wet
mantles, the smoke of them keeps their bodies in temperate
heat throughout the night.'

Moryson insisted that not only the ordinary Irish, but some
of the Old English lords in Ireland lived in this fashion, 'not
unlike wild beasts'. That this was not inventive malice on his
part is confirmed by the description given a few years earlier
by Don Francisco de Cuellar, the Spanish nobleman who was
washed up on the west coast of Ireland when his galleon was

wrecked after the defeat of the Armada in 1588. 'The custom of these savages is to live as the brute beasts among the mountains. They live in huts made of straw. The men are all large bodied, of handsome features and limbs, and as active as the roe deer. They do not eat oftener than once a day, and this is at night; and that which they usually eat is butter with oaten bread. They drink sour milk, for they have no other drink; they do not drink water, though it is the best in the world. . . in this kingdom there is neither justice nor right, and everyone does what he pleases.'

The accounts of these and other contemporary observers provide a reasonably clear picture; and as they happen to be the first batch of reports by eye-witnesses who can to any extent be relied upon, the question has to be asked whether the picture holds true for earlier times—whether, say, Strongbow's men, had they left comparable accounts, would have told the same story. In all probability, the answer is yes: but with a number of qualifications. First, all the writers were hostile witnesses—in de Cuellar's case, the antipathy being the more pronounced because he must have expected that the Irish both out of hatred of the English and out of reverence for the Catholic Church would have treated him much more kindly. Accounts of this nature, too, inevitably tend towards exaggeration, in the hope of arousing the astonishment of the reader; and even when they are restrained, they are apt to concentrate on the eccentricities, rather than on the normalities, that the observer has noticed. As early as 1629 an Anglo-Irishman, Geoffrey Keating, was jeering at English visitors for crawling around Ireland 'beetle-fashion . . . for it is the fashion of the beetle, when it lifts its head in the summer time, to go about fluttering and not to stoop towards any delicate flower that may be in the field, but to keep bustling about until it meets with the dung of horse or cow, and proceed to roll itself therein'. As Keating protested, in their anxiety to portray the quaint, the picturesque and the startling, English reporters often forgot to note Irish virtues; reverence for piety and wisdom, for example, and hospitality 'so great that it cannot be truthfully said that there ever existed in Europe folk who surpassed them in generosity or in hospitality according to their ability' (this last character-istic has been noted by later English travellers almost as frequently as Keating's strictures on them have been echoed by the Irish). Thirdly, these visitors did not understand the Irish language and had no conception of Irish culture; some-times they noted the Irish love of music, and skill as instru-mentalists, but of the range and depth of Irish culture they were ignorant. And lastly—most important of all—they arrived at the close of a long-drawn-out war, in which the more civilised and stable side of Irish life had been swept away. Moryson's insistence that not only the ordinary Irish, but some of the Old English lords were living like wild beasts is a fair indication of the change that must have come over the Irish social scene in the course of the sixteenth century. The helot class, peasants and labourers, had always been differentiated from their masters, the lords and their families; when both classes were in adversity, social distinctions lost their force. This substratum of society probably did not find conditions very much worse under their new masters than under the old; but it must have surprised and hurt the old aristocracy to find that no distinction was made between them and a submerged peasantry whose existence—apart from its value as labour—they had hardly recognised.

These qualifications made, it remains probable that the general impression left by the accounts of Spenser and the others of a pleasure-loving, leisure-loving, peripatetic, hos-pitable, hardy, rough, musical, unsettled warlike race of nomads would not have been very different had the accounts been written at the time of Strongbow's invasion. This assumption is borne out by the account of Giraldus Cam-brensis written at that time, though it is too highly coloured to be considered reliable. Giraldus was credulous, and the line between fact and fancy in his account is never easy to draw. Still the basic facts are clear. When he came to Ireland with Prince John in 1185, he found a damp country—

it seems to have been even damper then than now, being less efficiently drained—largely covered in forest. Communications were poor, but there were tracts of good pasture land, whose grass fed the flocks and herds which provided the natives with their livelihood. They grew oats but not in any quantity, preferring to avoid the labour of tillage, and of enclosing land for that purpose; they did not plant orchards, or build permanent houses; and they avoided, if possible, having anything to do with villages or towns—which were built and inhabited first by the Norsemen and then by the English.

The social structure Giraldus found had developed out of the fusion of pre-Gaelic, Gaelic and Christian ideas; it was based on the family group, grandparents, parents, children, who lived together, holding land in common. The clan system did not develop, though families allied themselves with kinsmen, or with neighbours—such groups of families forming a loose-knit hegemony under a sub-king; he in his turn, recognising a provincial king; and the provincial kings, a High King. This hierarchy was not feudal: there was no formal machinery for enforcing allegiance, and no land tenure system of the feudal type. The degree of national unity obtained varied; at no time did a High King command the allegiance of the whole country, and even Brian Boru, whom tradition was to single out as the most powerful holder of that title, was opposed by some of the local kinglets and ignored as far as possible by others. Tradition carves up the Ireland of old into five distinct provinces; but their boundaries were constantly fluctuating; the fortunes of their inhabitants swayed according to the exigencies of the military situation.

The whole country accepted rules of behaviour codified in the 'Brehon laws'; but these represented a climate of opinion rather than a set of formal instructions. Brehons—lawyers and arbitrators—expounded and interpreted the law; but it was not formally enforced by a judiciary, and the main sanction appears to have been public opinion, which was prepared to apply ostracism if the punishments—fines, usually recommended by the Brehons in their capacity as arbitrators—were not accepted. But the evidence of how the Irish political and legal structure actually worked—as distinct from how lawgivers felt it ought to work, or how casual observers like Giraldus Cambrensis heard that it worked, or how later historians liked to think it worked—is scanty. All that can safely be said is that the family unit was dominant, living its nomadic existence under its elected chieftain; largely self-contained, obtaining its clothes from its flocks of sheep and its footwear from the hides of its cattle; paying tribute in goods and services to the dominant figure in the district; enjoying a quiet and leisurely pastoral existence in times of peace, and a tip-and-run, raiding and counter-raiding existence in time of war.

But how, then, to account for the recollections of a more advanced form of civilisation, recited by the bards—minstrels, poets, and teachers—and recalled in the references to Tara's Halls and collars of gold in Tom Moore's lyrics? That a high level of craftsmanship existed at some stages is indisputable; the discoveries of archaeology afford the proof. But again, the evidence is insufficient. More research needs to be made before the mysteries are explained; it is only possible to write speculatively about Irish life before 1600. After 1600, however, the evidence becomes sufficiently abundant and trustworthy to provide a fairly consistent account of Irish social life, though the same reservations have to be made about travellers' tales: even about such painstaking observers as Arthur Young.

In the seventeenth century two things happened to alter the Irish economy. One was the spread of English rule and custom throughout the entire country, which destroyed the old Gaelic conception of land as a family property, and handed it over to individuals, and which also brought to an end—except in time of civil war—the old raid-and-counter-raid; enabling men (if they wished) to settle down to tillage in reasonable safety. The other was the introduction of the potato. Even in unsettled times, root crops had had a decided advantage over corn; they were less easy to destroy. But by the seventeenth century this was of less significance than the fact that the potato could support a much larger proportion of number of mouths per acre.

The potato did not lessen the importance of cattle. What it did was provide the population with its subsistence, while cattle formed its disposable income; and on this basis the Irish ought to have been able to look forward to a fair measure of prosperity. The fertile soil was capable of maintaining a high level of production. From the produce, related industries should have thrived—tanning, weaving and so on. They never thrived, because they were not permitted to thrive. As soon as any Irish industry began to flourish it attracted the jealous attention of its English competitors, who saw the Irish product replacing theirs in the Irish market and sometimes in the English market too. Their flocks of sheep, for example, ought to have given the Irish a thriving export trade in wool: but the export of wool to Britain was forbidden at first because the Irish were enemies; then, when the country was pacified, on the excuse that the Irish poor needed protection—preventing the wool from leaving the country would help provide them with clothing. Had the Irish been able to sell their wool, they could have bought clothes. As it was, they had to make their own out of the rough cloth they weaved. The cloth was good enough to command a reasonable price in continental markets when it could be sent or smuggled through to them, but most of it was kept for family use. The result was an almost complete absence of a money economy outside the towns. The rural population lived at subsistence level, going to the towns only when there was some small surplus to sell—victuals, as a rule—and taking in exchange such things as snuff, salt, and tobacco; money hardly entered into their lives.

The Acts of Parliament which prevented a money economy from superseding barter were normally the result of complaints that Irish goods were undercutting English products; but sometimes Governments would have their own reasons for placing restrictions on the development of Irish trade. Wentworth, for example, however anxious he might be to build up Ireland's economy in the expectation that the Crown revenues would thereby be increased, was also aware that a commercially prosperous Ireland might grow dangerously independent of the Crown. He therefore discouraged the Irish wool industry, in order to compel the Irish to continue buying their clothes from England 'for how can they then depart from us without nakedness?' Not all English rulers were as forthright as Wentworth about their motives; but they tended to adopt the same policy because it happened to satisfy economic as well as political needs.

The English at this time were stern mercantilists; they believed in exporting as much and importing as little as they possibly could, in the expectation of building up wealth through a satisfactory financial surplus on the year's trading. Not only did they object to the Irish producing goods which might be exported and compete with English products: they even objected to the Irish making goods for themselves, thereby depriving the English merchant of a potential market. What they were unable to realise was that unless the Irish had some outlet for their produce, they could not earn any money from it; and without money they would not be able to buy English goods, even if they wanted to. Any sign of life in Irish industry was enough to send the English merchants running to Westminster, there to secure new acts of Parliament, crushing the feared Irish competitor. One industry alone escaped this treatment—linen—partly because the linen industry was not sufficiently developed in England to satisfy home needs, partly because a toll was exacted on all exports of linen from Ireland; as the Irish were not permitted to export it direct except to England, it could be profitably re-exported.

Ireland, in fact, was treated as if she were an English colony; but whereas most of the English colonies had, or were to have, goods that England needed—sugar, coffee, tobacco, dyes and so on—Ireland had little that England required except linen, and food and water to victual passing ships. By the 1670's one of the very few other commodities she was permitted to export was 'servants'. Occasionally trade regulations would be temporarily relaxed, in time of English need—during the Great Plague, for example; but they would soon be re-imposed. The Irish were not even permitted to export their cattle to England after 1666. Later, the House of Lords urged William III to remind the Irish that 'the growth of woollen manufactures there had been, and would always be, looked upon with jealousy in England,' and that if the Irish were not careful laws would be passed 'totally to prohibit and suppress the same', and the Commons frankly stated that the wealth and power of England depended on her preserving a wool monopoly. The Irish, they pointed out, were wholly depen-dent on England and they had better be made to understand this. The Irish Parliament accepted the warning. It submitted to a new tax on all wool exports to England, sufficient to ensure it would not be able to compete with the British product, and to an outright ban on all exports of wool to other countries. The suppression of woollen manufacture was a blow from which the country's economy never fully recovered; it was too plain a hint to entrepreneurs that no industrial venture in Ireland would be tolerated if it was successful. Irish industry collapsed, and with it, trade. The only commerce which flourished on a large scale outside the linen trade was smuggling; for obvious reasons it is impossible even to estimate what proportion of the national income came from contraband, but all authorities are agreed it was considerable.

The low level of economic activity in Ireland had a further effect: it encouraged the Irish gentry to live most or all of the year in England as 'absentee landlords', taking no active interest in their Irish estates, and doing nothing to develop them. Why should they? What with the ban on the export of livestock and its by-products, and the lack of effective demand in Ireland, money spent on developing a property would have been wasted. The effects of absenteeism were already beginning to be felt in the seventeenth century. Most of the big Irish landowners had English property, or at least English connections: they were tempted to make England, with its greater social opportunities, their centre, and to use their Irish property simply for what revenue they could get from rents. Their money, which would normally have been spent locally on tradesmen's bills, was spent in England. There was not a sufficient smattering of resident aristocracy even to provide for the local courts: in Ireland a paid magistracy had to be established, for lack of suitable J.P.s.

The absentee's income from his rents would have been negligible but for the potato. The fact that it was easy to grow, and that it could be produced in tiny plots of land in sufficient quantity to sustain life, tended to force down the standard of living of the Irish tenant farmer; with each increase of rent he drew in his belt a little tighter, giving up such luxuries as butter or meat, and living on potatoes almost exclusively. He was unable to prevent this decline of standards, because if he was not willing to rent the land on those terms there were others who would; landlords or their agents fell increasingly into the way of letting land by 'cant' —by auction—which meant in effect that the man who was prepared to condemn himself and his family to the lowest standard of living got the land. He might, of course, compensate himself by working harder; say, by clearing bad land of stones, making it more productive. But this would only be of short-term benefit to him, because at the next 'cant' other prospective tenants, realising the improved productivity of the land, would be prepared to offer the landlord higher rents to move in onto it; and the improver, if he outbid them, would find himself as badly off as before.

The standard of living was pushed down still further by the fact that the potato was susceptible to blight. In some years the crop would be poor; occasionally it would fail altogether. A farmer who grows a variety of crops can, in the event of failure of one, switch to another; the farmer who is dependent entirely for his susbistence upon potatoes has nothing but the potato between him and starvation. Famine was always around the corner, and sometimes on the doorstep.

This was the condition of the country that goaded Swift into writing his *Modest proposal for preventing the children of Ireland from being a burden to their parents or country*. Rather than that Irish children should grow up thieves and beggars, as they normally did, he suggested they should be offered for sale for dinner parties: 'a child will make two dishes at an entertainment for friends, and when the family dines alone, the fore or hind quarter will make a reasonable dish, and seasoned with a little pepper or salt will be very good boiled on the fourth day, especially in winter. I grant this food will be somewhat dear, and therefore very proper for landlords, who, as they have already devoured most of the parents, seem to have the best title to the children.' In this, the most savage of his satires, and in other writings Swift portrays the miserable, shiftless, squalid life of the Irish at the time; every contemporary account agrees with his verdict. The journals of the Irish House of Commons are a protracted wail: whereas in the seventeenth century Ireland had enjoyed a few periods of expansion, from 1700, they complain, the land has been impoverished, industry left idle, commerce driven into decay. No way was open to remedy this state of affairs because English laws forbade the people to earn their own livelihood. It is impossible to get accurate figures for the economic state of the country because what few statistics were kept were systematically rigged for one purpose or another, and disagree with each other; and in any case they would not include the most important item—smuggling.But that almost every year the Irish parliament should have continued to criticize the wretched treatment Ireland was being given—and this although its members owed their position and prospects to keeping on the right side of the executive— is proof enough of the country's weakness. It could be argued, and was, that the Irish had brought their misfortunes on themselves by congenital laziness or incapacity. But as Petty noticed, this laziness proceeded from want of employment and of encouragement to work, not from natural indolence. He blamed the potato, which could be grown with very little effort; later observers blamed the whole system of government. Swift, for example, thought that laziness was the Irishman's misfortune, not his fault; it was the product of a multitude of discouragements—restraints, rather than natural disqualifications, were to blame. Richard Brinsley Sheridan was to go still further: he thought that the Irish had been calumniated as an excuse to degrade them; that the English by this means had tried to palliate their own inhumanity. As a later writer put it, 'We were idle, for we had nothing to do; we were reckless, for we had no hope; we were ignorant, for learning was denied us; we were improvident, for we had no future; we were drunken, for we sought to forget our misery.'

In the second half of the eighteenth century things began to show slight signs of improvement. As the English economy grew stronger, although the English merchants grew no less alarmed of Irish competition, they also became anxious to develop the Irish market; they were reluctantly coming to realise that it would be necessary to provide the Irish with the wherewithal to buy English goods. As population increased, it began to outrun the productive resources of the land; a more favourable eye was turned on the possibility of imports of food from neighbours—provided that they were kept at a price high enough not to undercut the prices which the English landed owners secured for their produce. In 1759, restrictions on the import of cattle into England were removed; the full effect of this change of policy became apparent in the 1770's, when England's involvement in foreign wars began to make her Governments more and more receptive to the idea of Ireland as a larder. After 1770 the amount of exports from Ireland, which had previously, with the exception of linen, been negligible, began to expand rapidly.

When Arthur Young made his tour of Ireland in 1776, the results of this improvement were already beginning to be noticeable; had he come ten years earlier, the picture might have been more depressing. Still, what he had to say was hardly encouraging. In the most fertile agricultural district in Ireland he found that the 'lower classes'—the tenant farmers—had 'such plenty of potatoes as always to command a bellyful'; they normally kept a cow and a pig and a flock of hens, which lived in the cabin with the family and the numerous lakes abounded in fish which any child could catch with a crooked pin. But, he said: 'Reverse the medal! They are ill clothed, and make a wretched appearance and, what is worse, are much oppressed by many who make them pay too dear for keeping a cow, horse, etc, and the wretched cabins, sometimes made out of sods and clay, have to house the live-stock as well as the family.'

Significantly, when a few days later Arthur Young found himself in County Armagh, in relatively well-to-do Ulster, he was able to claim that the people there were 'in general very well off as to living'—they were better clothed and, in addition to porridge, potatoes and bread, they could afford meat once a fortnight.

The oppression which Young noted was the result of the land tenure system. Few big landlords had any inclination either to live in Ireland or to concern themselves with their estates except to see that rents were paid. To avoid the difficult and sometimes dangerous task of rent-collection, they often farmed out rents to a middle-man; the landlord accepted a flat rate and allowed the middle-man to make his profit by screwing up the rents to a higher level—'rack-renting', as it was called. As the middle-men did not own the land themselves they had no interest in improving it; had they done so, and thereby obtained higher rents, the landlord would have turned the screw upon them. Their sole concern was to extract from the tenant every penny he earned above the subsistence level.

The improvement in the country's economic prospects, consequent upon the growing demand for Irish foodstuffs, was, therefore, of no benefit to the tenant. If he switched

from grazing to tillage, and grew corn, he might obtain a
higher profit per acre than he had done from grazing; but
of what use was that to him, when the profit was promptly
taken from him in higher rents by the landlord, or by the
landlord's middle-man? If the tenant protested that he ought
to get some benefit from his harder work, and refused to pay,
he was evicted. And unluckily for the tenant, the population
of Ireland was rapidly increasing at this time, putting more
pressure on the land. The Irish countryman, having no
alternative employment, was forced to pay the rack-rents
demanded, for if he did not, he knew there were other
hungry men longing to take his place.

One remedy, only, the tenant possessed: force. He could
put himself in league with other tenants locally, all of them
pledging to stand by each other, to resist eviction by refusing
to allow any other tenant to take up residence in a vacated
property. Land leagues—oath-bound secret societies—sprang
up in various parts of the country in the 1760's, under various
names. The 'Whiteboys' were the best known, their name
arising out of the Ku Klux Klan type of hooded garment they
wore to disguise themselves when they met to terrorise a
new tenant, or to take vengeance on a landlord by maiming
his cattle and burning his hay. Their objectives varied from
place to place and from time to time; in general, they waged
war on enclosures, on the substitution of pasture for tillage,
and on rack-rents; in particular they fought local evictions.

At times, and in places where they had a strong leader,
these Whiteboys not merely terrorised a district, they almost
administered it; the verdict of their 'courts' might be feared
more than decisions in the courts of law. The movement
threw up one or two political propagandists and, in alliance
with nationalism, might have produced a peasant movement
of real power. But the links between, say, the United Irishmen and the peasantry were negligible in the early stages of
the political movement: and although after they had been
driven underground the leaders of the Society tried to link
up with the tenantry, the Whiteboys developed little national-

ist spirit—though naturally it was assumed, not altogether unjustly, by the Castle, that agrarian warriors would prove useful rebel material in the event of a serious uprising, or of a French invasion.

♣ *Two* ♣

1782 - 1848

In contrast to her condition in the earlier part of the century, Ireland enjoyed relative prosperity under Grattan's parliament. That parliament owed its existence largely to the hostility aroused by English commercial policy; the Volunteers from the first asserted their determination to end the country's economic servitude: they pledged themselves to wear only clothes of Irish manufacture; they demanded free trade (the Irish Commons took the unprecedented step of voting supplies for six months only, to underline the demand); and they threatened civil war if it was not granted. The Lord Lieutenant reported that the situation was out of hand, and in 1780 the English Government had to give way, passing Acts which permitted the free export of Irish wool and some other commodities, and which allowed Ireland free trade with the colonies. It was assumed by the Volunteers that after the 1782 constitution was secured a still more positive national commercial policy would follow. The results of 1782, however, were disappointing. Foster's Corn Law, giving bounties on corn and stimulating the export trade, benefited Irish agriculture by encouraging tillage. The country's new political independence, too, limited though it was, encouraged entrepreneurs and attracted capital; wealthy families spent more of their time and money in Ireland; and for a time there was a general impression of economic well-being—less than a quarter of a century later, a writer recalled the period as a Golden Age, in which 'the nation started suddenly into wealth and power and intelligence'. Yet the prosperity was comparative only. The country remained poverty-stricken, by English or Continental standards.

What economic improvement there was, too, was destined to be transitory—whether Ireland had a parliament of her own or not. The demand for agricultural produce could be maintained only so long as wars and threats of wars made England a lavish-spending customer; the demand for industrial products, only as long as Irish manufacturers could continue to keep pace with the changes made by the Industrial Revolution. While machines continued to be worked by hand, Irish industry was able to benefit from new inventions. But as soon as the advantages of steam power were recognised, it was certain to suffer, owing to the need to import coal. For a time, however, advances in technique helped by government protection provided what seemed to be proof that a home legislature could revive Irish agriculture and industry—a conviction that was to do its part in creating and fostering separatism after the Union of 1800.

The Union gave the Irish industrialists what they had once clamoured for—assimilation into the English economy; mercantilist discrimination could no longer be used against them. But mercantilism by this time was dying. The Industrial Revolution put the English manufacturer in a position where he no longer required protection from competitors; he could undersell them in a free market. All he had to fear was that they might adopt protection against *him*; the Union, by preventing the Irish from taking such action, was a positive advantage to him. At first, a small measure of protection was left to Irish industry, but the last duties were swept away in the 1820's, and the Irish manufacturer was left to face his English competitors unaided.

Irish industry once again collapsed. The wool and silk trades, which had attained fair prosperity, were destroyed and the cotton trade did not long survive them. They were destroyed by the mass-importation of goods from Britain at lower prices made possible partly because of the growing availability of cheap power in Britain; partly because of her greater capital resources; partly because of her longer industrial experience. The linen industry survived in the Belfast region, where it was most highly developed; and some brewing and distilling firms continued to thrive, surviving even the shock of Father Mathew's temperance campaign of 1839 (the effect of the campaign was to reduce the consumption of spirits by well over half: beer suffered less as it was not then considered a really intoxicating drink). Otherwise, industries throughout the south fell into decay. Labour troubles accelerated the process. Up to 1819 skilled workers in Ireland earned rather more than their equivalent in Britain, because they were scarcer. In trying to maintain their position, their trade unions or 'combinations', in spite of stringent laws against them, often took strike action, and resorted to violence against employers or non-union workers. Not only were they unable to prevent a heavy fall in wages—the Irish cutlers' wage, for example, dropped from 50s. a week to 12s. a week—but in trying to prevent it, they weakened their industries still further, by keeping production costs too high for the goods to be competitive in a free market. Noting Ireland's chronic industrial unrest, too, capitalists grew unwilling to invest money in Irish industry; in any case, little money was available for investment. And the Union was to encourage still greater absenteeism; Dublin society, in spite of the efforts of Lady Morgan and of some Lords Lieutenant, went into a decline; and the better-off Irish families turned again to London as their social centre, taking their money with them.

If agriculture had continued to flourish, the collapse of industry might have been less catastrophic; but after the Napoleonic Wars ended in 1815, the demand for Irish agricultural produce began to slacken. This was the more serious because the population on the land was still rising rapidly. Landlords had been pleased to sub-divide part of their properties into more and more smallholdings so long as corn prices were high, in order to obtain the required labour force for tillage. But when after 1815 corn-growing began to be less profitable, and when the cattle trade offered better prospects, landlords were tempted to reverse the trend. The pressure of population made their task difficult. It was increasing faster in Ireland, at the time, than anywhere else in Europe; from about three million in the middle of the eighteenth century it rose to over six million in 1815 and over eight million in 1840—in spite of the fact that about thirty thousand people were emigrating to England every year. So great a population dependent on the one staple food meant that famine was always a danger.

Famines had not been uncommon in the eighteenth century; 1741, in particular, when an early frost had destroyed much of the potato crop, was remembered as 'the year of the slaughter'. But in the nineteenth century so dependent were the peasantry upon the potato that even a slight failure was enough to push them over starvation's edge: and famine became endemic. The danger was increased by the absence of any protection for the tenent from the landlord. Whereas in England a landlord letting a farm was expected to provide a dwelling, outbuildings, fencing and so on, as a matter of course, in Ireland he provided none of these things: the tenant received no more than the land itself. On it he had to build his own mud cabin—unless the previous owner had left one in a usable condition. The tenant was given no preference over other men covetous of his land; in fact when tenancies were put up for auction, the advertisement of the sale would usually assert that no such preference would be given—that the land would go to the highest bidder, even if he offered only a shilling or two more than the resident tenant felt he could afford to pay. Bernard Shaw has described what happened to the tenant who tried to improve his land, in *John Bull's Other Island*:

'That man Matthew Haffigan and his brother Andy made a farm out of a patch of stones on the hillside; cleared it and dug it with their own naked hands and bought their first spade out of their first crop of potatoes. Talk of making two blades of wheat grow where one grew before! Those two men made a whole field of wheat grow where not even a furze bush had ever got its head up between the stones. . . . What good was it to them? The moment they'd done it the landlord put a rent of £5 a year on them, and turned them out because they couldn't pay.'

The landlord in all probability knew nothing about the field —he was an absentee in London. But a landless man, seeing what the Haffigans had done, was prepared to hire the use of the reclaimed land at a higher price than the Haffigans were prepared to offer; and the Haffigans would have no redress. Even where tenants obtained a lease, the landlord could usually find some excuse to eject them. One expedient was for a landlord to neglect to send out demands for rent; if better prospective tenants came along, the occupants could be evicted for being in arrears.

In addition to rack-rents, the tenant was also required to pay tithes; and the fact that he had to pay them to a parson of a faith which he considered heretical helped to make tithes, rather than rents, the cause of the most serious agricultural unrest in this period, until legislation to end the old tithe system in Ireland was pushed through a reluctant parliament. But this was of little help to the tenant. It merely meant, in most cases, that he had to pay more in rent, or be evicted—unless the Whiteboys in his area were strong enough to terrorise landlords or their agents into caution. The Whiteboys enacted 'that whosoever shall attempt, directly or indirectly, to deprive us of our farms, shall be punished with death. That the landlord, middleman, or agent, who shall eject a tenant from his estate, shall be punished with death. That the landlord who demands a higher rent than that which we have fixed, shall be punished with death. That he who bids a higher rent for a farm, takes the place of an ejected tenant, purchases by auction or otherwise, goods that have been distrained, shall be punished with death.' Usually it was neither the landlord nor his agent who was affected (except by destruction of property); it was the incoming tenant, who suffered the penalty. Yet such was the demand for land, the absolute necessity of having it to avoid starvation, that not even these threats always frightened tenants away.

The poverty of the country was appalling. Commission after commission sat after the Union, culminating in the most extensive of all, the Devon Commission, which reported in 1845. All of them described the Irish situation in ugly detail—as did travellers from England and Europe who visited the country in the period. John O'Driscol, for example, who toured Ireland in the early 1820's, noted that 'where formerly there were flourishing villages, shops, tanyards, milk, etc., on a small scale, where beer was brewed and spirits distilled and the people were very comfortable and contented, there is now a very different scene presented to the eye of the observer. He sees only ruined houses, decayed and deserted villages without trade, tanyard, brewhouse, mill or any symptom or means of industry or comfort. As the people increased in numbers, the excise drew away from them the means of support and decent subsistence. They have been converted into outlaws, smugglers, and banditti. And the low murmur of preparation for some desperate and hopeless enterprise is heard throughout the country, on every hill, in every ruined village, and in all those cheerless dens of dirt and misery, called cottages in Ireland.'

But although descriptions of this kind were a commonplace, the government remained at a loss for a remedy. Some experts were inclined to blame the potato, because its failures were the immediate cause of famine. But as O'Driscol pointed out, the potato was not in itself to blame; indeed, its discovery could have helped to enrich the tenant, had he been able to reap the financial benefit of frugality by eating potatoes and using the price he obtained for his corn to improve his living standards. The essential evil was the land tenure system, whereby everything but bare subsistence was taken from the tenant in rent, leaving him without resource if his subsistence—potatoes—should fail him. And what was not known then—though it has been realised since—was that the more the peasant was forced down to subsistence level, the greater would be the increase in the population; the low standard of living actually encouraged early marriages and large families which could be sustained by the possession of a small plot of land and a few seed potatoes.

Even if the causes of the trouble had been fully understood by Governments, they would have been unlikely to take the necessary decisive action; *laissez faire* would have been invoked against it. The right of a man to do what he wants with his own was not often then contested, as it was later to be, on the score that the good of the community must override the rights of the private property owner; the argument of the common good had no effect unless it was reinforced by the prospect of profit—for example, in justifying the acquisition of land for railways. The test of the common good was not applied for the benefit of tenants; not until long after the Factory Acts in Britain had tempered the wind to the industrial worker, was the Irish peasant allowed to deserve any rights whatsoever.

The only occasion on which his needs were given some official recognition was during the Melbourne administration from 1835-41. The impetus came, not from Westminster, but from the Castle, while Thomas Drummond was Under Secretary. Drummond is now mainly remembered for a sentence in a letter he wrote in 1838. Thirty-two Tipperary Magistrates had written urging stiffer coercion in their county to put down agrarian outrage; Drummond, a hardheaded liberal Scot, disproved the magistrates' allegations, and concluded:

'Property has its duties as well as its rights: to the neglect of those duties in times past is mainly to be ascribed that diseased state of society in which such crimes take their rise; and it is not in the enactment or enforcement of statutes of extraordinary severity, but chiefly in the better and more faithful performance of those duties, that a permanent remedy for such disorders is to be sought.'

The letter so shocked the Lord Donoughmore, to whom it was addressed, that he suppressed it. When it came out months later, the Ascendancy were aghast: and their disgust was shared by *The Times*, which denounced 'this Jack in Office' who had taken upon himself to lecture landowners. Drummond's weakness and leniency were blamed as the cause of trouble. Unfortunately for the landowners' case, however, the next inquiry into the state of Ireland showed that under Drummond's administration, agrarian crime had substantially diminished. Drummond died young; even had he lived, on the return of Peel to office in 1841 he would certainly have been removed from office. In any case, the forces of disaster were beyond the control of an administrator, no matter how able. But the phrase, 'Property has its duties as well as its rights,' was to ring on down the years: in Ireland, Drummond is generally regarded as 'the only governor of Ireland under the English who governed justly, impartially, and with the desire to benefit'.

Drummond himself wrote a description of the Irish people which gives a clear picture of the problem that faced him in office. In his survey of the social and economic conditions of the country for a Royal Commission on Irish railways he described the differing conditions in the four provinces. In Ulster, he found the people better lodged, clothed and fed than the others; 'the wages of labour are higher on average. . . . They are a frugal, industrious and intelligent race, inhabiting a district for the most part of inferior fertility to the southern portion of Ireland, but cultivating it better.' In the south, the condition of affairs was 'in every respect inferior to that of the northern; their habitations are worse, their food inferior, consisting at best of potatoes and milk without meal.' Nevertheless the population was robust, active and athletic, and although ignorant 'eager for instruction, and readily trained under judicious management to habits of order and steady industry'. The inhabitants of the western districts 'are decidedly inferior to both, in condition and in experience; their food consists of potatoes alone, without meal, and in most cases without milk; their cabins are wretched hovels, their beds straw.' Poverty and misery, he concluded, had deprived these westerners of all energy; labour brought insufficient return to give motive to exertion; and the country swarmed with a wretched and indigent population.

The relative prosperity Drummond found in the North was the product of a variety of circumstances. Through the 'Ulster Custom', the predominantly Protestant tenants enjoyed certain rights not shared by the Catholic tenants of the south. As soon as an Ulster farmer was established in his holding, he acquired an interest in any improvements he made to it, and could demand a share in them when he left, or if he was evicted; and he was rarely evicted, except for non-payment of rent. These rights, enforced locally by public opinion, were accepted by Ulster less because landlords realised that the system gave better results (though in fact agriculture was more prosperous in the North) than because the Protestant tenants' agrarian organisations proved themselves even more formidable in enforcing them than the Whiteboys—where public opinion was insufficient. In spite of *laissez faire* disapproval (the Devon Commission denounced the Ulster Custom as 'hostile to the just rights of property') the tenants were strong enough to retain their privileges; they were never reduced to the same straits as the southern peasantry.

Industry, too, remained fairly prosperous in Ulster. The linen industry collapsed elsewhere in the country, but where it was concentrated round Belfast it had capital and experience at its command; by the middle of the century it had been successfully reorganised on a factory basis. Another Belfast industry that held its own was ship-building. Although Ulster was far from prosperous in the early part of the nineteenth century, she was well enough off relative to the rest of the country to create a different economic climate, and different economic interests. While southern nationalist thinkers, recalling the days of Grattan's parliament, were tempted to regard separation from Britain as the pre-requisite of economic recovery, the Ulstermen came more and more to look upon their trade connections with Britain as essential to their future.

Except in Ulster, and the district around Dublin, the condition of Ireland grew worse in the 1840's, as Government

Commission after Government Commission, traveller after traveller, depressingly testify. It was bad enough in 1839 for a French writer, Gustave de Beaumont, to say, 'Misery, naked and famishing—that misery which is vagrant, idle and mendicant—covers the entire country'; and three years later a German, Kohl, remarked that since he had seen Ireland, he considered that even the poorest of Letts and Esthonians lived well by contrast: 'with us and other nations lawless beggary is the exception; here is to be seen a people of beggars, unique of its kind, to be found nowhere else.' The frigid statistics of the Devon Commission confirmed their stories; in County Mayo, it revealed, 95 per cent of the population lived in mud cabins; for food, any change from potatoes and meal stirabout, a thin porridge, was unusual; milk was scarce; butter in some places unknown.

The Devon Commission came to the conclusion that Ireland's poverty was not due to the size of her farms; Armagh, with the smallest average size of farms, was also the most prosperous county. The real trouble, it decided, was the inefficiency of the farming; draining, manuring, rotation of crops and other refinements were urgently needed. But if they were to be obtained in the south, some form of tenant right would have to be introduced; and the Commission, in which the landowner influence predominated, disliked the idea. The Government would have been even more disapproving, had it been called upon to legislate on the basis of the Commission's findings; but as it happened, in the winter of 1845 the Irish problem began to solve itself far more ruthlessly and efficiently than legislation could ever have done; through Famine. The intervention of providence was so timely that in England it was spoken of by Malthusian-minded economists as 'nature's remedy'.

Although the potato blight which reached Ireland from the Continent in 1845 was only partial, attacking some fields and leaving others untouched, it was enough to bring starvation in many districts. Reports of famine reaching Westminster were at first discounted—not surprisingly, as within living memory there had hardly been any year without one. But as they grew more serious, an idea was born in the mind of the Prime Minister, Robert Peel. Peel at the time was being converted by Anti-Corn Law League propaganda for Free Trade. His difficulty was that the Conservative Party, which he led, was still protectionist. Could not this Irish famine, he thought, if it turned out really serious, be used as an excuse to repeal the British Corn Laws, on the pretext that the starving Irish might have cheap meal?

The argument was in fact fallacious. What the Irish lacked was not simply food; the corn which they had grown for their landlords was not affected by the blight on the potatoes. But they had no money to buy it; nor had they the money to buy imported meal, however cheap. The fallacy was pointed out to him by his colleague, the Duke of Wellington, who insisted that what the Irish lacked was not food but purchasing power. No attention was paid to him. The Corn Laws were repealed and, as a gesture, a million pounds' worth of cheap Indian meal imported into Ireland.

The winter that followed, although hungry, was no hungrier than many a previous winter had been for the Irish peasant. But in 1846 the blight returned, covering a much wider area. In a celebrated passage, Father Mathew, the temperance reformer, described how at the end of July, travelling from Cork to Dublin, he had seen the plant blooming in all the luxuriance of an abundant harvest: returning a week later, he had found only a wide waste of putrefying vegetation. From the whole country, similar accounts poured in; three-quarters of the potato crop was lost. O'Connell and the *Nation* urged that the ports should be closed to exports of corn, which could then be distributed among the starving peasantry. But Lord John Russell, who had succeeded Peel as Prime Minister, was an even more rigid adherent of *laissez faire*. His argument was that if corn could no longer be exported, the Irish farmer would receive no income from its sale; and that the whole mechanism of commerce would therefore be brought to a standstill. What he did not recognise, or did not admit, was that 'commerce' in the English sense did not exist in Ireland. The country had no army of industrialists, contractors, wholesalers and retailers, all of whose livelihoods might be jeopardised by government intervention. In any case Russell, like Peel, was concerned less with the reaction of the Irish than with English interests. To justify himself, he argued that intervention would be dangerous because 'those supplies which would naturally be a portion of the commerce of this country would be applied to the relief of the people of Ireland.' Only if the situation in Ireland became desperate, he said, might public works be sanctioned; provided that the money for them was found by a loan to be paid back by the distressed districts themselves at some later date; and provided that the works were unproductive, so that they did not cut across the legitimate field of any private enterprise.

The situation was in fact already desperate when he spoke. But for remarkable efforts in another legitimate field for private enterprise—charity—it would have been more desperate still. English public opinion began to be roused by horrifying reports from Ireland. An Irish Justice of the Peace, for example, wrote to the Duke of Wellington to describe the condition of a Cork district near his home: 'reaching the spot I was surprised to find the wretched hamlet apparently deserted. I entered some of the hovels to ascertain the cause, and the scenes that presented themselves were such as no tongue or pen can convey the slightest idea of. In the first, six famished and ghastly skeletons, to all appearances dead, were huddled in a corner on some filthy straw, their sole covering what seemed a ragged horse cloth, and their wretched legs hanging out, naked above the knees. I approached in horror, and found by a low moaning, they were alive, they were in fever—four children, a woman, and what had once been a man. In a few minutes I was surrounded by at least 200 of such phantoms, by far the greater number delirious, either from famine or fever. Their demoniac yells are still ringing in my ears.'

Again and again, O'Connell in speeches, the *Nation* in articles, demanded that the Government take the only obvious course: ban all export of food from Ireland. It quoted extracts from the shipping intelligence of the day, showing how from the Irish ports grain, flour, eggs, butter and meat were still being taken to England; and it ridiculed the argument that the Irish would be able to buy cheap food with the money earned by the sale of their produce. Little of that money returned; landlords, who received it in rents, spent much of it in England. A mounting toll of deaths from starvation—and of verdicts by coroners' juries of wilful murder against Lord John Russell—at last compelled the Government reluctantly to sanction expenditure on public works. They remained as unproductive as Lord John Russell had promised—ditches with no outlets, roads that ran nowhere in particular. After a time, their absurdity became transparent. All that they were doing was abstracting labour that ought to be put to some useful purpose. In the spring of 1847, the Government finally fell back on the remedy that had already been extensively adopted by charitable organisations, which had distributed huge sums collected in Britain for famine relief; soup kitchens were established, and within a few weeks three million people were being fed daily.

Even to this final act of grace the Government could not resist adding a clause to benefit the landlord: that outdoor relief should not be given to tenants of more than a quarter acre of land. Ostensibly the clause was designed to prevent the well-off competing with the needy for soup. But at the time, possession of one, or even of ten acres, was no guarantee of means. The choice for starving tenants lay between their survival or their holding; if they chose soup, that suited their landlords, who by this time were anxious to clear their property of useless, non-rent-paying tenantry, and convert it to pasture. Deprived of their land, the peasants' only resource was emigration. As a direct consequence of the Famine, a quarter of a million Irish men, women and children crossed to Britain; and a million left for America (usually in unseaworthy, squalid ships, on which the death rate from disease was high—one in six in 1847). In Ireland, over a million men, women and children died.

The Great Starvation seared itself on the national mind. The refusal of the English Government to take appropriate emergency action naturally came to be explained on the grounds that the English wanted the Irish to starve; a thesis made the more tenable by comments from such sources as the *Economist*, which thought the purge, however drastic, was salutary. When John Mitchel contended that there had been enough agricultural produce available in Ireland, had the ports been closed, to feed the population three times over, the figures were naturally pounced upon as evidence of England's black inhumanity. That there was no such conspiracy is made clear by the amounts subscribed in England for private charity; the Government's failure to take decisive action was based, not on malice, but on a misunderstanding of Ireland's needs, disastrously coupled with its belief in the sanctity of *laissez faire*. Even if the corn had been kept at home, it could only have been distributed by what would have amounted to a social revolution. Considering that the Government was in the hands first of Peel, always implacably blind where Irish affairs were concerned, and Russell, the surprise is that so much was eventually done; nothing like the final soup-kitchen organisation had ever been attempted, let alone successfully carried out, on a national scale before.

The closing of the ports might not have provided enough food to meet the crisis; at least it would have been a gesture of good will. That the gesture was not made may be said to mark the final collapse of the Union in any but an administrative sense. Was it conceivable, the Irish could ask, that the people of a British country could have been left to starve, while Governments refused to intervene? Of course not! If the British chose not to consider Ireland part of Britain, when such an emergency arose, they could hardly complain if the Irish did likewise.

♣ Three ♣
1848 - 1914

The Famine not only killed off or dispossessed tenants by the hundred thousand; it also bankrupted landlords who were dependent on their Irish rents for their living. To restore some semblance of economic order, the Government put through an Encumbered Estates Act, designed to facilitate the transfer of property cheaply to entrepreneurs—a new Plantation, designed to attract a new breed of landlords better fitted to put Irish agriculture back on its feet than the old chronic absentees. The Lord Lieutenant, Clarendon, backed the policy in the expressed hope that the prospect of good properties going cheaply would attract sturdy English and Scots farmers; but such men were put off by the gruesome tales they had heard of Ireland in the Famine years. Instead, more land fell into the control of the class which came to be known as 'gombeen men': petty shopkeepers who had acted in a small way as money-lenders as well as retailers, and who had saved enough, in spite of the Famine, to invest in property. A tenant, therefore, who survived the quarter-acre rule, often found himself under a landlord even more grasping, and much better qualified to know the degree to which the rent screw could be turned, than the absentees of old. This bore out Fintan Lalor's predictions. Lalor, coming late into the Young Ireland movement, brought with him the belief that the land of Ireland belonged of right to the people of Ireland: any laws which deprived them of ownership were null and void; landlords, whatever their race, were usurpers; and tenants would be justified in using any means at their disposal to re-establish their rights over their property—in fact, this ought to be their first duty. Although Lalor died soon after, his teaching was remembered.

For the time, however, the failure of the '48 rising discredited physical force as a way of solving Ireland's problems; and O'Connell's humiliation under the Melbourne Government was still too fresh in the memory for any great hopes to be placed on Parliament. But one of O'Connell's expedients, it was realised, had given useful results: his idea of legal—or at least ostensibly legal—associations, whose value had been confirmed by the success of the Anti-Corn Law League in Britain. The obvious basis for a legal campaign was the land, because agitation for Tenant Right might be expected to win support throughout the country—even from the Ulster Presbyterians, some of whose landlords were trying to do away with the Ulster Custom in order to clear tenants off their property. Gavan Duffy, the only Young Ireland leader remaining in Ireland, helped to organise a Land League and give it direction. Its aim was that 'the three F's'—a Fair rent, Fixity of tenure, and Freedom of sale:—approximately the Ulster Custom—should be given the force of law, and extended throughout the country. The League had political implications; there was more than a hint in it of Lalorism—the idea that the land should be the precursor of national agitation; and the decision was taken to test its rapidly growing popularity in the parliamentary field. But the League failed to appreciate the dangers inherent in its alliance with political and sectarian ambition; it failed to survive their disruptive influence. Its collapse enabled landlords to proceed even more harshly against the unfortunate tenant; provided with some of the better eviction facilities which they had long demanded, they took the opportunity to hasten the process of eliminating leases and substituting tenancies-at-whim. In this they had the full support of Governments; Lord Palmerston echoed the prevailing view when he referred to 'Irish tenant right' as 'Irish landlord wrong'. Rackrenting continued. In one notorious case, over a hundred tenants of Lord Digby, who had enjoyed tenant right for two generations, and had improved their land on the assumption that the right would be preserved, were told on his death that their rents would be raised to the rack level of their neighbours, and that if they objected, eviction proceedings would be taken against the lot of them.

Tenants retaliated with terrorism. As Sir George Lewis had described it to the Government: 'This system pervades the whole community . . . it is not the banding together of a few outcasts who betake themselves to illegal courses and prey on the rest of the community, but the deliberate association of the peasantry, seeking by cruel outrage to insure themselves against the risk of utter destitution and abandonment. Its influence, therefore, even when unseen is general; it is, in fact, the mould into which Irish society is cast—the expression of the wants and feelings of the general community. So far as it is successful, it is an abrogation of the existing law, and an abolition of the existing Government.' Great numbers of police had to be brought in to deal with agrarian outrage, enabling Friedrich Engels, visiting Ireland in 1850, to complain that he had never seen so many in any country, 'and the drink-sodden expression of the Prussian gendarmes is developed to its highest perfection here among the constabulary, who are armed with rifles, bayonets, and handcuffs.' Yet, the 1850's and 1860's were relatively prosperous; prices were rising for agricultural produce, and although higher rent pursued them the tenant could survive so long as they continued to rise. The landless men, with no prospect of securing farms, were the chief sufferers; the rapid expansion of cattle-rearing in place of tillage lessened the demand for their labour.

Only in Ulster did industry thrive. Belfast had established itself as a leading industrial city—from 20,000 inhabitants in 1800 it had grown to 100,000 in 1850. Its eminence in shipbuilding was assured by a combination of luck, judgement and inventiveness: the first Harland gained a reputation as a ship-builder who designed narrow-beamed ships to cut through the ocean waves, rather than toss over them; the

shipyards that were later to be 'Harland and Woolf' opened
in 1853. In the South, the only major industry to continue
to expand was brewing; again, through a mixture of luck and
judgement. In the eighteenth century the brewing of stout
and porter had been traditionally associated with London, so
much so that the legend was commonly accepted that only
from Thames water could quality stout be brewed, though
Thames water was not, in fact, used in the brewing process.
But in the early years of the nineteenth century the London
brewers lowered the quality of their product, partly in an
attempt to maintain profits by deceiving the excise, partly
because the dark colour of stout encouraged them to adul-
terate it without much fear of detection; and its reputation
dwindled. In Dublin, at least one firm—Guinness—stuck to its
standards, even though this entailed higher prices; and with
the help of some sharp business practices, designed to crush
rivals, succeeded in capturing not only most of the Irish
market but, eventually, a substantial market in Britain as
well. Other individual firms, including some distillers, kept
going; but apart from brewing no trade existed on any large
scale in Dublin, and the demand for labour was consequently
small. Emigration provided the only outlet for younger sons;
and they continued to leave for America in their tens of
thousands annually. From over eight million inhabitants before the Famine, Ireland was reduced to five million in 1851,
four million in 1871 and three million in 1914. To some
extent this emigration must have provided a safety valve. So
also did the relative prosperity of Irish agriculture in the
1860's which kept the tenant farmers from taking too keen
an interest in nationalism, preventing close links between the
tenant right and the nationalist movements during the
Fenian period.

By this time, too, the full force of *laissez faire* insistence
upon the rights of property had begun to diminish. There
was a growing admission that although in theory the rights
were absolute, in practice their enforcement ought to be
tempered with moderation. In a celebrated Irish law case in

1858, a clergyman sought to retain the value of improvements he had made to his property on the promise of a lease, a promise which had been broken; the Master of the Rolls, though admitting that he had no jurisdiction in equity, said—'I am bound to administer an artificial system; and being so bound, I regret that I must administer injustice in this case, and dismiss the petition.' In England the Fenian outrages aroused a greater recognition of the need to find ways to pacify Ireland, even at some sacrifice of principle. English commentators, too, could not help being stuck by the fact that 'principle' was not nearly so important as Irish landlords made out; the Irish land system was not basically different from England's, but the more equitable English custom of a dual ownership by landlord and tenant had not been allowed to develop in Ireland. A correspondent employed by *The Times* in the late 1860's, though himself an Irish landowner and a conservative, summed up the trend of opinion when he wrote that the law of the land throughout the United Kingdom favoured the landlord; 'but in England its harshness is practically nullified by the circumstances that in that country the permanent improvements on estates are made, as a general rule, by the landlords, and that tenants shield themselves from the law by contract, and take care that when they hire land they shall be repaid should they add to its value. In Ireland, however, where in most cases what is done in the way of improving the soil is by the tenant, not by the landlord, and where the tenant, in the majority of cases, has not risen to the status of a free contractor the law is in the highest degree unfair; it refuses to protect what really is the property of the tenant added to the holding, and exposes it to unredressed confiscation.' The fact that the law was for the most part enforced by members of the landlord class, in their capacity as magistrates, made the tenant's position still less secure.

But the Irish landlords had helped to slit their own throats. By substituting tenancies-at-whim for leases, wherever possible, they had created a huge class whose main enemy was landlordism. In 1870, out of 680,000 farms in Ireland over 525,000 were occupied by tenants-at-whim, who were still called upon (as a rule) to provide all their own capital and equipment, farm buildings and fencing, for none of which could they claim compensation if they were evicted. The class might be expected to seize any opportunity that arose to fight and, if possible, to destroy landlordism in Ireland.

In Gladstone, however, an English Government had found a leader who was prepared to reverse the traditional policy towards Ireland. His reaction to the Fenians had been to decide that an attempt must be made to remedy Irish griev-ances, rather than simply to stamp out the disaffection that they provoked. Coming into power in 1868, he turned his attention to the land, sponsoring, in 1870, what was intended to be a definitive Land Bill. It proved to be the precursor of a land revolution.

Gladstone had no intention of accepting the tenants' full demands; he considered that full acceptance of the three F's would be incompatible with property rights. All he was concerned to do was to extend the Ulster Custom sufficiently to remove discontent in the South, and thereby to eliminate the constant drain on resources that the need for a large constabulary represented. The plan was to give the tenant compensation 'for disturbance' if evicted, and 'for improve-ments' if he left of his own accord; and penalties were threatened against rack-renting landlords. The real aim of the Act, however, was to encourage the revival in Ireland of the English system of leases—of long-term contracts between landlord and tenant which, it was assumed, would promote a friendlier relationship, and in time partnership, between the two. But it was too late; the damage had been done. The subtle legal twists of the Act were incomprehensible to the peasant mind; it was regarded with suspicion. And before long, its prospects were finally wrecked by another dispensa-tion of providence. The harvest of 1877 was poor; that of 1878, the worst since the Famine. Nor was scarcity com-pensated for by higher prices; export prices slumped, too.

The Irish tenant, carrying the rent burden on top of his ordinary production costs, was ceasing to be a match for his competitors from the New World and from certain European countries, where the occupant of the land was also its owner. Landlords, however, tried to keep up the accustomed level of rents; their tenants, hard pressed, could not find the money; the cycle of evictions and threats of reprisals intensified; and the land was thrown again into confusion.

Inevitably, the tenants began to combine against the common—landlord—enemy; and a leader appeared in Michael Davitt. Davitt, who had been jailed for his part in the Fenian conspiracy, had converted himself during his imprisonment to a variant of Lalorism. Although at heart a Fenian, he liked Lalor's idea of an agitation aimed primarily to restore the land of Ireland to the people of Ireland; not simply by a transference of the deeds of ownership to the tenants, but on a system akin to that expounded by Henry George, with the community owning the land, and the occupiers holding their portions in trust for the people of Ireland. This refinement of Lalorism would not have commended itself to the land-hungry peasantry, but they were all in favour of Davitt's preliminary step—the destruction of landlordism. Davitt chose the County of Mayo, the most over-populated, poverty-stricken, rack-rented and eviction-prone of all, for his starting point, and found himself rapturously received. In August 1879 Davitt founded the Mayo Land League; when two months later the Irish National Land League was set up, Parnell became its president.

Parnell's accession was significant. It meant that the League was committed to constitutional methods, at least in theory, to achieve its ends; for he insisted that its aims must be such that he could reasonably put them forward at Westminster. Accordingly, the League's formal emphasis was more on the need for fair rents than for the destruction of landlordism; but as the agricultural slump worsened its members' informal speeches grew less moderate, and so did their actions. Whatever Parnell might say in the Commons, in his speeches to the League he left his hearers in no doubt that all depended upon their own determination; they must band together to resist exorbitant rents and evictions. And after several months of what amounted to a state of siege between land-lords and tenants, Parnell made a speech in which he both satisfied and stimulated the campaigners: the 'boycott' pronouncement of 1880.

'Now, what are you to do to a tenant who bids for a farm from which another tenant has been evicted? I think I heard someone say, "shoot him!" I wish to point out to you a very much better way—a more Christian and charitable way, which will give the lost man an opportunity of repenting. When a man takes a farm from which another has been evicted, you must shun him on the roadside when you meet him; you must shun him in the shop; you must shun him on the fair-green and in the market-place and even in the place of worship, by leaving him alone, by putting him into a moral Coventry, by isolating him from the rest of his country, as if he were the leper of old.'

The process was first put into formal operation against an estate on which Captain Boycott was the landlord's agent; from him it took its name. The League adopted the idea whole-heartedly, and the mass of the tenantry fell in behind it. Clashes between them and landlords, landlords' agents, police and military were common. Commoner still was silent destruction of life, limb and property. 'Moonlighters' roamed the countryside, dealing with eviction cases as they thought fit, or as opportunity offered: cattle were maimed, women shaved, agents thrashed or even brutally murdered. The military and police retaliated with their own brutalities, and soon landlordism was in a state of siege. The cost of preserv-ing landlords and agents in the security to which they felt themselves entitled steadily mounted; eventually, the British Government was compelled to recognise that this was not just another temporary crisis—that the war would not cease until sufficiently attractive terms of peace had been offered. There was only one possible way out: amendment of the

1870 Land Act. Its deficiencies were by this time obvious;
it had failed to achieve its stated aim of preventing the ex-
ploitation of tenants by their landlord. Compensation 'for
disturbance' applied only if the 'disturbance'—eviction—of
the tenants was not held to be their fault; the courts were
prepared to rule that it was the tenants' fault if the eviction
was for arrears of rent; in this bad harvest period, most
tenants *were* in arrears; and consequently the Act afforded
them small protection. Gladstone, back in power in 1880,
decided to amend the Act, to allow compensation for disturbance in selected cases even where non-payment of rent
was the cause of eviction. The Land League denounced the
amendment as a sham, cynicism which appeared justified
when the Lords rejected the amendment. Gladstone realised
that the problem would have to be attacked more radically;
but he decided that he must first establish his good faith by
striking at the men who had brought the law of the land
into contempt. The Government thereupon resorted to the
ultimate power of coercion available to it; *habeas corpus* was
suspended, and the League's leaders, among them Parnell,
were imprisoned.

Meanwhile, a Commission had been investigating the
operation of the 1870 Land Act, to find out where it had
gone astray. Its findings were remarkable, in that they condemned the whole *laissez faire* basis of land ownership in
Ireland. In its view, Ireland 'swarmed with a home-keeping
people, without manufactures, colonies or commerce, dependent upon tillage, and holding on, for life and living, to a
soil of which they were not the owners'. Therefore, 'the
economic law of supply and demand is but of casual and
exceptional application in Ireland. It is generally admitted
that to make it applicable the demand must be what is called
"effective"; in this instance it may be said that, whatever was
the cause with the demand, the supply was never effective.'
To the Irish tenant, tenancy was 'not a matter of the chaffer
of the market, but almost of life and death'; yet English
governments had imposed on Ireland land laws that were

utterly at variance with the state of public opinion. As a result not only the courts that administered them, but the Government that enforced them, had been brought into odium.

The moral was plain. The land war could only be brought to an end by bringing the law into line with public opinion, even if this meant sacrificing certain principles which most British politicians, including Gladstone himself, had regarded as sacrosanct. The Bessborough Commission said, in effect, that everything which the Gavan Duffy Land League had asked for should be granted. The Land Act of 1881 accepted its advice. Apart from some reservations on Free Sale, the three F's were given legal standing throughout Ireland. Freedom of contract between landlord and tenant in the old sense was abandoned; a Land Commission was set up with power to fix 'fair rents'; and the principle of dual ownership of the land by landlord and tenant was established. The Land Act of 1881 did not finally satisfy the peasants; its basis, indeed, was soon to be undermined by new legislation. But it effectively crushed landlordism; and with landlordism went Lalorism, because the incentive for a land war was largely removed. 'The long-scourged tenantry of Ireland might now sing aloud', a member of the Irish party ecstatically wrote, 'with the freed bondsmen of Port Royal,

We last night slaves
Today, the Lord's free men.'

The 1881 Act was allowed through by the Lords for the same reason that they had condoned Catholic Emancipation; the state of Ireland made it impossible for them to reject it. But they complained in passing it that it would be mischievous in its operation; and so, in a sense, it was. Under the Act, the landlord became little more than a receiver of a rent over which he had no control. To him the Act was plainly socialistic, striking at the root of the rights of property, and justifying him in refusing to make any improvement to his estate. It destroyed his power for good as well as his power for evil. He could not longer exchange an indolent tenant for a useful one, nor was it worth his while to put capital into his estate, knowing that he could not be certain of obtaining any return from it. The tenants too, were dissatisfied with the condition in which they found themselves. They had no capital to improve their land; in any case, they were reluctant to use what little money they possessed for that purpose, because of their experience of rack-renting, which continued to influence them long after they became the owners of their own property.

This general dislike of the Act encouraged a Conservative Government to adopt a fresh policy in 1885. For some time past English radicals such as John Bright had been advocating peasant proprietorship as the cure for Ireland's ills. The 1870 Act had offered a government loan of two-thirds the purchase price to any tenant who wished to become the owner of his land, and the 1881 Act pushed up the proportion to three-quarters; but there was little response; the peasant had neither the capital to provide the remaining one-quarter, nor the security on which to borrow it. By the Ashbourne Act of 1885, however, the State undertook to advance the whole sum required, the tenant/owner-to-be paying interest at 4 per cent. Conservatives felt able to justify this move on the grounds that dual ownership, apart from other unsatisfactory features, was dangerous in principle. It would be better to complete the transaction by transferring the property to the tenant, and paying the landlord compensation. To the Irish landowner this might appear rank bribery of the tenants; but, deprived of his control over rents, he was tempted to make the best of a bad bargain, accept his money, and depart.

At first, tenants did not swarm in great numbers to take advantage of the offer. They had been conditioned to mistrustfulness for so long, that they could not believe there was no catch. Not until over twenty years later was the full peculiar significance of the 1885 Act pointed out by a German commentator, Dr. M. J. Bonn: that under no circumstances did a purchasing tenant have to pay more in interest than he would have had to pay in rent. 'An Irish tenant therefore (by use of English credit) becomes an owner by the process of paying for 49 years a rent 28 per cent less than that of his neighbour, who is under a judicially fixed rent. . . . Under these circumstances, the purchase policy became an extremely popular one. The popularity does not imply that the Irish tenant felt the irresistible impulse to become a proprietor; it only proves that he felt himself moved by a keen aspiration towards paying 30 per cent less rent than he did before.'

In 1891, a fresh Land Act provided £33,000,000 in additional state credit to buy out more Irish landlords, and it also created the Congested Districts Board, a semi-state, semi-independent organisation designed to provide whatever special treatment might be needed for those areas of the west and mid-west that were most overcrowded and poverty-stricken. These Acts only whetted the tenants' growing appetite. As time went on and they began to understand that they were not being duped—that the land was really theirs for the asking—the grants were found to be far too small: and at the turn of the century the demand grew for more financial assistance from the Treasury.

By this time even the landlords were agreeable. A meeting was held in Dublin in 1902 between the representatives of both landlords and tenants, with Lord Dunraven in the chair; although a Unionist, he was prepared to accept that a satisfactory settlement could be reached 'only by the substitution of an occupying proprietary in lieu of a system of dual ownership; that the transfer must be by purchase on equitable terms; that purchase price must be based upon income, and that income should be second-term rents or their fair equivalent; and that the State might reasonably be asked to bridge the gap, if any, between the price that owners could afford to take and the price that tenants could afford to give'. On this basis he drafted a report, and to the general surprise it was unanimously accepted by both sides. By accepting it, the landlords countersigned the Ashbourne death warrant. They recognised that tenants could buy themselves in at an amount not exceeding what they were paying as rent, and which might (if the State could be persuaded to bridge the gap) be less. In short, the curious situation noted by Bonn was now ratified by all sides.

One more step was needed: powers to deal with, obtain and distribute land on which, owing to previous evictions, no tenant remained; for the Land Acts had done little to help landless men, or tenants whose holdings were too small to be economic. An attempt was made by William O'Brien, a Nationalist M.P., to organise a new type of Land League for their benefit; its chief demand was that the 'ranches'—the popular term of abuse for large estates on which there were no tenants, because the tenantry had been evicted earlier—should be divided up to satisfy local needs. An Act passed in 1909 introduced compulsory acquisition of untenanted land to relieve congestion; and the principle that an owner might use or abuse his land in any way he liked was finally abandoned.

Within a few years, these Land Acts transformed the Irish social scene. Poverty had remained endemic in the poorer regions; Sir Henry Robinson, a genial Castle civil servant, was later to recall in his memoirs that he had tended to scoff at stories of Irish misery, thinking that they were mere propaganda, until he saw it at first hand in the 1890's—one district in particular remaining in his memory, where 'the people were living skeletons, their faces like parchment.' After the turn of the century conditions rapidly improved. Poverty remained; but there was rarely absolute want. On the other hand, the majority of farms were small; too small to provide much more than a bare subsistence living unless capital was available or—as was happening in other countries similarly placed—until it could be provided by co-operative organisations. For obvious reasons, the tenant farmers did not themselves possess capital. Even when they were able to save, the money was not spent on the farm; it was set aside for dowries for the daughters, or gifts to the younger sons (even if the farm were large enough for a part of it to be split off as a marriage portion, or to provide for younger sons, subdivision was forbidden). Loans were hard to come by;

the banks considered farm revenue a poor risk. Nor was a farm good security for a loan, because banks knew that they would not be able to sell out a defaulting farmer, however gross his defection, without causing great local indignation; probably the sale would be boycotted. In any case, the new landowners were not accustomed to dealing with banks. Many of them had had little experience of money in any form. It was to become a stock joke that the first time money came into some houses was when the Old Age Pensions Act was passed.

The farmers' best hope would have been in the development of co-operatives, to provide the services, equipment and marketing facilities that they could not themselves afford. The idea of co-operatives was not entirely new in Ireland. Robert Owen, visiting Dublin in 1823 to spread his co-operative gospel, had been surprisingly well received; the possibilities of co-operatives were widely discussed at the time, and some actual experiments were carried out. William Thompson turned his Rosscarbery estate into a co-operative settlement, preaching economic determinism and the just distribution of wealth; and a co-operative colony was established at Ralahine, County Clare. Its objects were 'the acquisition of a common capital; the mutual assurance of its members against the evils of poverty, sickness, infirmity, and old age; the attainment of a greater share of the comforts of life than the working classes now possess; the mental and moral improvement of its adult members; the education of their children.' The experiment for a time was successful; among other things, the colony was responsible for the introduction of the first reaping machine to be used in Ireland. But before it had time to prove itself its founder, Arthur Vandeleur, lost his money gambling; the administrators of the estate broke up the community when he went bankrupt.

Even had it been a complete failure Ralahine would not necessarily have invalidated the possibility of co-operation among Irish tenant farmers. Yet it was not until near the end of the century that Sir Horace Plunkett, a younger son of the sixteenth Lord Dunsany, attempted to introduce it on a national scale. Plunkett had picked up the idea in England, where he had been educated. It was particularly applicable to the butter trade, for Irish butter, still made by age-old primitive methods on the farm, varied too much in quality to be able to compete in the English market with the new mass-produced, mass-marketed product beginning to arrive from the Continent. Plunkett saw that what was needed was an organisation that would collect and grade the farmers' milk, process it into butter and market it. A co-operative creamery was started in 1889, soon to be followed by others which provided a satisfactory source of income to dairy farmers who became members.

As a founder member of the Board set up to deal with the congested districts of Ireland, Plunkett became still more convinced of the rightness of his theories. He conceded that the Board was a most useful innovation, but insisted that it had one fundamental defect: it ignored the social aspects of the problem. So in 1894 he set out to provide a remedy by founding the Irish Agricultural Organisation to watch over and encourage the whole co-operative movement in Irish agriculture. His long-term aim was to wean the Irish farmer away from his old notion that land ownership was an end in itself, and to make him realise that agriculture to be prosperous must look upon farming as an industry and as a business, as well as a way of life. Compared to any other industry, farming in Ireland was hardly out of the stone age; considered as a business—the marketing side—it was also archaic. It was not, properly speaking, financed at all. Even as a way of life, too, it needed organisation if it was to hold the people of the land; better education, in particular, must be given—a predominantly city-type education should not be foisted on unreceptive country children. If these things were understood, farmers would realise that they would have to abandon their intense individualism and combine with their neighbours wherever joint action could prove more profitable and more pleasurable than individual action. For example, farmers in combination would be able to get equipment and machinery

cheaper—at wholesale prices, if they ran their own distributing agency; they would be able to buy equipment for com-
munal use that would be outside the purse of individuals,
and would, in any case, be wasted on a single small-holding;
and their products could be standardised for marketing, to
win a better reputation and, consequently, a better price in
England.

Plunkett's arguments were irrefutable: but he laboured
under disadvantages in trying to put them across. The
individualism of the Irish peasant made him a difficult person
to contact, let alone interest in new ideas. He was often
financially tied, too, to the local gombeen man, to whom he
would be chronically in debt; and gombeen men were of no
mind to allow rivals to install themselves locally in the shape
of co-operative stores on the British pattern. Plunkett was a
Unionist, but he was mistrusted as deeply by his fellow-
Unionists as by the Nationalists; both did their best to im-
pugn his motives and to condemn the co-operative principle. As for the republicans, they considered Plunkett
simply as an adjunct to the British kill-Home-Rule-by-kind-
ness policy: the better his ideas, the more they resented him.
Yet the co-operatives spread until by the time of the Great
War there were nearly a thousand of them in various parts of
Ireland. Only in creameries, however, did they achieve real
success; outside the milk-producing areas their influence
remained small.

Apart from the influence of Plunkett, the kill-Home-Rule-
by-kindness policy lowered—or at least gave the appearance
of lowering—the political temperature in Ireland by creating
a new, more tolerant atmosphere, not at all to the liking of
the separatists. It also created a new atmosphere in England.
In the first place, the influence of the Irish landlord element
began to diminish. The Irish Ascendancy ceased to be as
influential in England as it had been—particularly in the
House of Lords, where Irish peers had often given their
prejudices legislative sanction. The country also began to
become increasingly unprofitable. The policy of repression

had been expensive, entailing the maintenance of what amounted to a standing army of constabulary; but at least while outrages continued, the expense could always be justified in parliament as essential. But money pouring out of the Treasury to maintain this, that and the other venture in Ireland could not be justified on these grounds; and Chancellors, always hungry for savings, were anxious to be quit of it.

The absurdity of the situation was underlined by the report of the Financial Relations Commission in 1896. For a long time the fiscal arrangements made in the 1850's had been suspect; and in 1893 Gladstone had ordered an investigation into the financial relations between the two countries. It reported in 1896 that on the most optimistic reckoning Ireland's means were no more than one-twentieth of the rest of the United Kingdom; yet she had been contributing nearly one-twelfth of the United Kingdom's revenue. If (as could be argued) taxation should be levied in proportion not to the total national income but to the surplus remaining when the community's bare necessities have been paid for, the proportion that Ireland, as much the poorer part, should pay would have been far smaller—perhaps one-fortieth. Irishmen had been arguing this for years; the significance of the report lay in the fact that it was produced by an English Commission and could not, therefore, be discounted as patriotic vapouring. It could not be refuted; it could only be ignored. But even in England, it could not be ignored completely; by encouraging the Treasury to continue to look upon Ireland as a liability, it created a habit of mind less inimical to the idea of Home Rule. The fear that Home Rule might lead to discrimination against English goods remained, but it was so long since the Irish industry had been competitive on any serious scale, that the threat was not taken too seriously. Had it not been for the Ulster problem, in fact, Home Rule might have slid into existence without serious trouble.

Outside Ulster, Irish industry had remained feeble. But early in the century the journalist D. P. Moran began trying to goad Irish business men out of the state of chronic apathy into which they had fallen, by assuring them that there was a market for Irish produce, if only they would put their backs into a campaign for persuading the Irish that home-produced goods were not necessarily inferior to imported goods. Although the campaign was hard going, it helped to stimulate some interest and pride in Irish goods. The employers, however, were soon absorbed in a struggle with organised Labour. Larkin and Connolly were denouncing them for the starvation wages that they paid to their workers. A series of labour disputes in Dublin led to strikes, provoking a federation of Dublin employers to break trade union activity in the country by refusing employment to members of Larkin's Union. Strikes, lock-outs and more strikes were the result; the employers held firm, provoking 'A.E.' to publish his impassioned open letter accusing them of disrupting the social order which they ought to be helping to preserve. 'The men whose manhood you have broken', he wrote, 'will loathe you, and will always be brooding and scheming to strike a fresh blow. The children will be taught to curse you. The infant being moulded in the womb will have breathed into its starved body, the vitality of hate. It is not they—it is you who are blind Samsons pulling down the pillars of the social order.' His prophecy was soon to be verified: a Citizen Army of workers was formed, and began to drill; when the strike was finally crushed, the army remained, and, led by James Connolly, fought alongside the republicans in 1916. But after 1916 neither the land, nor industry, nor Labour made any vital contribution to the country's development until the Treaty; all causes were subordinated to the struggle for independence.

Part Three
CULTURE AND RELIGION

♣ One ♣

To 1688

To an English schoolboy, 'history' traditionally consists of recorded events, mainly extracted from written sources. The study of history through archaeology has been comparatively neglected; he may be aware of the existence of Stonehenge; of Roman remains at Uriconium, and of the local museum's collection of old pottery; but he rarely relates such relics to the history he is learning from books. For an Irish boy, however—if he happens to be interested in the subject at all—archaeology (and the legends which grow out of it) is history. The historian Alice Stopford Greene wrote of the way he can be 'stirred by what he has seen in his country home. There was, perhaps, beside it a Danes' Fort, a Giants' Ring, one of the two thousand mounds piled up in Ireland by human hands, a Rathcroghan, or a mighty Ailech of the kings, where legendary monarchs sleep on their horses waiting for the day that shall call them to ride out. He may have lived by a burial place of the great chiefs, by a round tower, by a high cross deeply carved, by some island of giants, rich in ruins and sculptured slabs. He may have been taken to the Irish Academy and seen the Psalter of Columcille; or to Trinity College to look on the book of Kells; or to the National Museum to be turned loose among the carved rocks, the copper cauldrons, the golden diadems and torques, the mighty horns of bronze, the heavy Danish swords, the weights for commerce, the marvels in metal and enamel work, the Tara brooch, the Ardagh chalice, the Cross of Cong, the long array of crosiers and bells and

L

shrines and book-covers. He may learn by chance that his country is the wonder of Europe for the wealth and beauty of its relics of the past.'

The discoveries of the archaeologists still cannot provide a very clear picture of early life in Ireland, but what it does give is distinctly clearer than the picture that can be extracted from the early annalists. Their work is full of contradictions, obvious falsities and much wishful remembering; they are purveyors of legend, and although the legends are charming, they spill over so often into fantasy that they cannot be expected to provide much accurate information, unless new research in psychology provides some aid to the interpreter—and, even then, it will be the minds of the legend-mongers, rather than of their heroes, that will begin to be understood. For the present, as Sean O'Faolain says in his study *The Irish*: 'myth and history, dreams and fact, are forever inextricably intermingled. It is therefore impossible to form any clear picture of this primitive Ireland.'

A picture, however, does not have to be absolutely clear to be revealing. Folklore and legend are the conscious expression of unconscious cravings or fears which were—and often still are—much stronger than more rational promptings. To this day, there are parts of Ireland where the inhabitants would not allow a thorn brush to be cut down; to do so would be felt to court bad luck—even by those whose faith or reason does not encourage them to harbour such superstitions; just as many sceptical English citizens continue to 'touch wood' or perform other acts of propitiation to primitive forces, as a form of emotional insurance. That these unconscious forces have profoundly influenced Irish history is not to be doubted; it is as yet impossible to analyse their effects, but they can be seen at work in the Gaelic revival at the end of the nineteenth century, when it brought a strong sense of Irishness to many of the men who were later to take part in the 1916 rising, and in the war of independence—so much so that it is commonly held that the country's independence could not have been won, had the Gaelic revival not come when it did. Such contentions can never be proved: it is enough to bear them in mind.

The archaeologists will in time have much more to contribute to the reconstruction of the early Irish scene. But it is not yet possible to gauge the full significance of 'the golden diadems and torques, the mighty horns of bronze'—the collection of Bronze Age gold in the National Museum is the most important of its kind in Europe—which have been inflated by legend into evidence of a high Irish civilisation; its echoes still heard in the lyrics of Thomas Moore, with his vision of Tara's Halls, lofty, noble—a mystical Government building. More concrete evidence is available from a later period; the sites of monasteries, and the round towers (eighteen of them survive in good condition, presumably owing their survival to the need to build them strong, to give sanctuary in times of raids). In early Irish history, evidently, there must have been periods of calm, when individual chiefs gathered around them the workmen who produced such notable work in gold and other metals; and then later the monasteries provided the opportunities for craftsmen of many kinds. But these things cannot be taken to reflect the ordinary life of Ireland.

It is not possible even to say when the Gaels first arrived, bringing with them the distinctive language and culture that have since come to be known as Irish. They presumably found an earlier culture already installed; and the two had merged, with the Gaelic element predominant, before Christianity came to the country in the fifth century A.D. Traditionally it was brought there by St. Patrick; but the story of St. Patrick is a good illustration of the difficulties that await an historian groping his way in search of reliable evidence.

As the story has usually been told, young Patricius was a Roman citizen living in the West of England. At the age of sixteen he was captured by pirates, who brought him back as a slave to Ireland, around the year A.D. 405. A few years later he escaped to the Continent, and became a priest. In a vision he heard Irish voices calling to him to bring the gospel to them; in 432 he answered them by setting out on the mission which before his death less than thirty years later resulted in the conversion of almost the entire country. Around the stories of his Christian saintliness and piety, the usual pagan ivy began to cling; in many a local district of Ireland sites were and still are displayed where he worked a variety of improbable miracles, and his banishment of snakes from Ireland became a legend on a national scale. But these things were less disturbing to scholars than some intractable discrepancies over dates. In 1942, a Celtic scholar, T. F. O'Rahilly, brought forward an accumulation of evidence to show that the discrepancies could be explained by the assumption that there was not one Patrick, but two; historians had confused them, but there was still *the* St. Patrick; even if some of the acts attributed to him had actually been performed by another, his reputation could stand unchallenged. More recently, however, further research has revealed that much of the hitherto accepted evidence about Patrick is untrustworthy. Early historians, apparently, faked it. They put in Patrick's name as the first bishop of Armagh, though he had no connection whatsoever with that see. Apparently, Armagh wished to claim jurisdiction over the whole island; and to do so, thought it advisable to claim direct descent from Patrick, already generally acknowledged to be the first missionary of Ireland. According to Professor James Carney, 'the upholders of Armagh did the only thing possible in the interest of the see and of ecclesiastical unity; they co-opted Patrick posthumously, as a foundation member, but in such a manner that modern scholarship need not be deceived.' No doubt the controversy will continue; whatever the outcome, these conflicting theories are enough to demonstrate the need to avoid too uncritical an acceptance of early sources of information.

The significance of St. Patrick would remain even if later scholars proved that he never existed; his influence on later generations of Ireland rests not on what he did, but on what they believed he did. If the myth had not grown up around him, Irish Christianity might not have become the force it did become in the centuries that followed, when it kept Christian culture alive during the chaotic period of the barbarian invasions. Before the end of the sixth century, Ireland had become the chief centre of Latin learning, from which went the teachers who spread the Christian revival back through Britain and Europe. Among them was Columba, a priest whose personality belied his name, 'the dove'. Resentment against him in Ireland forced him to leave for the rocky islet of Iona, there to found a monastery which for centuries was one of the centres of Celtic, Classical and Christian learning and piety: it was from Iona that Scotland and much of England were converted.

The greatest of the Irish missionaries was Columbanus, an apostle of the ascetic way of life, who founded in the Vosges, in Switzerland and in Italy monasteries which were to have a profound influence on the revival of Christianity and of classical culture; he and other Irish scholars did much to collect and preserve writings that would otherwise have been lost. There was also John Scotus—'John the Irish'—one of the most striking personalities at the Court of Charlemagne, who left what has been called 'the only philosophical and theological synthesis of the early middle ages'. The work of such men, and of the scholars they left behind in the monastic centres in Ireland, meant that—in Professor Kuno Meyer's words—'for once, at any rate, Ireland drew upon herself the attention of the whole world, as the great seminary of Christian and classical learning.'

The influence of these men on Europe is to some extent calculable; because their works, or the results of them, can still be seen. Their influence on Irish life is harder to judge, for in Ireland they were not missionaries, imposing themselves on their surroundings, but teachers and preachers, forming an integral part of their environment. Much of what they left in the way of records, too, was later destroyed by the Norse invaders. But enough evidence remains to justify Pro-

fessor Corkery's verdict that the fusion of the cultures, Irish
and Classical, in native and church schools, was 'the greatest
thing that has ever happened in Irish history. Thinking in
terms of tradition, which includes history and literature, and
in terms of soil, which includes politics, one can almost say
that if this companionship had not come about, one or the
other culture must have wilted; in which case, the Ireland
that Europe was so significantly to come to know, as also the
Irish that we ourselves actually know, would never have
been.'

For the monks, even if at first they may have been inclined
to be contemptuous of the old language, eventually gave it
body by translating it from the spoken into the written word,
providing it with a conventional spelling; their work made
possible a written, as well as an oral, record of traditional
song and story. From the lyrics, romances and legends of
fresh beauty, to the intricate convolutions of the Book of
Kells, the evidence which remains is distinctive and remarkable; and Ireland was the first nation north of the Alps to
produce a whole body of literature in her own speech.

The Golden Age was cut short by the Norsemen, who
began to appear around the coasts towards the end of the
eighth century; and as they grew bolder, their attention was
naturally attracted to the monasteries, with their treasures.
In the two hundred years of raids the Norsemen were able to
carry away much that was valuable, and to destroy the records
that the monasteries possessed. Under the strain of Norse
pressure, too, the Irish ecclesiastical structure, built as it
was on the monastic foundation, was undermined; it never
fully recovered.

The dominant influence of Irish Christianity in England,
too, had been broken by the Synod of Whitby in 664. The
questions to be decided there were in themselves unimportant—the style of monks' tonsure, and the date Easter should
be celebrated. But the decisions taken represented a decisive
defeat for the Irish view, in favour of the view of Rome. The
Irish themselves eventually accepted the Synod's decision,

and in doing so, further weakened their position. Their Church structure was different from England's, where the now familiar system of dioceses, under bishops, had already evolved. In Ireland the monastery was the centre, with the Abbot as the most important figure; bishops, who were attached to important families, were often little more than superior chaplains, numerous and of little account. After the Norman invasion, the chaotic state of Irish church discipline and organisation, which had led to considerable laxity in observance, attracted the adverse notice of the English churchmen; from Canterbury, Lanfranc called for reform, and Rome looked favourably on his proposals. The Irish re-former Malachy also tried to introduce Roman reforms, managing to prepare the way for the national Synod which met in 1152 to re-establish the Catholic faith, to purify and correct the people's morals, and to divide the country into Sees, with the Primacy at what was supposed to be Patrick's centre, Armagh. But in his visits to Rome, Malachy—as it was his interest to do—had given so scarifying a picture of conditions in Ireland that the Papacy was inclined to favour anybody who could promise even more radical treatment. The assumption of Irish over-lordship by Henry II, therefore, was not displeasing to Rome; on the contrary, Henry claimed that Pope Adrian IV had actually commissioned him, by the Bull 'Laudabiliter', to subdue the Irish and impose reforms on them; and whether or not the Bull really existed, there is no reason to suppose that the Papacy was anything but gratified by the success attended English arms in Ireland.

Inevitably, the reforms tended to anglicise; both religious and secular institutions lost their Irish flavour. The state of war which existed in the country, too, militated against the survival of the Irish tradition. But it survived; to the alarm of the English administrators, it tended to replace Norman-French and English, rather than vice versa (just as the English vernacular had replaced Norman in England), where the two languages came into contact. The Statutes of Kilkenny in 1366 reflected this fear; they berated the colonists who had drifted into Irish ways, and imposed penalties unless they gave them up. But the statutes were ignored. 'Many of the Norman houses', Professor Corkery says, '—the Old English, as they called themselves—"lived Irishly", as the phrase went.' They gave their children an Irish education; some of them set up their own 'bardic schools'—for the bards were teachers, not simply itinerant minstrels. Brehon law was practised almost universally; and the finest specimens of bardic poetry come out of these two centuries of resurgence. In 1541, the Earl of Ormond had to translate the Speaker's Address into Irish so that a predominantly Old English parliament could understand it; by this time Irish had spread back all over the country—though not through the towns. The towns never became Irish; their citizens remained absorbed in their commercial affairs, language to them being simply a medium of commerce. The result was that the towns developed no distinct culture of any kind; in other lands, art and literature are often associated with an urban atmosphere, in Ireland they flourished only in the country.

The Church, too, lost contact in its higher levels with the Irish. Bishops tended to be English; king's men, out of sympathy with the Irish people, unable even to converse with them—which was to prove important, at the time of the Reformation. The Tudors were able to weed out opposition among the Old English in Ireland by wars and executions and plantations, and to replace them on their estates by more amenable settlers or by relatives tamed by an upbringing at the English court; and they could wipe out the monasteries and the bardic schools, slaying the teachers, burning the records and looting the treasures. But the Tudors could not prevent Irish from being talked: nor, as their representatives were ignorant of the language, could they use it for the purpose of converting the Irish to the new Anglican faith. Once again in Tudor times the traditional church and the traditional language found themselves in alliance—an alliance of desperate circumstances. Had the English been able to use the Church, as they were later to do, as an ally against nationalism, the story might have been very different; but the bishops who joined the Reformed Church, cut off from contact with their language, were helpless; and with the disappearance of the Irish schools, monastic and secular, there was, in any case, no instrument which they could use to spread the reformed religion.

By this time, too, the English were facing a more positive nationalism than they had found before. The revival in Irishness had provided a new outlook, expressed in the bardic poems which anthropomorphised Ireland into the figure of a beautiful but sorrowful maiden, much grieved by her persecutor—England. This changing attitude must have helped Hugh O'Neill in his efforts to secure a unified military command; and have made it impossible for the English to carry out Henry VIII's idea of conquest by persuasion. Naturally the English came to identify Irish culture with the resistance that they were trying to stamp out; and the Irish came to accept the identification, so that when the 1641 rebellion broke out there was a romantic gloss on the aims of the Confederates, who looked back to the Irish past as to a Golden Age.

The Church, too, was inseparably bound up in this new nationalism. Before the Reformation there are very few signs of strong feeling in Ireland for the Papacy as an institution. The higher ecclesiastics accepted the Act of Supremacy; Jesuit missionaries sent tentatively to Ulster in 1542 met with a discouraging reception, and soon departed. But they stayed long enough to realise that the Irish were antagonistic to the reformed Church, and untouched by Protestantism. The only effect, therefore, of the Statutes which followed Elizabeth's accession—the Act of Supremacy, securing the power of the Crown over the Church, and compelling all office holders to take the oath to the Queen; and the Act of Uniformity, introducing the Book of Common Prayer and compelling clergy to follow its ritual, was to cut the people off from the conforming clergy, and to make them turn instead to the missionaries that began to arrive from Rome. Sometimes these

missionaries were horrified to find that the Irish were barbarous, ignorant, superstitious and much given to vice: but
this was hardly surprising, considering that the whole Irish
ecclesiastical structure had been destroyed by Henry VIII,
and that the faithful had since lacked any guidance. They
flocked to the missionaries to receive it; and the missionaries'
zeal, Spenser noted, made a marked contrast with the laxity
of the Established clergymen; 'they spare not to come out of
Spain and from Rome by long toil and dangerous travelling,
where they know peril of death awaits them, and no reward
or riches are to be found.' Within a few years the Catholic
Church was firmly in control over the whole countryside,
and well-positioned to assume control of the cities, too, had
the English authorities lacked the force to prevent it. By
contrast, the Established Church was demoralised. Many
benefices were empty: others could count on no congrega-
tion; churches were falling into ruin; and the clergy, for the
most part, contented themselves with securing more revenue
by pluralism, and enjoying it, if possible, away from their
livings. Little attempt could be made at proselytism, as the
clergy spoke no Irish. The Book of Common Prayer was not
translated into Irish until the reign of James I; and not until
Charles I's reign did Bedell translate the Old Testament into
Irish and establish an Irish catechism. 'Whatever disorders
you see in the Church of England,' Spenser said, 'you may
find in Ireland, and many more; gross simony, greedy
covetousness, fleshly incontinency, careless sloth, and generally all disordered lives in the common clergy.' Priests be-
haved as if they were laymen, taking other jobs, and neither
reading the scriptures, nor preaching, nor administering
communion. The only real interest they took Spencer thought
was in collecting tithes, dues and offerings.

The Acts of Supremacy and Uniformity were enforced as
best as the administration could, with the appropriate penalties; and as the dispossession and plantation policy was in
full swing at the time, land and faith were brought together
in common resentment, to become the issues which set

off the Desmond rebellion. But Catholic rulers, such as Philip of Spain, tended to regard Ireland less as an ally than a piece to be moved in their political games. Suspicion of his motives made the Irish leaders mistrustful of foreigners, even of Jesuit influence; there was no real unity of purpose; all the Desmond rebellion achieved was crushing defeat, and the provision of more land for plantation.

Unable to convert the people to the reformed religion, the authorities were increasingly tempted to fall back on more rigorous persecution of Catholics; Elizabeth's reign provided the Church with a few martyrs, one of them an Archbishop of Cashel, tortured and executed in 1584. On more than one occasion Mountjoy came out strongly against the repressive policy: writing to Court in 1603 he expressed his conviction that 'a violent course will do little good to win men's consciences. . . . The bringing of the Inquisition lost the King of Spain the Low Countries, and of their provinces they have lost almost all with their excessive violence in prosecuting the contrary religion. I am of the opinion that all religions grow under persecution: it is truly good doctrine and example that must prevail.' Cecil paid no attention to the advice; but the death of Elizabeth opened the way for James I, who was believed to favour religious toleration. So confident were the Irish Catholics that he would repeal galling enactments that in some towns they simply took over, opened up their old churches and joyfully observed their old religion. But Mountjoy was not prepared to concede their right to take the law into their own hands; although his views on toleration might have been acceptable to James, James was in no position—particularly after the Gunpower Plot—to make concessions, and both Mountjoy and his successor, Sir Arthur Chichester, were instructed to enforce the Acts of Supremacy and Uniformity.

By this time, the Catholics were sufficiently numerous and well-established even in the cities to make government, without their co-operation, impossible. Some compromise had to be reached: and throughout James's and Charles's reigns—

and again in Charles II's—an uneasy bargain was struck
whereby toleration was connived at—as it was in England—
rather than openly granted; the amount varying according
to the willingness of the Irish Catholics to provide the King
with money, and the state of anti-Popery feeling in England.
In the same period, an attempt was being made to inject a
little life into the Established Church. Before the end of
Elizabeth's reign a university had been founded in Dublin;
and for a time there appeared a possibility that it might become a useful centre for proselytising. But the Church had
fallen too far into decay. Sir John Davis, in 1610, reiterated
Spenser's earlier criticisms: 'the churches are ruined and
fallen down to the ground in all parts of the kingdom. There
is no divine service, no christening of children, no receiving
of the sacrament, no Christian meeting or assembly, no, not
once a year: in a word, no more demonstration of religion
than amongst tartars or cannibals.' An individual enthusiast
like Bedell might make some local impact; his popularity in
his diocese, which survived even the religious passions inflamed by the 1641 rebellion, suggests that a really earnest
campaign in the vernacular might have produced results a century before. By Stuart times it was too late. The Established
Church evolved into the Church of the Ascendancy; a political
and a social force, and through the medium of Trinity
College, Dublin, destined to exert a powerful cultural influence, but endowed with little religious significance.

Of more importance in this period was the emergence of
dissenting Protestantism after the plantation of Ulster,
developing into a fully-fledged Presbyterian organisation at
the time of the Commonwealth. By the Restoration, it was
strong enough to maintain itself against the Establishment;
although theoretically a Presbyterian was subject to the same
disabilities as a Catholic, Governments were inclined to
recognise for political purposes the difference between the
two. After the 1670's the Presbyterian Church was even
conceded a small annual state grant, the *Regium Donum*—'less
as a mark of favour than as a precautionary bribe'.

The uncertain position in which the Catholics found themselves never knowing from one day to the next what tribulations the future had in store for them, and the absurdities of a situation where breaches of the recusancy laws were sometimes connived at, made it inevitable that they should take advantage of any English weakness; and the Irish rebellion of 1641 had some of the features of a crusade. As in Elizabethan times, there was an underlying disunity. The Old English and the Irish alike were both Catholic: but the Old English were prepared to remain loyal to the Crown—in the hope that Charles I, if he asserted himself over parliament, would reward them with toleration—while the Irish leaned towards a separatist policy, designed to set up an independent Catholic state. The divisions went deep, leading to rivalries and hatreds even stronger than those that were felt for the parliamentarians, the common foe. Dissention contributed to the rebellion's failure, and at the same time helped to destroy what remained of the old Gaelic Ireland.

The Irish language had not been directly attacked after 1603, though its stamina had been sapped by plantation: some bardic schools had managed to survive, and there was a faint prospect, had the rebellion driven the English out of Ireland, of a revived Gaelic Society. Owen Roe and other leaders of the Confederation were distinctively Irish—a feature which cannot have escaped Cromwell when he prepared to drive the Irish 'to hell or Connaught'. By his Plantation the old Irish aristocracy were almost eliminated, and the Irish who remained were pushed so far away from the centres of Anglo-Irish life that any chance of the old language and customs regaining their hold, as they had so often done in the past, was destroyed,

With the Restoration the pattern of James I's and Charles I's reigns was resumed, though more erratically. Charles II had greater sympathy with Catholicism than the earlier Stuarts; but he was even more concerned for his own safety. On the one hand, many of the Catholic gentry were restored to their lands; the viceroy, Ormonde, in an attempt to encourage the Old English who had supported him at the time of the rebellion, looked favourably on a scheme to enable Catholics to gain toleration by acknowledging the king's temporal power; and although the scheme fell through, the penal code was not heavily enforced against them. On the other hand Titus Oates's Popish Plot provoked a spasm of even more blind intolerance than had the Gunpowder Plot; one victim was Oliver Plunkett, Archbishop of Armagh, who was brought to England, tried and executed. But on balance, Catholicism quietly reasserted itself during the reign; and when James II came to the throne in 1685, appointing Richard Talbot, brother of the Catholic archbishop of Dublin, as Lieutenant-General in Ireland, Catholics were ready to move in to most of the positions of authority in the administration, the army and the courts, with little disruption of business.

The change-over was alarming enough to send Irish Protestants hurrying to England, there to play on the fears that led to the invitation to William of Orange, and the revolution of 1688. James's failure to reassure the Protestants who remained—for many more of them fled across to join William when he arrived in England—helped to bring about his own defeat. It was Protestant fears that led to his closing of the gates of Derry, and its prolonged resistance to siege; resistance which, in turn, helped to give William time to muster the forces with which he won the Battle of the Boyne.

♣ *Two* ♣

1691 - 1829

The Treaty of Limerick in 1691 granted the Irish Catholics such privileges 'as they had enjoyed under Charles II'—in itself an indication of the amount of toleration which connivance had then secured them—'and as were consistant with the laws of Ireland'. The second phrase offered an easy escape from too scrupulous obedience to the first; William, though anxious that the Treaty clauses should be honoured, was unable to insist that it should be honoured. Connived toleration ceased; the Penal Laws took its place. They were easy to enforce because the Catholics no longer had any respected or influential body of social opinion to sustain them. The Old English, both as Loyalists and Catholics, had naturally answered James's summons to a parliament in Dublin; they had fought in his cause; and most of them, outlawed after his defeat, flew with the Wild Geese to make new, and often distinguished careers on the Continent. Such few remnants of the Old Irish as had survived Cromwell also disappeared.

William's Irish parliaments were aggressively Protestant. Rejecting the safeguards written into the Treaty of Limerick, they embarked on fresh legislation against Catholics. The code that came to be known as 'the Penal Laws' had as its object less the conversion of Catholics than the ensuring that, unconverted, they remained powerless. It altered the laws of descent, substituting Gavelkind—compulsory division of a holding between all the sons of the family—for primogeniture, unless a son was prepared to turn apostate, in which case he was entitled to the whole property, and maintenance suitable to his rank. It changed the laws of property, forbidding Papists (the legal term then normally used for Catholics) to purchase or lease land, except on short tenancies. It forbade Catholics to teach. They were not allowed to possess arms, or a horse worth more than £5—not that many of them can have had such a horse. An Act of 1704 permitted the Catholic clergy their freedom but only if they registered; apparently in the belief that it would be better for the Government to know its enemies, so that they could be offered a life pension if they joined the Church of England; those who did not register were to be transported. All Catholic prelates were ordered into exile, in the hope that ordinations of new priests would cease—a hope that was not fulfilled.

The effect of this persecution was to bring the Catholic Church and the Irish people once again into the melancholy intimacy of suffering. The priests not only stayed with the people; they became part of the people, as they had been in Elizabethan times; and the people survived the century of penal legislation with their faith undiminished. Here and there cases of apostasy were remarked, but they were few —hardly more frequent than they would have been had no penal laws existed; and some of them were of design, the convert pretending to enter the Established Church in order to save Catholic property from division or spoliation or loss.

Catholics had little inducement to become converts out of admiration for the Established Church. Swift was as shocked as Spenser had been at what he found, when he first arrived at his first Irish parish; sadly he described the Church's debility, of its internal dissensions and of its financial weakness. His own church had no parsonage, and was in ruins. He was later sarcastically to put the blame on the curious fact that although only the most pious men were selected as Irish bishops, in England, on the way to Ireland they were invariably kidnapped and killed by highwaymen, who appropriated their credentials and went to Ireland in their place. Sometimes the bishops did not even both to cross the Irish sea; they left their Sees empty. Those who came to Ireland often involved themselves in politics, as a lucrative sideline. They were usually English; it suited English Governments to retain political control in Ireland, and bishops were accordingly selected for their political pliability. The Primate, as the subject of highest rank in Ireland, took his place at the head of the Lord Justices, from whose hands patronage was distributed, and into whose hands power fell. Archbishop Stone, who virtually ruled Ireland from 1747-1764, was a typical representative; a crafty politician, adept at securing the passage of controversial Bills with the help—as he admitted—of the gentle lubrication of wine. The Church as a result was able to wield enormous secular influence. As a religious body, its record was uninspiring.

The Dissenters, however, established themselves still more firmly in Ulster during the eighteenth century, in spite of the hostility of the Anglicans, who tended to feel about dissent even more bitterly than they did about Catholicism. William III had tried to help them, in return for their assistance against James I; he renewed and increased the *Regium Donum*, and tried to secure them a Toleration Bill; but the Anglicans were sufficiently influential in parliament to have it rejected. Nevertheless, the Dissenters on the whole had little to complain about while William lived. After his death, a sacramental test was imposed which kept them out from administrative posts; their ministers were not even allowed, as registered Catholic priests were, to perform the marriage ceremony. In desperation they began to emigrate in their thousands to America. By the time of the American War of Independence, they formed a sixth of the United States' population, fired with hearty anti-British sentiments; those who stayed behind were also fired by resentment of their treatment, a fact whose significance became clear when Wolfe Tone, forming his Society of United Irishmen, chose the Dissenters of Belfast as his first allies.

The city and the country Dissenters had divergent interests. The city men wanted to free themselves from galling restric-

tions, and for that purpose they were willing to ally themselves with members of any religion, Protestant or Catholic.
But the Presbyterian farmer, however great his dislike of
Anglican landlords, was also deeply mistrustful of the Catholic
landless men who would hasten to bid for his farm, should
his landlord evict him. Some Ulster landlords were anxious
to have a Catholic tenantry because Catholics were willing
to forgo the protection of the Ulster Custom, which gave
tenants rights over their land. The dissenters were prepared
to fight for these rights; they banded themselves into armies
to terrorise landlords or intruding Catholic tenants, in
defence of tenant right. Arthur Young in his *Tour in Ireland*
refers to the 'Hearts of Steel', a body who 'began in 1770
against rents and tithes, and from that went to all sorts of
grievances. It was in reality owing to the impudence and
levelling spirit of the Dissenters.' But he admitted that they
had a just grievance: tithes. He thought the tithe farmers a
bad lot—an opinion he was frequently to repeat. Later, the
Peep-o'-Day-Boys formed an anti-Catholic organisation in
County Armagh, to prevent Catholics from bidding for
Protestant farms. The organisation was to have far-reaching
consequences; in 1795 it clashed with members of the
Catholic counter-movement, the Defenders, at the Battle of
the Diamond, where a score of Defenders were killed;
following the battle, the Orange Order was founded, to protect Protestant tenants from Catholic infiltration on to the land.

The Defenders were only one of many similar Catholic
organisations which sprung up, sometimes locally, sometimes
over wide areas, among the tenants of the South. The first
of them had been the original 'Tories'—landowners dispossessed by Cromwell's plantation, and not allowed back by
Charles II. They had hung around their old homes, making
raids or biding their time. Later there were the Rapparees
and the Whiteboys. Usually the land was at the root of their
activity. The Whiteboys sprang up as a consequence of mid-
eighteenth-century evictions. Although they were sometimes
accused of having links with England's enemies through the

Wild Geese, they were normally considered simply as terror-
ists; but it is possible that they had more significance. They
were Irish speakers; their organisations may have helped to
breed and to preserve the Irish songs and verses that come
from this period. Most of them are melancholy, looking back
to a more glorious past—a past, they hoped, which would
be recreated when the Wild Geese returned in strength.
Some of them are of high quality; evidently the Irish peasantry at this time was not absolutely crushed by the weight of
its economic, political and religious burdens; the last distilled juices of Irish tradition were being squeezed out by
oppression. And the poets of the time, although unsophisti-
cated, obviously had literary knowledge and ability far above
the level of the boors and clods whom they described—their
landlords. Corkery in his *Hidden Ireland* likens them to Burns,
but without Burns's affectations; the aloof Egan O'Rahilly;
the vagrant, feverish Owen Roe O'Sullivan; the entertaining
Brian Merriman.

But the Irish tradition began to weaken as all hope of a
revival dwindled. The remnants of the Catholic aristocracy
were too scattered to keep it alive even as a pastime, and the
Anglo-Irish, it has been said, were as indifferent to the
tradition of the older Ireland 'as a European trader is to the
native language and culture of Burma or China'. They were
not even aware of the existence of any cultural activity; nor,
to judge from what is recorded about Anglo-Irish Society at
the time, would many of them necessarily have been aware of
it even if it had been in English. They were on balance a
thoroughly disreputable, unscrupulous, hard-drinking bunch
of blackguards who lived in Ireland only because dissipation
was easier and cheaper there than in England. Ironically they
have left a fine legacy behind them in the Georgian country-
and town-houses which are Ireland's architectural pride. It
would be pleasant to feel that the peaceful beauty of Georgian
Dublin reflects the civilisation that gave it birth; but it gives
a far less accurate picture even than Jonah Barrington's
memoirs, which in their flights of fancy are more true to his

irresponsible environment. The architect responsible for Dublin's noblest civic buildings, James Gandon, was an Englishman; and of his patrons the one responsible for the finest of them, the Custom House, was John Beresford, a citizen scrupulous only in his devotion to his own financial interests and to the preservation of the oligarchy that protected them.

Perhaps this is to paint too black a picture of the Ascendancy life in eighteenth- and early nineteenth-century Ireland; there were compensatory features, which can be found in the pages of Mrs. Delany's journals, or the letters of the Fitzgerald family. And one art flourished as it has rarely flourished since classical times: oratory. It is impossible now to judge the effect of the speeches of Grattan, John Philpot Curran or William Plunket on their audiences, or to compare them as orators with their fellow countrymen Burke and Sheridan in England. But an extract from Curran's defence of the freedom of the press in the trial of the United Irishman, Hamilton Rowan, may give some indication—bearing in mind that it was not simply the content of his speeches, but his use of the human voice as an instrument, that won the undisguised admiration of his contemporaries.

'What calamities are the people saved from by having public communications left open to them? I will tell you, gentlemen, what they are saved from, and what the Government is saved from. I will tell you also, to what both are exposed by shutting up the communication. In one case, sedition speaks aloud, and walks abroad. The demagogue goes forth; the public eye is upon him; he frets his busy hour upon the stage; but soon either weariness, or bribe, or punishment, or disappointment bears him down and drives him off, and he appears no more. In the other case, how does the work of sedition go forward? Night after night the muffled rebel steals forth in the dark, and casts another and another brand upon the pile; to which, when the fatal hour of maturity shall arrive, he will apply the flame. As the advocate of society, therefore, of peace, of domestic liberty, and the lasting union of the two countries, I conjure you to guard the liberty of the press, that great sentinel of the state, that grand detector of public imposture; guard it because when it sinks there sinks with it, in one common grave, the liberty of the subject, and the security of the Crown.'

For the most part, however, the Anglo-Irish were unprepossessing, and those of them who are remembered, are remembered chiefly for their courage in breaking away from the traditions of the society which had nurtured them: Grattan, Tone, and Lord Edward Fitzgerald. But none of these men had—as Davis was later to have—a sense of their Irish background; they neither knew nor cared about the hidden Ireland, still sighing under Ascendancy's feet. One of the very few who knew something of it was Burke; his mother had been a Catholic, and he had his first instruction in the classics in a hedge school. He brought with him to England not only the wider vision that distinguishes him from even the greatest of his contemporaries, and a casual unscrupulousness in financial matters characteristic of the Anglo-Irish of his day, but also a conviction that the Catholics had been the victims of gross injustice: he more than any other man was responsible for their emancipation from the Penal Laws. 'A *nation* to be persecuted!' he sarcastically told his Bristol constituents, ridiculing the idea that the Irish Catholics could be suppressed indefinitely: in such circumstances, he insisted, it was 'prudent to be just'.

Such of the Catholic aristocracy as remained in the country owed their survival either to pretended apostasy or to their social contacts—influential Protestants protecting them. In the cities, a small Catholic middle class remained in business, where their religion was not an outright bar to entry into business, though it was often a handicap. Their main anxiety was not to attract any unfavourable notice. Such agitation as there was on their behalf, therefore, was mainly conducted by Protestants; a Catholic Committee formed around 1760 achieved little, and it was left to the members of the patriot party, in particular Grattan, to take up their cause. The Government was even more alarmed at the prospect of an alliance between Catholics and Volunteers than of the revival of popery; by 1774, the international situation was sufficiently menacing for the decision to be taken to come to terms with the Catholics, and the Catholic bishops agreed to repudiate the temporal power of the Papacy, in return for a general relaxation of the Penal Laws. These were modified still further four years later, and abandoned altogether in the flush of Volunteer enthusiasm in 1782.

Although the Volunteers were committed to a policy of toleration for the Catholics, they were divided on the issue whether Catholics should enjoy the franchise; and in any case the Junta which came into power after 1782 was determined that they should not have it. Although no longer labouring under penal code, Catholics continued to suffer from various disqualifications.

They were accordingly tempted to take the hand Wolfe Tone held out to them, after he had founded the Society of United Irishmen. The Society, like the Volunteers earlier, was not united on the question of concessions to the Catholics; in his journal Tone records the views of the objectors—that the Catholics if emancipated would establish an inquisition, demand back their old properties, and insist upon setting up an exclusively Catholic government, incapable of enjoying or extending civil liberty. But Tone was resolute—much more resolute, he was quickly to find, than most of the Catholic Committee. They were naturally anxious to secure concessions; but they lived in terror of getting mixed up with anything that the government might decide was revolutionary or seditious, and use as an excuse to reimpose the penal laws. They counselled moderation, caution. Tone, who became assistant secretary of their Committee, tried to coax them into action, but it was hard work. Their bishops, particularly, were terrified of anything that smacked of resolution. They were reluctant even to approach the English Government, for fear they might give offence or embarrassment; but eventually. largely owing to the energy of a Catholic radical John Keogh, they plucked up courage, pushed out their more timorous colleagues, and appointed a sub-committee to present an address to King George III. They were graciously received; so graciously that, as Tone had feared, they came away prepared to accept very much less than the full emancipation they had intended to demand. Pitt, sensing this, seized his opportunity. He instructed the Irish Junta to put forward a further relief bill, giving Catholics owning freehold property worth 40s. the vote and other concessions, such as allowing them to take degrees and commissions in the army. The Junta was alarmed; but as Pitt had foreseen, the effect of the Act was to content the Catholics. They dissolved their committee in a flurry of votes of thanks, and Tone found himself not with the powerful body of devoted followers for which he had hoped, but only a gold medal and a bonus.

For the next few years the Catholics were more concerned to prove themselves worthy of the royal confidence, than to pursue other political aims. Those who had looked favourably on the Society of United Irishmen, repudiated it when it was proscribed; such Catholic support as the Society received was found mainly among the Defenders, who had gained nothing from the Act of 1793. It was an object lesson to the authorities in the value of timely and tactfully made concessions; and it was followed up two years later by the establishment of a seminary for Catholics at Maynooth. Again, the motive was not generosity. The French Revolution had cut the Irish priesthood off to some extent from its normal resource—a continental education; Pitt was astute enough to realise that if he could establish and endow a seminary in Ireland, it might be able to secure the priesthood's loyalty. These conciliatory gestures had the effect of keeping the Church—as distinct from the Defenders and individual priests, who in some cases fought with the rebels—from any contact with the United Irishmen in 1798 and it helped to win the Church's support for the Union two years later.

In case the memory of benefits received should not be
sufficient, Pitt promised further concessions to the Catholic
bishops if they supported the Union. They did; only to hear
that the king's conscience, which had begun to plague him as
he grew older and madder, was an insuperable obstacle. The
Union, in fact, hardly recognised the existence of the Catholic
Church. Pitt had said he would grant Emancipation (by which
was coming to be meant the right of the Catholics to sit in
parliament), commutation of tithes and provision for the
priesthood. Instead of holding out for these claims, he resigned when the King opposed them; and the Government
which succeeded quickly made it clear that it had no intention of honouring them.

In the meantime, the result of Catholic defection had been
to leave the United Irishmen heavily dependent on dissent in
the North for their support. The feud between the Catholic
and Protestant tenantry—the Defenders and the Peep-o'-
Day-boys—was a handicap, but in the towns the movement
continued to find its most staunch support from the Dissenters. The Government had tried to conciliate them in
1780 by the removal of the Test clause that prevented them
from holding office. But they still resented the hold which the
Established Church maintained, through the Junta; and they
were dissatisfied with Grattan's continued failure to keep
alive the spirit of the Volunteers. The news of the French
Revolution encouraged them to believe the time had come
to make themselves felt in Ireland. They were not, however,
united enough or strong enough to play a decisive part in
1798. The old split between those who desired to confine
themselves to constitutional action and those who felt that
force was required reasserted itself; many of the leaders were
arrested and imprisoned before the rebellion broke out; and
those forces which took the field were easily defeated.

After the Union, the emancipation campaign languished,
until a new Catholic Board was set up. Like its predecessor, it
consisted at first mainly of the Catholic gentry, with a few
well-to-do merchants like Keogh; but by 1810 it had been

joined by some younger men, more vocal and resolute, of whom the ablest was Daniel O'Connell. Again, the Board tended to divide into two groups, the moderate urging caution and the progressive, of whom O'Connell quickly assumed the leadership, urging action. They split on the question whether the Crown should retain a veto on episcopal appointments made by the Pope—which the bishops had earlier accepted, but about which they were changing their minds. O'Connell led the opposition to the Veto with much vehemence, disrupting the Board in the process; by 1815 the Emancipation campaign had virtually collapsed, and for a few years defied his efforts to revive it. He started up yet another Catholic committee; but it remained puny. As late as 1823 he was able to obtain the necessary quorum for a committee only by press-ganging a couple of priests from the shop below into coming to the meeting. But at this point he hit upon an idea which was to provide him with the support he needed.

O'Connell had an Irish, rather than an Anglo-Irish background. He had little use either for Irish as a language or a culture, but he spoke, as it were, the English of the people: he was a Catholic and a countryman, and he understood the masses better (not that he had much affection for them) than any other Irish politician until the—very different—de Valera. He realised intuitively that the masses must be given a stake in the Emancipation campaign; and he provided them with a chance to place it, at the rate of a penny a month, in a Catholic Rent collected at church doors. Within a few months the Rent was bringing in £1,000 a week. After some hesitation the hierarchy, led by Bishop Doyle, came in behind the movement; so did most of the priests, and within a couple of years the Association had expanded from a small Dublin committee to a nationwide organisation, which not only fought the political battle for Emancipation, but took up Catholic causes big and little throughout the country.

The Government of the day grew alarmed. It was divided on Catholic claims; but even those who, like the Lord

Lieutenant, Wellesley, were well-disposed, wanted to deal
with the Catholic question in their own time and on their
own terms; they did not care to have concessions extracted
from them by pressure. They were further alarmed by the
intemperate language which O'Connell used—often about his
own supporters, when they thwarted him. To the end of his
life he never realised that wounding phrases thrown off
casually in the heat of controversy might alienate good friends
and leave an indelible impression on opponents, justifying
them in their belief that he was a man not to be trusted; by
his intemperance he lost the support of the dwindling liberal
Protestant element and of the Castle Catholics. His strength
in the country, however, was sufficiently great to overcome
this handicap. The Clare election in 1828 was gained by his
winning-over of the Catholic 40s. freeholders, who hitherto
had voted as their landlords directed. It proved to be not
merely a flamboyant gesture, but a declaration of war on the
constitution; and parliament had to surrender.

♣ *Three* ♣

1829 - 1921

Politically, the gain to the Catholics from Emancipation was small; psychologically, the effect was enormous, because victory had at last been won not by leaders from the Ascendancy class, but by the people. But the Emancipation campaign also finally demonstrated that there were no longer any prospects of an alliance between Dissenter and Catholic in Ireland. Before 1800 they were companions in misfortune; both suffered from Anglican oppression, and the hatred of the common enemy was sometimes sufficient to make them forget mutual differences. After the Union the British adopted a different policy. In 1802 the Government handsomely increased the *Regium Donum*, enabling reasonable salaries to be paid to Presbyterian ministers—provided they were known to be loyal: payment was not as of right, but for services rendered. That this policy was deliberate is clear from the correspondence of Castlereagh's secretary, who boasted that Presbyterian ministers would be 'henceforth a subordinate ecclesiastical aristocracy whose feeling must be that of zealous loyalty, and whose influence upon their people will be as surely sedative when it should be so, and exciting when it should be so, as it was the direct reverse before'.

After the Union, too, the collapse of industry in the south, contrasting with the comparative prosperity of Ulster, gave the inhabitants of the industrial core of Ulster divergent interests from the southerners. Whatever might be his sentimental pull towards Irishness, the forces tugging him the other way were to prove the stronger; for Presbyterians as well as Anglicans were alarmed at the rebirth of aggressive

187

Catholicism, reflected in Daniel O'Connell; they rebuffed him, and he found himself unable to make any progress in the North. Except for a brief period when the land war seemed likely to provide Protestant and Catholic tenants with grounds for an alliance against landlordism, dissent ceased to be potentially a nationalist force. Quite the reverse, in fact; Presbyterianism rapidly became anti-liberal and anti-Catholic, rallying, with a few exceptions, to Unionism when Home Rule became a political question—much to Gladstone's chagrin, as he had assumed that dissent in Ireland could be— as he hoped to keep it in England—politically Liberal.

When Emancipation was secured O'Connell turned his attention to a campaign for repeal of the Union. But there was another campaign ahead of far more immediate concern to the bulk of his followers in the country—against tithes. Tithes had been the most galling, if not the most oppressive, of the Irish peasant's burdens. Their object had originally been to provide the clergy with payment for the economically unproductive but spiritually necessary services which they rendered to their parishioners. But where, as in the greater part of Ireland, the Established clergy were of a different religion to their parishioners, any spiritual consolation they had to offer was either valueless or—if pressed on the parishioners—an incitement to apostasy. It was also objectionable for other reasons. Tithes were not fixed; they were re-assessed each year, so that farmers found the profits they hoped to make in good years appropriated by the parson or by his agent, the tithe proctor. Just as land agents were often more hated than landlords, because they were encountered by the tenantry at first hand, so the tithe proctor was often more hated than the parson who employed him. Stimulated by the success of the repeal campaign, the Catholic tenantry began to band themselves together to resist tithes; the military had to be called in to assist in collecting them; scuffles and pitched battles followed, of which the 'Wallstown Massacre' of 1832, in which four men were killed and many wounded, was the most notorious. It soon became

clear that the cost of collecting tithes was becoming greater
than the amount that could be collected; and the Melbourne
Government managed—in spite of the opposition of the
Lords, who thought it was truckling to violence—to pass an
Act in 1838 converting tithes into a rent charge payable by
the landlord at 75 per cent of the former tithe rate. The
change benefited the Protestant clergy, who found it easier
to secure their money, and the landlords, who had it in their
power to extract the full 100 per cent in rent out of the
tenants; all that the tenants got out of it was the knowledge
that they were henceforth paying for what they considered
heresy only at second hand.

In this period, too, the State accepted the need to provide
education for Catholic children, for the first time. Schools
had been provided as far back as in Elizabethan times, but
they were invariably Protestant, and few Catholics would let
their children go to them. In the time of the Penal Laws, no
Catholic had been allowed to teach in a private house or a
school, or 'publicly'; the best children could hope for was a
nearby hedge school, where they could receive the rudiments
of an education under the sky. When the Penal Laws were
relaxed, Catholic private schools quickly sprang up, mainly
for families who could afford to pay for their children's
education; and in 1811 the Kildare Place Society was founded,
with the aim of doing something for families without means.
The original intention was to avoid proselytism; even
O'Connell was, for a time, a member. But soon charges were
made against the Society of proselytising on the sly, and it
collapsed.

In 1828 a Select Committee of the House of Commons,
appointed to see what could be done, advised that the remedy
would lie in schools where the pupils could be segregated
according to their beliefs, for purposes of religious instruction. But the assumption was that some basic Christian instruction—bible readings—could be given to all comers. The
exact nature of this instruction aroused heated controversy
when the Whig Government brought in an Irish Education Bill

in 1831, at the height of the repeal agitation; the wrangle provoked Greville to write bitterly in his memoirs: 'while the whole system is crumbling to dust under their feet, while the church is prostrate, property of all kinds threatened, and robbery, murder, starvation and agitation rioting over the land, these wise legislators are debating whether the brats at school shall read the whole bible, or only parts of it.'

The Bill established a system from which—in the opinion of the Chief Secretary, Edward Stanley—'should be banned even the suspicion of Proselytism'. A Board was appointed not to set up schools itself, but to give grants to local managers for the building and maintenance of such schools and to help pay the salaries of teachers. The composition of the Board was not calculated to give great confidence to Catholics that Stanley's assertion would be proved correct. Out of the seven members, only two were Catholics; one a Castle employee, and the other the Archbishop of Dublin, Dr. Murray, a man so mild that when he was blackballed by the Ascendancy element for membership of the Royal Dublin Society, in 1835, he insisted that no protests should be made. The Protestant Archbishop of Dublin, Dr. Whately, on the other hand, was a forceful character who was determined to use the new 'national schools', as they came to be called, as an 'instrument of conversion'—his own words. 'The education supplied by the National Board', he wrote, 'is gradually undermining the vast fabric of the Irish Roman Catholic Church.' He also made sure that the schools were not in any sense Irish, removing from the textbooks verses containing dangerous nationalist sentiments like Scott's 'Breathes there the man?' and 'freedom shrieked when Kosciusco fell.' The schools' music manual, too, banned Irish airs, including Thomas Moore's, but left:

> *I thank the goodness and the grace*
> *Which on my birth has smiled*
> *And made me in these Christian days*
> *A happy English child.*

In these circumstances, the 'no proselytism' pretence could not be maintained; but in any case the Catholics were soon dissatisfied with a system that prevented their faith from being a positive force in education—in the National Schools even private prayer was excluded.

Although by the 1860's nearly a million children were being provided with a National School education, the system was neither popular nor efficient; and when Gladstone became Prime Minister in 1868, the Powis Commission was set up to re-examine it. The Commission decided that the system as it stood was unworkable: undenominational education was too unpopular. Accordingly, discrimination in favour of lay schools as against schools run by religious orders, was abandoned; denominational schools for both Protestants and Catholics were permitted to take advantage of State aid for primary education. (Catholic secondary education was already largely in the hands of the religious orders, who alone had had the resources to undertake it after the relaxation of the Penal Laws.) In other words, the policy of the Government, which had been to prevent the Church from dominating education, had achieved precisely the contrary result; Catholic education was by the end of the century firmly under Church control.

There remained the problem of University education. Peel had earlier put forward one unsuccessful scheme; Gladstone had another, his desire being to create a University for Ireland. Elizabeth had hoped to do this, too, but her University had become the Protestant Trinity College, Dublin; and its Protestantism had been little altered by the admission of a few Catholics as students. Gladstone's original proposal was for a secular university. There was never the least prospect that the Catholics, fresh from their victory over undenominationalism in the schools, would accept it. Nor was Trinity College anxious to be subjected to the control of a Government Board. So strong was the opposition the measure aroused that it helped to discredit the Government at Westminster, where it was defeated, and soon afterwards broke up.

By that time, however, Gladstone had accomplished what

at the time appeared to be a decisive step; the Church of Ireland had been disestablished. By the middle of the nineteenth century it had become less a prey to abuses than it had been in the days of Swift, but its Establishment as the national church had become even more absurd with the decline in the number of Anglicans, who were only one-eighth of the population. In many districts the Anglican parson ministered only to himself: more than twenty parishes in Clare, for example, contained no Protestant at all. The more zealous the pastor, too, the more suspect he became of trying to proselytise.

Disestablishment had the support of the Nonconformists in England, who were anxious to see the Church of England disestablished also, and who hoped the Irish Church would serve as a useful precedent. It also suited Gladstone: although a champion of the Church of England, he was prepared to argue that it had no right to impose itself on the Irish. Disestablishment, in fact, provided a useful rallying cry for all the diverse political elements in Britain, Nonconformists, Radicals and Whigs, who had for a time been demoralised by Disraeli's political cunning. In 1868 Gladstone was able to carry resolutions in favour of Disestablishment against the Tory Government; and the following year, in office, he put an Irish Disestablishment Bill through parliament, with little serious opposition. The connection between the Church of Ireland and the state was finally severed.

Although the Act did little more than give legal recognition to a situation that already existed, its passage gave heart to the nationalists; they saw in it the first crack in the structure of the Union; for the Act of 1800 had stated that the Church of Ireland must be considered an essential and fundamental part of the Union. From their relations with the Catholic Church, however, the nationalists could take little comfort. On balance, the Church had corporately shown itself, if not positively in favour of the Union, at least mistrustful of any efforts to undermine it: in 1828 Bishop Doyle, one of the most popular and influential members of the Irish Hierarchy,

Plate 6. Cork: the River Lee (Irish News Agency)

PLATE 7. The Custom House, Dublin (Irish Tourist Board)

had told a committee of the House of Commons: 'if we were freed from the disabilities under which we labour, we have no mind, and no thought, and no will, but that which would lead us to incorporate ourselves most fully an essential with this great kingdom'—the United Kingdom. And the Church was hostile to the Young Irelanders, particularly in their revolutionary phase.

Peel's act of 1845 endowing Maynooth more liberally— by which he hoped, as Pitt had, to secure a better, more loyal, priesthood—helped to weaken still further the links between the Church and the separatist movement; particularly as 1848 reminded the hierarchy of the risks of revolutionary activity developing into anti-clericalism. Although Papal policy varied according to what party was powerful at the time, in general the Vatican was inclined to mistrust Irish nationalism, in case it led to a situation where a leader might arise who was prepared (as O'Connell had been, on occasion) to put his nationalism before his Catholicism. Besides, the Vatican saw in Irish Catholicism a weapon that might prove useful within the United Kingdom—a possible base, if all went well, from which to launch a new counter-Reformation in Britain.

By this time, too, the Church was losing its close connection with the Irish peasantry. So long as the Penal Laws had been enforced, the priest might be revered, and was generally obeyed; but he was not considered as somebody apart. As late as 1825 O'Connell could tell a parliamentary committee of the dangers inherent in having a priesthood 'so much under the influence of low people as they necessarily are when all their relatives are in the very lowest stage of society'. When a priest arose who combined a ready sympathy with a forceful personality, such as Father Mathew, the temperance reformer, this close connection with the people helped to make his influence enormous—on a par with O'Connell's. But gradually the new secondary schools, some of which were seminaries, began to turn out a more anglicised product, talking only English, knowing only English culture. By the 1820's, the influence of the new-style priests, though it had not spread throughout the country, was strong where strength was most effective, around Dublin. Maynooth, too, came to be regarded as a stronghold of English influence; as late as 1909 a Professor of Gaelic there lost his job because of his too fervent support of the introduction of compulsory Irish into Education at all levels.

Nationalism, on the other hand, gradually came to see the old Irish tradition as a potential ally. The United Irishmen had paid little attention to it, in spite of their need to secure the Defenders, its last repository, as allies. Their newspaper, the *Northern Star*, published Irish poems, and a few individuals espoused the language cause, but the movement as a whole gave the subject little attention. O'Connell tended to despise Irish, because he thought it stood in the way of nationhood, being too primitive for modern needs. The first real indication that the Irish tradition might become a nationalist rallying cry was given by Thomas Davis in *The Nation* in 1843: 'a people without a language of its own is only half a nation. A nation should guard its language more than its territories— 'tis a surer barrier and more important frontier, than a fortress or river.' *The Nation* continued to pay much attention to the past, glorifying it in the stories and ballads of Davis and the verse of James Clarence Mangan, Samuel Ferguson and others. But the impetus the Young Ireland gave was counteracted by the effects of the Famine. Before 1845, a third to a half the people of Ireland spoke Irish in the household; twenty years later, death and emigration had reduced the proportion to about one-fifth; and the Fenians, though individuals were well-disposed, accomplished little for the language. All the indications were that as a living language it would continue to disappear, for the National Schools made no provision for teaching Irish until 1879, and then only to the extent of a concession that it might be taught as an extra-curricular subject.

It began to look as if Irish might soon become the preserve of antiquarian societies—the groups of scholars who busied themselves with the subject, most of them regarding it as a learned hobby, all the better for becoming more esoteric by ceasing to be commonly heard. But in 1876 a Society for the Preservation of the Language was formed, the first with a practical rather than an academic purpose; and from the young men attracted to it, the Gaelic League emerged in 1893. The League was suggested by Eoin MacNeill (who was later, significantly, also to suggest the Irish volunteer movement) and organised by Douglas Hyde, a Protestant in the Davis tradition, who had been brought up in an Irish-speaking district, and come to love the language and its literature with a quiet force that was to lift him even across the barrier of his Ascendancy background and his Trinity College environment. The objects of the Gaelic League were to preserve Irish as the national language of Ireland; to extend its use as a spoken tongue; to facilitate the study of existing Gaelic literature; and to encourage the cultivation of a modern literature in Irish. The movement caught on as if the country had been waiting for it impatiently for centuries. Branches sprang up by the hundred, Irish texts were published and avidly read; Irish newspapers, Irish customs, Irish dancing, Irish games (the Gaelic Athletic Association had actually preceded the League, and they began to work together) were produced with varying, but on the whole marked, success. Rapidly, what had begun as an Anglo-Irish pastime developed into a national movement.

There was little that was anti-English in the movement. As Hyde put it, when he spoke of the need for de-anglicising Ireland he did so not as a protest against what was best in the English nation, but 'to show the folly of neglecting what was Irish and hastening to adopt, pell-mell and indiscriminately, everything that is English, simply because it *is* English'. The League had no politics. Yet its effect on nationalism can hardly be over-estimated. As a later historian has said, 'the language led inevitably to other things, to Irish music, Irish customs and traditions, Irish place-names, Irish territorial divisions, Irish history; it emphasised the separateness of

Ireland as nothing else could; it brought with it national self-respect, a feeling of kinship with the past, the vision of a persistent and continuing tradition going back beyond human memory. The Gaelic League was not alone a re-discovery of the language but a re-discovery of the Nation, a resurrection of the Gael.' It was certainly one of the greatest influences on the men of 1916; particularly on Pearse, who only a few months before the rising had written that Ireland must be 'not free merely, but Gaelic also'.

The League even became strong enough to exert some influence on the Irish educational system; in 1901, Irish was at last put on the curriculum as a modern language—on the same status as, say, French—and three years later the Education Commissioners allowed its use during ordinary school hours in Irish-speaking districts. This was not quite so generous a concession as it sounded. The Commissioners appear by this time to have become convinced that Irish was vanishing; one way of facilitating its disappearance, and of relieving them from well-intentioned but irritating criticism by the Gaelic Leaguers, would be to teach children English through the medium of the vernacular. Previously the attempt to teach English to Irish-speaking children through the medium of English had not given good results; the new plan was to allow the younger children to learn in Irish, in order gradually to wean them to learning English, and later to learning through the medium of English, as they grew older. In 1907 the demands of the Gaelic Leaguers secured a further modification, allowing Irish something approaching parity in schools in districts where Irish was commonly spoken; by this time the Commissioners' views were being borne out by the continued decline in the Irish-speaking areas, which continued until the Treaty. All that the League could claim was that the decline might have been still faster without its intervention.

An internationally famous by-product of the League was the Irish National Theatre. Members of the League had toyed with the idea of writing and producing plays in Irish, and

Irish literary societies had been founded in London as well as in Ireland; but it was the Anglo-Irish element that eventually took action. In 1898, Lady Gregory recorded in her diary that she had entertained the poet, William Butler Yeats, to tea; Yeats had been full of playwriting, and wanted to take a little theatre somewhere and produce Irish romantic drama. The idea blossomed, and contributions were solicited for an Irish Literary Theatre, with the intention of building up a new school of dramatic literature. 'We hope,' the prospectus ran, 'to find, in Ireland, an uncorrupted and imaginative audience, trained to listen by its passion for oratory—we will show that Ireland is not the home of buffoonery and of sentiment, as it has been represented, but the home of an ancient idealism.' In 1899, English actors were brought over to give a season of plays by Anglo-Irish writers in Dublin, an experiment successful enough to be repeated; three years later the writers Yeats, Martyn and Lady Gregory came to terms with a group of Irish actors—the brothers Fay, who had their own company—to form the Irish National Theatre Society. Among their early performances were the first productions of plays by J. M. Synge. Soon the company attracted a sponsor, Miss Horniman, who presented it with a theatre: and 'the Abbey' opened on 27th December, 1904, with Synge's *Shadow of the Glen*, Yeats's *On Baile's Strand* and Lady Gregory's *Spreading the News*.

Although the Abbey quickly built up a literary reputation, it did not begin to attract the general Dublin theatre-going public, still drawn to English plays and musical comedies, until 1907, when the first night of J. M. Synge's *The Playboy of the Western World* provided the useful publicity of a riot. Synge, the demonstrators thought, had reneged on the Irish movement; he had portrayed an Ireland which, if not identical with the usual English pigs-in-the-parlour view, was too close to it for comfort. The effect of the row was that people began to go to the Abbey who had previously thought it simply a coterie theatre; and when *The Playboy* was taken to London it was hailed as a masterpiece. Although Synge died in 1909, and Miss Horniman withdrew her support, the company was, by that time, well enough established to stand on its own feet; among other productions, it put on Shaw's *The Shewing up of Blanco Posnet* in Dublin at a time when the Lord Chamberlain was refusing it a licence in England. Apart from the plays, the Abbey actors also made a deep impression; the brothers Fay, Sara Allgood, Maire O'Neill and many others created a distinctive style of acting in which simplicity and lack of stagey artifice were underlined by fine voice control; a tradition that has since almost vanished from the theatre, in Ireland as well as in England, but which helped to account for the Abbey's influence at the time.

That the Abbey became for some years the most influential theatre in the English-speaking world can most easily be accounted for by the fusion of Irish and Anglo-Irish cultures. They provided the warmth of the language, the freshness of the approach, and, most important of all, the undercurrent of dedication which, in their very different ways, Ibsen and Shaw were bringing to the Theatre. Nor was it only in the Theatre that the fusion had results. Out of it came the writings of Padraic Colum, James Stephens—one of the most delightful of fantasists—and, above all, Yeats. Yeats had already won a place for himself in the literature of the English language with the milk-and-honey lyrics of his youth, for which he might be remembered, had he written nothing else, as a potential Tom Moore. But with the impact of the Gaelic Movement and the Abbey Theatre his range widened; and the shock of the 1916 rising, in which many of his friends and acquaintances were imprisoned or executed, had a profound effect on him, disrupting his club world

All changed, changed utterly
A terrible beauty is born

and goading him on to 'The Second Coming' and the tremendous achievement of his old age.

The Gaelic revival gave an opportunity to the Protestant Ascendancy to resume its contact with the nationalist move-

ment; but they made only insignificant use of it, partly because Protestantism had by this time become much more
closely identified with Unionism, in the course of the Home
Rule controversy—out of which the Orange Order was able to
retrieve its declining fortunes.

After the Union, the Orangemen had for a while possessed
the viceregal ear; their influence at the Castle was considerable until Wellesley was appointed Lord Lieutenant, and even
under his rule in the 1820's the Order was powerful enough
to make it impossible for him to secure convictions for libel,
where Protestants were defendants. But Emancipation was
one setback, and the arrival of Thomas Drummond as Under
Secretary in 1835 another. Previously it had been safe for
administrators and even judges openly to boast of their
Orange convictions; but when the Deputy Lieutenant of
County Tyrone toasted 'the Battle of the Diamond' at a ban-
quet, Drummond saw to it that he was officially reprimanded
for commemorating 'a lawless and most disgraceful conflict'.
The Deputy Lieutenant sent back an insolent reply; he was
promptly removed from his post. Although Drummond's
policy was reversed by Peel's Tory Government in the 1840's,
the Orange Order did not recover its influence until Home
Rule days, and then only in Ulster. Gradually a division arose
between the Protestants of the North, who formed a homogeneous society, and the Protestants of the South, who had
no particular sympathy with their Northern co-religionist
(they did not even like him). Although to the last the
Northerners objected to Partition, and even refused to vote
for it (it was imposed on Ireland by English votes alone) on
the ground, among others, that it would leave the Southern
Unionists at the mercy of Rome, the fact was that so strong
an emotional partition already existed, long before 1920,
between the Protestant North and the Catholic South, that
the Southern Protestants were certain to be regarded as ex-
pendable in any settlement that could be reached.

Religion undoubtedly was the decisive factor in Partition.
The Northern Protestants' loyalty to the Crown would not

have prevented them from rebelling against it if an attempt
had been made to impose its authority on them against their
will; and their economic ties with England, though strong,
need not have debarred a Home Rule solution, provided that
some guarantee of Imperial Preference for Ulster's two main
industries had been forthcoming. The fundamental reason
why the North would not accept Home Rule at any price
was simply the fear that Home Rule would be Rome Rule.

The fear may have been irrational, but it was not entirely
unjustified; the Ulster Protestants, who since the Union
of 1800 had held aloof from nationalism (with a few exceptions, such as John Mitchel), could hardly be expected to
realise that nationalism was a stronger force in the South
than Catholicism. In any case they might argue that Catholicism would prove the more powerful in the long run, and
they could point to the activities of ultramontane prelates
like Cardinal Cullen as examples of what could happen once
the Catholic Church established itself as master in its own,
Catholic house.

Cardinal Cullen had been largely responsible for the per-
petuation of the break between the Church and the separatists;
already apparent in 1848, it continued through the Fenian
period and has lasted in a modified form to the present day.
Most of the Fenian leaders were Catholics; but they con-
tinually felt themselves compelled to put forward the argument that was later to become republican stock: that the
people must learn to draw a clear line between ecclesiastical
authority in spiritual and in temporal matters. Through
editorials in their newspapers they urged the hierarchy not
to attempt to retain the authority it had been forced to
assume over an ignorant, crushed peasantry in earlier centuries; 'it would be an unwise father who would endeavour
to subject his children, after they have reached the years of
discretion, to the same discipline which was good for them
during their boyhood.' But Cardinal Cullen's warnings to
Catholics to have nothing to do with Fenianism only grew
more frequent. This hostility was to persist; partly because

the Irish Republican Brotherhood, which survived the collapse
of Fenianism, was perforce a secret revolutionary society, and
as such unacceptable to the Church, but mainly because the
Church in Ireland at its higher levels was becoming anglicised
—still with the Vatican's approval, because a Catholic Ireland
remained more valuable to Rome within the United Kingdom than outside it. Cardinal Manning's correspondence gives
an illuminating example of this attitude: at first he felt some
sympathy with Irish aspirations, and in 1873 expressed the
view that a measure of Home Rule might be beneficial on the
same principal as vaccination against small-pox; but ten years
later he had realised the potential advantages of a bloc of
Catholics at Westminster, and was opposed to any change.

The price the Church had to pay for this anglicising process was a loss of contact with the people. Where the Church
and the nationalist movement clashed, the Church often
found that appeals, and even injunctions, were of little use.
In the early stages of the formation of Davitt's Land League
in 1879, one of his meetings was formally denounced in a
letter to the press from John MacHale, Archbishop of Tuam,
himself a moderate nationalist and a respected figure. The
meeting was none the less well-attended; Davitt found that
his plans were not impeded by archepiscopal disapproval.
Where the Church co-operated with the Irish parliamentary
party the effect might appear to be formidable—it aroused
considerable alarm in England, where the popular assumption
was that the electorate was entirely under the thumb of the
priesthood. But the influence melted like butter over the fire
of Sinn Fein after 1916. Diatribes from pulpits could not
divert the republicans from their course, nor deprive them
of public sympathy, not even when reinforced with the
Church's most formal condemnation; although the weight
of the Church was thrown against them, it appeared to influence public opinion little—except where Church and
public opinion were allies—as over conscription.

The antagonism meant that the Church also tended to lose
touch with Irish culture and the language, just at the time its

support was most needed—and where it would have been most valuable to both parties, the Gaels and the Church. The Gaelic League was suspect as an offshoot of Fenianism and as a 'front' for republicanism; this led to disputes between the League and the hierarchy, some of them creating considerable bitterness. A few bishops and many priests had separatist sympathies; a few, such as Archbishop Croke, might be recognisably Irish-minded; but the Church as an institution gradually drifted away from its old Irish moorings.

This is not to suggest that it became English. An old antipathy between English and Irish Catholicism was never healed; Irish Catholicism tended to develop its own characteristics, differentiating it from Catholicism in any other part of the world. Its puritanism, particularly, astonished Catholic visitors from other countries. Various explanations were put forward: the most convincing, that it arose out of the social circumstances which discouraged early marriages in Ireland. When the old cottier system began to disappear after the Famine, Irish peasants found themselves forced to postpone marriage until they inherited or purchased a farm; they could no longer rely on living on potatoes from a small plot of land, and finding casual labour in the district. Usually they were unable to marry until into their late thirties, or forties. The temptations that years of celibacy imposed on them could obviously only be resisted with the help of a powerful moral code; priests felt it necessary to push sexual license to the head of the ordinary sins against which they preached; and also to seek in every way possible to remove the occasion of sin, such as mixed gatherings for dancing or other relaxations, which elsewhere would have been thought innocent enough.

At the same time, Irish Catholicism retained its old element of paganism. To some extent the Church had absorbed pagan custom and superstition, as it did everywhere: 'wishing wells' became 'holy wells', and ancient legends were revised to bring in some saint, usually Patrick, as the protagonist. But the Church did not succeed in eradicating the countryman's convictions about the supernatural. Preaching failed to cure him of his fear of banshees or his respect for the powers of the 'little people'; and although he might be willing to commit mortal sin in the eyes of his Church by yielding to some temptation, no amount of temptation would induce him to plough up a thorn bush, or to commit any other similar crime against the dictates of his atavism. This did not mean that he had any the less fervent belief in his Church and creed; on the contrary, it even strengthened him in it, in the hope of placating a possible ally. But there could be no question which held the stronger—because it was the deeper—power over him. When the countryman lost the use of the Irish language, however, this paganism became incongruous. By 1921 culture and faith in Ireland were both at sea, detached from each other and from the common people who had nurtured them, no longer comfortably established in their old powerful homogeneity.

Part Four

AFTER THE TREATY

After the Treaty

♣

Here's to you, men I never met
Yet hope to meet behind the veil,
Thronged on some starry parapet
That looks down upon Inisfail,
And sees the confluence of dreams
That clashed together in our night
One river, born from many streams,
Roll in one blaze of blinding light.

'A.E.'s wish had been granted: the many different nationalist streams had formed one river, and the river had reached the sea. What followed was the saddest incident in the country's sad history: civil war.

For the practical purpose of fighting the English the country had been to all intents united, outside the Protestants of the North, the Anglo-Irish, and the Castle Catholics and some members of the Ascendancy, even, recognising the inevitable, had come to see the need for a settlement even at the cost of breaking the English connection. There was more general unity of nationalist purpose in 1921 than there had ever been. Theoretically all the groups comprised in Sinn Fein had the same aim: an all-Ireland republic. But by accepting Lloyd George's offer to negotiate in 1921 it could be argued that they had tacitly conceded that an all-Ireland republic was unattainable. For by this time a Six County unit had already been established in Northern Ireland and Partition—the division of the country—was an established fact, which Lloyd George could not have altered even if he had wanted to; and he did not. By accepting his offer of a truce, therefore, the Nationalists were preparing to abandon the principle of an all-Ireland Republic for the sake of ending hostilities.

De Valera did not see it that way. He did not believe, or did not realise, that acceptance of a truce had such implications. But to vice-President Griffith, a separatist rather than a republican, the negotiations offered an opportunity to win independence for Ireland: that this would mean abandoning advanced doctrinaire republican positions worried him not at all. Collins's attitude was even more practical. As military leader of the republican army, he realised that the struggle could not go on indefinitely; already his forces were being worn down, and he knew it would require only a little more effort on the part of the English finally to crush resistance.

Unlike Griffith, Collins did not think there was any necessity to reach a definitive agreement: he assumed that what was needed was not so much immediate freedom as the means to obtain freedom later. He was consequently prepared to examine proposals which might provide this stepping stone.

It was to prove a sad mischance that de Valera did not go to London for the final negotiations; Griffith and Collins were eventually persuaded by Lloyd George to accept—and to induce the other members of the Irish delegation to accept —a Treaty which was totally inacceptable to him. Griffith felt that Lloyd George's final Home Rule proposals put Ireland's future in her own hands, which was all he had fought for; and Collins was impressed by Lloyd George's dire threats about what could happen to Ireland if the terms were not accepted. But de Valera considered them a betrayal, because they made no provision for a republic. The proposals were put to the Dail; by a small majority it sided with Griffith, and ratified the agreement; and at the General Election which followed, the British terms were endorsed by a decisive majority of the electorate.

By refusing to recognise that after 1917 there was no longer any prospect of making Ireland a willing part of the United Kingdom, the English had driven the militant wing of

PLATE 8. Gathering Turf (Irish Tourist Board)

PLATE 9. The Lower Lake, Killarney (Irish Tourist Board)

the separatist movement to identify itself with doctrinaire republicanism, as a symbol of defiance. The republicans argued that the Treaty had no moral validity, accepted as it had been under duress; and that in any case it broke faith with the Irish separatist tradition, handed down from Wolfe Tone through the Fenians to Pearse. There were many men, including the bulk of the republican army, who had come to think of the cause they were fighting for as much more than administrative separatism—men who considered themselves pledged to fight on—even against fellow-countrymen—until an all-Ireland republic was won; the attempt to bring the fighting to an end before it was won, however estimable in intention, appeared to them a betrayal. Nor was the people's verdict, expressed in the General Election, decisive. De Valera had already forecast that a 'snatch election' might be won because 'a war-weary people will take things which are not in accordance with their aspirations'; he could argue that when the people recovered they would feel ashamed of their cowardice, and despise the leaders who had persuaded them to accept this 'most ignoble document'. But it was one thing for de Valera to denounce the Treaty; another for him to decide what to do to prevent its provisions being put into force. While he hesitated, the issue was decided for him by the republican extremist wing of the army, who repudiated the settlement; and out of sporadic outbreaks of violence between pro-Treaty and anti-Treaty forces grew the civil war.

For over a year, men who had fought together against the English fought one another with far greater bitterness. Many more republicans were executed by the new Irish Government brought into being by the Treaty than had been executed by the British in the war of independence: some of the victims being men who had been high in the councils of Sinn Fein before 1921—Rory O'Connor, Liam Mellowes, Erskine Childers. Property was destroyed, houses burned, men and women murdered, or executed in reprisal for murders, in an orgy of fanatical destruction. In the end the Government proved resolute and ruthless enough to survive. De Valera, who had assumed the leadership of the republican forces, called off armed resistance in 1923; not before the hatreds that stemmed from this period of 'the Troubles' were quite strongly enough established to colour political sentiment to the present day.

In the meantime, the terms of the Treaty had been put into operation, and the Irish Free State had come into being. Griffith died in 1922, and Collins was killed in a civil war ambush; the leadership of the Government devolved on William Cosgrave. Cosgrave had been condemned to death for his part in the 1916 rising, his sentence like de Valera's being commuted to penal servitude for life; he showed unexpected talent as an administrator, and to him is generally conceded the credit for establishing the Free State as an economic and administrative unit, with his colleague Kevin O'Higgins, while Richard Mulcahy was stamping out republican resistance.

The Dominion status which the Free State received under the Treaty gave her, among other things, control of her land but not her sea defences; bases were retained by the English in some Irish ports. And there was one other unusual stipulation: the two Houses of Parliament, Dail and Senate, were to be elected by proportional representation—a device intended to provide the Protestant and Unionist minority with parliamentary spokesmen. But otherwise administration in general followed the British pattern, as did the new Irish judiciary. In the decade following the Treaty, Ireland took her place as a co-equal member of the Commonwealth, eventually joining in the consultations that led to the Statute of Westminster, with its formal recognition of the new independent status of the Commonwealth countries.

Even after he had given up the attempt to overthrow the Free State by force de Valera was not immediately prepared to recognise the new constitution to the extent of converting the republicans into a parliamentary party. Only after the 1927 General Election, which the Republicans contested (to find themselves still in a minority) did he face realities.

Previously he had argued that the Oath of Allegiance, which every member of the Dail had to make to the Crown, was an insuperable bar to him or his followers, as republicans, taking their seat. Suddenly he changed his ground; asserting that the Oath might be taken, but disregarded as an empty formula, he brought his followers into the Dail.

It was significant that in spite of the inconsistency of his action, de Valera's reputation among his followers was hardly affected. The die-hards of the Irish Republican Army had withdrawn their allegiance from him when he first decided to enter Free State politics; other republicans jibbed at his decision to take the Oath, in order to enter the Dail; but the bulk of the republican electorate followed him. The I.R.A. became a small underground force, compounded of idealism and irresponsibility, losing public sympathy and backing; its members occasionally made raids for arms, or to pay off old scores, but it gradually ceased to be a decisive force in affairs, as did the rump of Sinn Fein. By contrast, de Valera's new Republican party rapidly gained public confidence. There was something about de Valera himself which inspired it, in spite of his recent political misjudgements and erratic twists of policy. Those around him knew that these twists were not the rationalisations of expediency, but the effort to bring idealism into line with bleak realities; and the gnarled integrity of the man came across at public meetings (though he was no orator)—particularly to the youth of the country, less immediately affected by bitter memories of the civil war than some of their parents. In 1932 he was able to win a majority at a General Election, and to take office.

That he could win an election was due to the gradual subsidence of extremist nationalism. One of the arguments most frequently used in Britain to deny independence to the Irish was that their nationalism was so hysterical, fierce, and uncontrollable that it would be dangerous to let them off the leash. The answer had been given by Bernard Shaw: 'nobody in Ireland of any intelligence likes nationalism any more than a man with a broken leg likes having it set. A healthy nation is as unconscious of its nationality as a healthy man of his bones. But if you break a nation's nationality it will think of nothing else but getting it set again.' Shaw in this case was proved an accurate prophet. So long as extremist nationalism remained in full force, as it did in 1921-3, it was capable of making the Irish just as dangerous to themselves as English politicians had warned. But as soon as the Cosgrave government settled down to provide its competent, if not inspired, administration, nationalism of the perfervid type began to die out. De Valera's political instinct was sound when he realised he must abandon the doctrinaire republican position; in doing so he reflected, rather than caused, the change of heart of the majority of his supporters.

He had promised to get rid of the Oath of Allegiance at the first opportunity, and he did. The English Government made no move. But when de Valera announced his intention also of withholding the land annuities, retaliatory action promptly followed. The land annuities represented the interest on the loans given to Irish tenants under the Land Acts to help buy themselves into possession. The Irish Free State Government had continued to collect them and pay them over to England. Republicans had often argued that to ask the Irish farmer to pay for land which had been filched from him was unjust, and that the annuities should in any case have been included —as had originally been the intention—among the 'public debts' from which Ireland was freed by the Treaty. But de Valera's decision to appropriate the annuities (amounting to some £3 million a year) provoked the Colonial Secretary in the National Government to declare an economic war: to impose retaliatory duties on imports of agricultural produce from Ireland, his design being to collect in customs over the amount lost by the annuities. De Valera in his turn imposed tariffs on English imports. He was not sorry to have an excuse to do this; for his Government at the time was initiating a new economic policy designed to make Ireland self-supporting, to achieve economic as well as political independence.

The first objective of the new political economy—in which Sean Lemass, de Valera's second-in-command, was to become the dominant figure—was to diversify the country's production. In agriculture, tillage was encouraged in an attempt to wean the farmers from their dependence on cattle; in industry, entrepreneurs who were prepared to set up new factories or expand old businesses were promised protection, in the form of tariffs or quotas on imported goods. Cosgrave's Government had taken one or two tentative steps in the same direction; but it had achieved little. Under the first few years' of de Valera's Government progress was much more swift.

By this time the party political pattern was growing more akin to the American than to the British system, with de Valera occupying a rather similar position to Roosevelt, and his party, to the New Dealers. The division between the two main parties, still on Treaty and anti-Treaty lines, more closely resembled the division between Republicans and Democrats than between Conservatives and Labour. For a time in the mid-Thirties the Treaty party, still led by Cosgrave, flirted with fascism in the garb of a 'Blueshirt' movement; which grew up to preserve freedom of speech (Cosgravite meetings were often broken up by republicans in the late twenties and early thirties); later, the blueshirts threatened to develop along the ugly Mussolini pattern, until de Valera firmly outlawed them. De Valera also maintained the outlawry of the I.R.A. whose members, if captured, could be tried and sentenced by a military tribunal from which there was no appeal to the ordinary courts. His methods caused liberal opinion some concern, but in the event they helped to preserve the structure of democracy. The I.R.A., suffering from internal strife, gave comparatively little trouble to the Government; the Cosgravites returned quietly to their old party ways, losing only face and some electoral support. Before the war broke out the two party system was again well established. Proportional Representation did not result in a spectrum of parties on the French pattern; although from time to time new ones were formed, none of them reached a sufficient size to challenge the two main parties; and the only other established contestant, Labour, was in decline.

The Labour Party had constituted the formal opposition in the Dail during the early years of the Free State, while the republicans held aloof from politics; but it lacked a leader of the calibre of Connolly. Larkin remained, but his talents lay in demagoguery; he was too unstable to provide the movement with its direction. It was unable to win support in the country, except in those districts where farm labourers existed in sufficient numbers to be brought into the trade union movement; and even in the towns, the workers were more attracted to de Valera's Republicans with their New Deal policy, than to Socialism. Labour, too, suffered from internal dissentions, beginning with a violent dispute between Larkin and his old Union, and developing into a series of quarrels between the Right and the Left wings; quarrels which flared up to rend the party whenever it looked like reasserting itself. Occasionally it would hold the balance of power, but not until after the war was it able to extract much advantage from the leverage it obtained in this way: and by then it had drifted so far from the course set by Connolly that it was not recognisable as a Labour Party on the normal social democratic pattern.

*　　*　　*

De Valera was not content to abolish the Oath, seize the annuities and reorganise the national economy; he wanted to create a new Constitution that could be regarded as home made—rather than imposed by the circumstances of the Treaty. One of his early actions was to give the office of Governor General to an amiable cypher, in order to demonstrate that no more heed would be paid to the office than to the Oath; then an 'External Relations Act' was passed abolishing the office of Governor General, and removing all reference to the King from the Constitution, though the Crown was still recognised for purposes of diplomatic accreditation; and finally, the 'Free State' was itself abolished. In 1937 a new Constitution removed the *de jure* distinction between the Free State and Northern Ireland; it referred to Ireland—'Eire' in the Irish version—the assumption being that its clauses would apply to the whole island, though temporarily they might remain enforceable only over the 26-County area formerly designated the Free State. The change had one immediate—and to de Valera, irritating—result; the English press, delighted to have the distinctive four-letter word 'Eire' instead of 'Irish Free State' promptly appropriated it for the purpose of describing the 26-County unit. To the majority of Englishmen, 'Eire' became, and remained, a synonym for Southern Ireland, rather than for Ireland as a whole.

The new Constitution codified changes that had already been made, but added little that was new, except to create judicial machinery for testing the constitutional validity of legislation on the United States model. It was too remote from everyday economic and political realities to have much appeal to ordinary voters; after inspecting it, they declined to give de Valera an overall majority in the General Election of 1937, and he could only stay in office with the unwelcome support of the Labour Party. The following year, however, he had better wares to offer; a settlement of the economic war. Neville Chamberlain had decided that the policy of appeasement should logically be extended westwards; a friendly Ireland, he thought, might prove a useful ally, rather than the positive danger to British security which, in the angry mood the economic war had engendered, she might have become. For a lump sum of £10,000,000 in lieu of the annuities, Chamberlain was prepared not only to call off the economic war, but also to hand over the bases—the 'Ports', as they were known in Ireland—that had been retained by the British Navy since the Treaty. At one blow, de Valera secured both the prospect of greater agricultural prosperity and the opportunity to maintain Ireland's neutrality in the event of war; for although a desire to preserve neutrality was already shared by all parties, there had been a feeling that its preservation would not be possible if one of the combatants retained bases on Irish soil. With the Chamberlain agreement in his pocket de Valera promptly went to the country, and was again returned with a decisive overall majority.

In the circumstances there was never any doubt, when war broke out the following year, that Southern Ireland would try to stay out of it. The justification usually given for her neutrality was that although the Allies, in 1939 as in 1914, were pretending to fight for democracy, self-determination and the rights of small nations, one of them—England—was holding in subjection parts of a small nation—Ireland—against the small nation's will; and so long as England continued to do so, Ireland could not fight by her side. The real reason was simpler; no Government which proposed to enter the war could have stayed in office. The mood of the country was overwhelmingly against participation. At times it looked as if the Allies, driven by necessity to resume control of 'the Ports' in order to survive the Battle of the Atlantic, might feel compelled to retake them by force; but had they done so, they might not only have created for themselves a formidable potential fifth column among the tens of thousands of Irishmen who had volunteered to fight in the British forces, but would also have met with the violent hostility of the Irish in Ireland. Realising this, the Allies decided that the risk was too great. The British would not even permit the Northern Ireland Government to introduce conscription, for fear that there would be widespread, organised and armed opposition to it among the Roman Catholic minority.

Throughout the war Southern Ireland maintained her neutrality strictly, imposing a censorship of the press mainly to prevent manifestation of pro-British feeling, and interning with impartiality all those members of the Allied or Axis armed forces, mostly airmen, who arrived (though the English airmen who force-landed near the Northern Ireland border were sometimes helped to make good their escape). De Valera was even punctilious enough to express his condolences

to the German Embassy on the death of Hitler, an action
which provoked some resentment in England; but as Churchill
remarked in his speech after VE day, feeling in Britain against
Ireland for her neutrality was largely counterbalanced by
recognition of the war services of her volunteers, who collected between them, among other things, a notable batch
of V.C.'s. In Ireland, too, admiration for the British stand
in 1940 was succeeded by gratitude for their restraint in not
trying to bully or blackmail Ireland into the war, which it
would have been possible to do by withholding supplies; at
the end of the war the British stood decidedly higher in Irish
esteem than the Americans, who had been less tolerant.

De Valera received further mandates from the electors
during the war; and even in 1948, when the first post-war
General Election was held, his was still so decisively the
largest party that it seemed he must settle in for a further
period in office. But after sixteen years in opposition, the
opposition parties were in a mood to sink their differences,
and form an inter-party Government. Cosgrave, who had
retired, had been succeeded by General Mulcahy; but Mulcahy was *persona non grata* to too many of his party's new
allies to be appointed Prime Minister. The leadership was
given to a lawyer, John A. Costello, who celebrated his
elevation to office by announcing soon afterwards, in the
course of a tour of Canada, that he proposed to make Ireland
a republic. Costello himself, and the Cosgravite party of
which he was a member, had hitherto fought elections on the
Treaty—Commonwealth—ticket. What prompted his sudden conversion to republicanism remains uncertain; but he
was able to convince his party of the need to declare a
Republic in order to 'take the gun out of politics'.

The I.R.A., still an illegal organisation, was not then a
very powerful body; but it had had spells of activity, the most
notorious being a campaign in England just before the second
world war. Beginning almost as a military operation directed
against strategic installations, it later degenerated into a
squalid type of guerilla activity, with home-made bombs

planted in letter-boxes and cloakrooms. Men capable of adopting such methods were rarely shrewd enough to evade detection for long; the campaign was quickly crushed and most members of the I.R.A. were interned either in England of in Ireland, North and South, during the war. Costello argued that the I.R.A. might make itself felt again; by declaring a Republic he hoped to deprive it of its incentive. In fact the inauguration of a 26-County Republic made little difference to the I.R.A., because its objective remained a Republic for all-Ireland. After 1949 the I.R.A. ceased to use violence in the South: their raids for arms took place in the North or in Britain; but if the Government hoped the I.R.A. would wither away, it was to be disillusioned. A more sensible reason for the declaration of the Republic was that the Treaty of 1921 had virtually ceased to exist. Partly through de Valera's legislation, partly by the growing divergence between English and Irish ways—during the war, particularly— the links between the two countries had corroded; a 'Commonwealth' party had become an anachronism. Costello was in effect switching his followers from the Griffith to the Collins line. Had it not been for old antagonisms, which had kept the pro and anti-Treaty controversy alive long after it had ceased to bear relevancy to Irish conditions, the change could have come about much sooner. Nevertheless the fact that Costello's party had fought the election on the Treaty ticket gave the sudden switch an appearance of political expediency, if not dishonesty.

Constitutionally the change made no perceptible difference in Ireland: it formally cut links that had in practice been severed by de Valera years before. Nor did it noticeably affect relations with Britain: Irish citizens were still allowed to enter British ports as British citizens, rather than through a door marked 'aliens', and the political break was not reinforced by the setting up of an independant currency. The declaration of the Republic did, however, move the English Labour Government to give a more formal guarantee to Northern Ireland of the British Government's continued care and protection, thereby confirming the impression that had been voiced in Ireland that the declaration of a 26-County Republic had pushed the chances of all-Ireland unity still further into the remote future.

The conversion of the old Cosgrave party to republicanism removed the only significant difference between the two main political parties. They were still divided on personalities; not only did the same Treaty and anti-Treaty faces glower at each other across the floor of the Dail, but the sons and nephews of Treaty and of anti-Treaty men appeared to take their seats beside their fathers and uncles: such names as de Valera, O'Higgins, Cosgrave, Larkin, Connolly, Childers reappeared, perpetuating the old divisions. The apparent absurdity of Treaty and anti-Treaty feud being prolonged into the second and even the third generation provoked some ridicule, notably from the *Irish Times*, which continued to reflect the views of the class that had once formed the Ascendancy. Illogical though it might be, it served a purpose. By providing a structure within which the democratic party political system could take root, and establish itself; and as the passions and hatreds of the 1922 period gradually died down, the parties which emerged were in practice little more illogical than the parties of the United States. In the period 1948-51 the inter-party cabinet revealed that it was able to carry on in spite of its administrative inexperience, inevitable after its members had been so long in opposition; and although the alliance disintegrated in 1951, letting de Valera in again, the parties were able to re-assemble their forces in opposition, and resume office a couple of years later. Once again 'A.E.'s 'many streams' had merged, this time to provide Ireland with a workable democratic system; by 1956—and, indeed, long before—the argument that the Irish, chronically 'agin the government' would be unable to govern themselves, had been refuted.

But although Irish nationalism had thus been given its justification in the eyes of the world, it had yet fully to justify itself in the eyes of the Irish themselves. They had known all along that the notion of their incompetence and irresponsibility was absurd. But they had hoped to display more than a mere ability to govern themselves; they had expected that the removal of the brake of English interference would permit a great leap forward, economic, social, and cultural. The results of self-government were to prove disappointing.

From 1922-32 the Cosgrave Government was more concerned to prove that it was responsible, efficient and reliable, than to embark on any hazardous experiments. One action only it took which captured the public imagination: the 'Shannon Scheme' by which the State provided the funds and the organisation to harness the waterpower of the longest river in the country. It was a courageous step, as orthodox prejudice remained against state trespass into private enterprise. There was no particular reason why the Irish people, with their bitter memory of the way that the sanctity of *laissez faire* had been invoked to justify their starvation in the Famine, should wish to retain it after the Treaty; but they found themselves with no alternative. If the first need of the new State was to prove its competence, the Government could not afford to make drastic changes in the existing economic structure—even if it had any clear idea of what changes were desirable, which it had not. The Cosgrave Government's first instinct was to preserve the system that the British had left behind—merging it cautiously with some of the institutions that Sinn Fein had created and operated between 1916 and 1921, but in general following the British lead—until a Commission of administrators, economists, financiers and business experts had had time to investigate what changes might profitably be made when the new State had settled down.

Disappointingly, the experts' report had little to say. The Free State had been granted fiscal autonomy by the Treaty largely because the memory of the period of Grattan's parliament had convinced Griffith—who convinced his fellow delegates—that whatever else they might concede, they must retain the right to protect and develop their own agriculture industry and commerce. The report of the Fiscal Inquiry Committee in 1923, however, stressed the need for caution, pointing out the damage that might be done if the State interfered clumsily in the complicated, delicate structure of business, and arguing that too strict a regulation of imports might have a detrimental affect on exports—particularly of farm produce. A few tariffs were imposed to help Irish industry, but so cautious was the Government that it even devolved its responsibilities on to a quasi-judicial Tariff Commission, the idea being that application for Protection would then be judged on their economic merits, rather than on their vote-catching possibilities. The Commission conceded that there was a case for Protection for a few more industries, ranging from margarine to rosary beads; but other applications were rejected, and no general protective policy was applied.

In retrospect it is easy to criticise so timid a policy; but the Free State Government was unlucky enough to ask for expert advice on economic matters at a time when economists in the U.S. and Britain as well as in Ireland, were still wedded to what proved to be disastrous deflationary notions, whose fallibility was finally exposed by the slump of 1929. By 1932 the imperfections of the policy—in particular its failure to provide the country with any decisive social advance to contrast with conditions under British rule—encouraged de Valera to abandon it. The Tariff Commission was allowed to lapse; the Government announced that anybody who could make out a *prima facie* case for establishing an industry in Ireland would be assisted to do so, regardless of what orthodox economists might think of its prospects; and business men found that almost any application to establish a new industry or develop an old one could count on receiving Protection sufficient to restrain, and sometimes virtually to eliminate, the competition of imports. Heavy duties were imposed at the outbreak of the Economic War on coal, cement, and electrical, iron and steel goods; and in 1934 a Control of Imports Bill gave the Government power to introduce quotas, restricting the import of such goods as tyres, shoes, sugar, motor cars, clothes, soap and many other commodities. The general level of tariffs, which had been under 10 per cent under the Cosgrave Government, had risen to 35 per cent before the war.

Like Cosgrave before him, however, de Valera was anxious not to give the impression of economic heterodoxy. He, too, appointed an investigating body, the Banking Commission, to advise on economic prospects and policy—hoping that his party's policy might give the immediate and striking results necessary to convert the financiers, economists and businessmen to a less staid outlook. They showed themselves as wary as before. The Commission's report in 1938 pointed out that although urban employment has undoubtedly increased, the gain had been at the expense of a rising cost of living for the whole community, partly through taxation—state expenditure had risen by over 25 per cent in the first five years of de Valera's Government—and partly in higher prices that had to be paid by the consumer for Irish goods, sheltered from competition by tariffs which made the imported product more expensive still. The benefits of industrialisation, it considered, were largely illusory.

The Government paid little attention to the report, and when supplies from England of manufactured products were abruptly cut off by the outbreak of war in 1939, it could even boast that the industrialisation policy had provided Ireland with assured supplies of some goods which might otherwise be unobtainable (though shortage of the necessary raw materials handicapped Irish industrialists, so that they were not able to take much advantage of this good fortune). After the war, therefore, the industrialisation policy was resumed.

It continued to come in for severe criticism, often from independent sources that could not be suspected of political or academic bias. In 1952, for example, a report on Ireland was issued by an American research organisation which the Irish Government had asked to make a survey of the country's industrial potential. It noted that industrial production had steadily mounted; but in the language that seems inseparable from such documents, it argued that 'it is obvious that the tempo of overall accomplishment toward dynamic improvement will be severely handicapped so long as the agricultural segment remains static in real production terms'. Its advice to the Government was to pay less attention to industry, which still provided only a small fraction of output and employment, and do more for agriculture, for which Government programmes, though there had been no dearth of them, had been under-financed and ineffective.

Another report by a firm of U.S. consultants, published shortly afterwards, examined some of the individual industries that had grown up, in relation to their prospects of earning dollars by exporting. Its general verdict, though politely phrased, was highly critical. The industries, it pointed out, suffered from several economic and psychological disadvantages. They were under-capitalised, not simply from lack of money but from lack of initiative: 'we have discovered no inclination among Irish producers to take any sort of risk.' The prevalence of family-owned businesses made for a smug, we're-doing-all-right attitude; Irish industrialists suffered from 'a persistent illusion concerning the superior quality of the Irish product'—an illusion wholly unjustified, for the Irish product was too variable, lacking high standards or quality controls.

The main reason for these failings lay in the fact that industries had to be built up almost from nothing, in face of competition from well-entrenched competitors in England and in other countries. The Protection policy, though it might give employment, was unable to promote efficiency; indeed, it had the opposite effect. An entrepreneur starting up a new business behind a tariff had no strong incentive to improve efficiency and reduce costs; for if he did so, and began to make heavy profits, the chances were that he would be criticised by the left wing in the Dail (which was vocal, if not influential) for using the public's money to feather his nest. The Government would in any case be tempted to lower the tariff by which he was protected from competition, where it had the chance, in order to reduce prices to consumers.

A few new firms employed go-ahead methods, and a few old ones continued to expand. But the most striking contribution to Irish industry came not from private enterprise but from state sponsored companies, set up with Government money under Government nominees, but given considerable autonomy, and encouraged to develop along their own lines.

Out of the Shannon Scheme grew the Electricity Supply Board, which eventually took charge of the generation, transmission and distribution of electricity throughout the country. At first it relied on a combination of hydro-electric plants and coal and oil-burning power stations; but in the 1950's the first of a chain of peat-fuelled stations began operating, at a cost which soon fell below the expense of generating electricity from imported coal.

These stations were the culmination of a remarkable experiment initiated by Sean Lemass after the Republicans had come into power in 1932, as part of the self-sufficiency plan, to exploit the country's vast peat resources. Before 1932, peat—turf, as it is generally called in Ireland—had provided the countryman, since the destruction of the forests, with virtually his only fuel. For centuries it had to be cut from the bog by hand, by local labour; but the establishment in 1934 of *Bord na Mona*, a public corporation, to develop the country's peat resources, led to a great improvement not only in productivity but in utilisation. Machinery was employed to cut the turf or to extract it in a milled state; for use either in the power stations or, manufactured into briquettes, for domestic and industrial purposes. Peat is so moisture-laden that it has only half the calorific value of coal, and many technical problems of converting it to a useful fuel remained intractable; but within twenty years of its foundation Bord na Mona had established itself as one of the most advanced industrial undertakings of its kind in the world.

Other state-sponsored companies grew up and began to thrive in this period; among them Aer Lingus, the national air line, and Irish Shipping. The Government also appointed a Board to handle tourism, which after the second world war brought more money into the country than any other industry, except cattle-breeding. On balance the record of the state companies was more impressive than that of private enterprise; satisfactory enough to dispel the notion that the Irish were wholly unbusinesslike, and incapable of managing their economic affairs.

These achievements, however, could not disguise from successive Governments that they were still faced with two of the evils which independence had been designed to cure: a high level of unemployment, and a high rate of emigration.

A Commission was set up by the Costello Government soon after it came into power in 1948 to investigate the problem of emigration; but its report, though setting out the problem clearly, did not offer any very helpful solution. Emigration had continued with only a slight abatement after the immediate exodus following the Famine. It came as an unpleasant surprise to the Cosgrave Government that the emigration flood did not at once dry up when Ireland won her independence; and it was even more disheartening for de Valera's Government to find that its self-sufficiency remedy was also useless. In the year 1950 over 40,000 men, women and children emigrated, nearly 1.5 of the population; and Ireland achieved the distinction of being the only country in the world whose population declined in the first half of the twentieth century.

The discovery that the provision of more jobs in industry at home did not discourage emigration lent weight to the views of what had come to be known as the 'pull' school, who believed that emigration was the result of the lure of bright lights—of London with its gangs of men digging for gold in the street, and of Boston with its jobs for the Irish boys—rather than of any particular deficiency in the Irish economy. But the 'push' school, who preferred to believe that emigration was caused by young men and women leaving from exasperation or boredom or poverty, did not accept this interpretation. They argued that the policy of creating work by industrialisation had been misguided; the cost of creating employment for men in industry was so high that it had deprived agriculture of the money it needed for development, so that as many men had been driven from the land as had been absorbed into industry. The net economic gain to the community was nil; in fact, the figure ought properly to be considered as a net loss, because agriculture in expanding might itself have given birth to a flourishing export trade, out of whose proceeds a home industry could have developed without artificial state aid.

The story of agriculture in Ireland in the first quarter of a century after the Treaty is almost uniformly depressing. The Cosgrave Government contented itself with rounding off the policy embarked upon by the British in the Land Acts, until the last trace of landlordism had been wiped out; it did little positive for the farmers, who continued in their conservative ways, concentrating on the production of livestock, particularly cattle. But de Valera, partly urged by a wish to encourage agricultural self-sufficiency, partly driven by the exigencies of the economic war, set to work to induce farmers to take the plough round their land, growing animal feeding-stuffs which had formerly to be imported, and wheat to reduce the country's dependence on imports for its daily bread. To this end, imports of feeding-stuffs were restricted, and guaranteed prices were offered to the farmer to reconcile him to undertake the labour of tillage; and it was hoped that the results would be spectacular.

To the Government's surprise, this policy failed to increase the total of agriculture production, which actually declined. The decision to call off the economic war was an admission of defeat, in that the Government realised its policy was not having sufficiently striking results to persuade the farmer his sacrifices had not been in vain. But a year later the outbreak of the second world war, by restricting imports, put back the clock; as Professor Joseph Johnston commented 'the Govern-

226

ment was compelled to do from necessity what it had formerly done from choice, and concentrate once more on growing crops for direct human consumption', though in the meantime it had probably realised 'that its effort to promote a tillage economy based on a declining and semi-bankrupt animal husbandry, was disintegrating the national economy as a whole and destroying the natural fertility of the soil'.

The destruction was caused by the reluctance of the Irish farmer to spend money on fertilisers, which during the war were in any case hard to obtain. After the war, when they came on the market again, agricultural production crept back to its pre-war level—but little higher. Although the inter-party Government took advantage after 1948 of funds placed at the country's disposal under Marshall Aid to embark on an ambitious land rehabilitation scheme, the effect on net productivity remained disappointingly small. That farmers as a class were distinctly better off in the 1950's than they had been at any previous time in the country's history was mainly because of rising prices for farm produce, and because of slightly more efficient production methods, which pushed up output per farm worker, not because of any general increase in productivity from the land, which was providing little more than it had in the days of English rule half a century before.

By 1956, in spite of all that had been done, the country's economy was still heavily dependent on the cattle trade; a trade that was in any case unsatisfactory, in many ways, from the Irish point of view, because it relied heavily on the export of store cattle 'on the hoof' for fattening in England, a system which deprived the country of native industries that could have been developed if more cattle had been slaughtered in Ireland, and their by-products put to good use. There were disturbing signs, too, that even the cattle trade's expansion was not as rapid as it should have been. The total numbers of cattle rose very little after 1921; nor was there any great increase in other forms of livestock. In fact all the signs of a primitive, farm-yard economy were maintained, with farmers content to graze a few stores in their fields, and to have a pig and a flock of hens living on kitchen scraps and what they could get by foraging.

Most of the causes of this stagnation can be traced to the events of the previous century. It is never easy to decide to what extent mental attitudes are conditioned by collective memories handed down through generations; but the evidence for this in Ireland is very strong. The farmer remained reluctant to put capital into his farm, even when he came into full ownership. His parsimony might be justified by the need to provide a dowry for his daughter and, if necessary, assistance to his land-hungry younger sons; but it was also attributable to the memory of rack-renting days, with their implication that money spent on improving a farm was money thrown away. The traditional land hunger of the peasant also lingered on. When the Land Commission no longer had any landlord-tenant ties to sever, it had to turn its attention to the needs of the numerous landless men, who were insisting that 'ranches'—estates, large by Irish standards, which were not being worked by the owners as farms—should be compulsorily acquired and divided up, more rapidly than in pre-Treaty times. So great was the demand that the estates were divided into farms too small to be economic—unless they were very heavily capitalised, and the landless men who came to them rarely had any capital. They were reluctant, too, to pay the heavy interest required to secure loans. So in most cases the dismemberment of potentially profitable estates into unprofitable small farms merely condemned their owners to a lifetime of unrewarding toil.

Agricultural economists were quick to point out these errors. They calculated, for example, that whereas Danish farms were capitalised to the extent of about £25 an acre, the amount of capital sunk in Irish farms at the same time was little more than £1 an acre. The disparity was reflected in the value of crops grown per 100 arable acres; in Denmark in 1950 it was £1,880: in Ireland, £370. It was also reflected in the use of artificial fertilisers (of which the consumption in

Ireland remained very small) and of yields per acre, which in spite of the great natural fertility of the Irish soil were in general lower than other European agricultural countries. Although the essential elements of a flourishing rural economy were present in Ireland, a fertile soil and plenty of labour, in the absence of ambition, organization, and capital they were being squandered.

Part of the trouble, as the Banking Commission pointed out in 1938, was misguided government policy. To grow feeding-stuffs at home, in order to dispense as far as possible with imports, was superficially an attractive policy for a country anxious to become self-sufficient; but as the cost of growing the feeding-stuffs was high, the inevitable result was to push up prices, and jeopardise the prospects for exporting Irish agricultural produce of all kinds. Irish produce would, in any case, have been hard put to it to survive in competition with say, Danish, Dutch, and New Zealand products in England, because of the inability of Irish farmers to get together to make the necessary arrangements for collection, grading, marketing, and distribution. The small size of farms in Denmark had not proved an insuperable obstacle to development largely because of the co-operatives through which farmers sold their produce; but in Ireland, after the Treaty, the co-operative system failed to extend its range outside the dairying industry. Again, the prejudice against the idea can be traced back to nationalist mistrust of Sir Horace Plunkett. For many years no political party in post-Treaty Ireland was prepared to give the support to Plunkett's co-operative organisation, still in existence, which was needed to overcome hostility and apathy. An attempt to overcome it by voluntary effort, through a new organisation based on parish units, proved fairly successful where it was tried, but it spread very slowly. Although proof that co-operatives could greatly benefit the farmer was eventually given by the growth of the sugar-beet industry, in which the principle was adopted, they failed to penetrate at all where they were most required, in the livestock trade.

While agriculture suffered from the inability of farmers to realise how much they stood to benefit from modernisation, the Irish fisheries also failed to develop as a result of the innate conservatism of the fishermen. That the demand for fish in Ireland continued to fall until it was lower than any sea-girt country in Europe, was sometimes ascribed to the fact that fish is the food associated with the Catholic's friday fast, and consequently rarely eaten, outside towns, except on one day of the week; but the real reason was that the arrangements for catching, collecting and distributing fish were far too haphazard to encourage the housewife to regard it as a standard part of the family's diet. The falling-off in demand made the fishermen all the more reluctant to allow modern methods of sea-fishing to be developed; the inshore fishermen who traditionally formed the backbone of the industry had only small boats; and as they could not get to the best fishing grounds, they realised that their livelihood would be jeopardized if they were faced with competition from an efficient fleet of deep-sea trawlers. Governments for many years chose to defer to the inshore fishermen rather than develop more efficient methods; with the result that the fishing industry—far from recovering as it had been expected to do when the Treaty gave Irish Governments the opportunity to adopt their own policies—continued to decline until a more energetic Government campaign for its revival was begun in the 1950s.

Inland fisheries fared little better. Writers from Fynes Moryson on had noted the great possibilities offered by the galaxy of lakes, and their connecting rivers and streams, in every part of the country: but again, it was not until the 1950s that a beginning was made on a national scheme to exploit their possibilities. In the first thirty years of the country's independence their potential was virtually ignored.

The results, in fact, of successive Irish Governments' efforts to utilize the country's natural resources on sea and on land during the first thirty years of independence were meagre. One reason was that although the Irish Free State was given fiscal autonomy under the Treaty, she had little real financial independence. The bulk of her trade was with the United Kingdom; she had little shipping of her own; British companies were firmly entrenched in the Irish market; and the link with sterling discouraged any break with financial orthodoxy. A great weight of economic inertia held her back; and the efforts of Governments were not enough to thrust it aside. As a result, although the ordinary country family was better-off than in 1921, its living standards were still so low relative to those obtainable by work in the towns that the younger generation continued to flock from the land. The relatively high prices obtainable for farm produce after 1939—particularly for cattle—prevented the drift from the land from becoming an avalanche; nor did the old land hunger quickly disappear; an ambitious eldest son might live on with his parents, even though his status was little higher than that of a labourer, in the knowledge that when they died he would come into the property. But the disparity between living conditions in the Irish countryside in 1956, and what they might have been expected to become by that time, was chastening.

So grave did the situation appear to be that the idea even got around, and was widely publicised in America, that the Irish were a dying race. The idea had been put forward some years before by observers who saw how rapidly the population was dwindling through emigration; and it was revived in the 1950s by the Reverend John O'Brien, a Professor of Notre Dame University, who published a symposium on the subject entitled *The Vanishing Irish*. It was easy for the Irish Statistical Office to disprove the wilder notions in the book; by 1950, as it happened, the population had actually risen slightly again, in spite of emigration. But some of the incidental facts the controversy elicited made painful reading. Ireland, it transpired, had the lowest marriage rate of any country in the civilised world. The average age at which men married was 35—considerably higher in rural areas—a curious situation for a country which venerated the family as an institution. Various guesses were made of the cause, in the symposium: Sean O'Faolain suggested that the Irishmen's natural impulses were either 'sublimated by religion, exhausted by sport, drugged by drink, or deflected by either an innate or an inculcated puritanism'; and other writers attributed the low marriage rate to economic and social causes—in particular the scarcity of land, which made it hard for a young man to marry until the death of his parents brought him into possession of a farm, by which time he might be afflicted by the caution of the middle-aged in making his choice of a wife. Whatever the causes, the effects were obvious—the flight from the land of younger sons, and still more, of daughters, who had no mind to wait around until some 'boy' (as landless men were called until well into old age) came into a farm and felt sufficiently well off to propose to her. Successive Governments were, of course, aware of the problem long before the Emigration Commission described it in detail; but they could do nothing without disrupting the traditional small farm pattern, or without imposing on the farmers regulations that he would resent. Out of prudence, they decided simply to do nothing.

Another disillusionment the country was to suffer in the years after the Treaty concerned the Irish language. One of the Cosgrave Government's early actions was to set up a Commission of Enquiry into its preservation; and that there should be no doubt of the Government's intentions, the Commission was reminded that 'by the Constitution of the Free State, Irish is expressly recognised as the national language. We believe that the Irish people as a body recognise it to be a national duty, incumbent on their representatives and their government as on themselves, to uphold and foster the Irish language.' The people were not given any opportunity to confirm the Government's belief, but probably they were willing to support any reasonable proposals that the Commission might make. Its findings were gloomy. The number of Irish speakers in the country had continued to shrink, and the 'Gaeltacht' areas—where Irish was the vernacular—were losing their Irish speakers fast. In any case, English was spreading through the Gaeltacht, because it was recognised as indispensable for young men who might desire jobs away from their homes. The 1926 census confirmed this estimate; it revealed that less than a fifth of the population could claim to be Irish-speaking, and of those less than half lived in the Gaeltacht areas.

By this time, the Government had taken steps to try to reverse the trend towards the disappearance of the language. In 1922 it laid down that the work of infants, and as much as possible of schoolwork in general, should be taught through the medium of Irish; and although shortage of trained teachers delayed the application of the principle, it was gradually introduced throughout the National School system. Secondary Schools were encouraged to teach Irish by the offer of grants, which were raised if the teaching was through the medium of Irish; so that by 1950 nearly half the examination papers for the annual certificate examination were written in Irish—a development encouraged by the award of extra marks, and by parental realisation that a knowledge of Irish was becoming essential for entry into many careers.

This policy had the desired effect of arresting the decline in the number of Irish speakers; by 1936 there were over a hundred thousand more of them in Ireland than in 1926. But it proved unable to arrest the decline of the Gaeltacht areas, whose Irish-speaking population still diminished; nor could it cause any perceptible increase in the amount of Irish actually spoken by adults. After a quarter century of endeavour, it was still easily possible to go from one end of a year to the other without hearing Irish spoken.

Various reasons were put forward to account for the failure of the language campaign (for failure it was widely held to be, though some enthusiasts persisted in accounting the results achieved as satisfactory). Two, in particular, were often heard: that there was little real enthusiasm for the language in high places—in parliament, or among the hierarchy; and that the attempt to revive it by making it a school subject was as foredoomed to disappointment as the hope that Latin might be revived by making it a school subject. And as for insisting that children from English-speaking homes should be taught through the medium of Irish, its only effect, the stock joke ran, was to make them illiterate to two languages.

But the fundamental reason for the campaigners' inability to do more than check the rate of decline of Irish lay in the intensified competition of English. Until the first World War there were many parts of Ireland where families who could speak no English suffered few disadvantages, except when younger sons or daughters migrated in search of work. By the 1950s, English language newspapers, periodicals, broadcasts and films had spread throughout the country. The new literacy provided by the national schools had little to feed off except English; Irish language publications tended to be respectable and dull. Broadcasts in Irish attracted few listeners; investigators found that at times when Irish programmes were on the air the bulk of Irish listeners switched to sponsored programmes from Radio Luxembourg, or to the B.B.C.'s Light Programme. An Irish film producing unit was out of the question, on account of the cost; and Irish plays, though occasionally attracting attention by their novelty, usually proved failures at the Box Office. The result was that men and women had little inducement to keep up their Irish after they left school.

The enthusiasts were inclined to put most of the blame on the Government for its lack of drive; but the Government was in a difficult position. Although up to a point the electorate were behind the language campaign, they would have objected if it became an inconvenience. The issue of documents—say, of all application forms—in both Irish and English was acceptable; the issue of documents in Irish only would have caused confusion and resentment which no democratically-elected Government would care to face. The small minority of politicians who were enthusuasts for the language were reluctant to do anything that would create antagonism to it; and this provided a good excuse for the apathetic

majority to do nothing with a clear conscience. The same
was true of the Church. A minority of Catholics held that the
Irish Church and the Irish language were inextricably linked,
and should remain so. They argued that Englishness and
materialism were similarly linked, not because of any particular propensity in English, but because its use as a language
brought in the flood of materialist, and even pagan culture of
English Sunday newspapers and American films. If Catholicism
could again ally itself with the language, this stream might
be dammed; so long as the Church held aloof, allowing Irish
to continue to be taught merely as a secular tongue, it was
depriving itself of its most valuable ally.

The most eloquent of the sponsors of this view, Father
Denis O'Flynn, Professor of Modern Irish at Maynooth, went
further; he suggested that by cutting itself off from Irish the
Church was cutting itself off from its own roots. If it allowed
the people to forget all about the early church in Ireland,
what real influence could it expect the example of Irish
saints to have on spiritual life? 'St. Patrick himself has become a plaster statue. Valiant Columbanus is no more than a
name, to be confused with gentle, no less valiant, Columba.'
But the hierarchy remained unconvinced. It accepted state
demands for the teaching of Irish, but did not throw itself
whole-heartedly into the campaign. As a result, Father
O'Flynn sadly admitted in 1950, 'Irish has come to be a joke
with many of our young people . . . I have to say that during
the past ten years I have heard Irish being spoken spon-
taneously by young people only twice.'

One of the reasons why the Church failed to throw its full
weight into the movement lay in history; the connection
between the language and separatism. The Church had always
condemned the Irish Republican Brotherhood as a secret
revolutionary organisation, as it had condemned the Fenians;
and after the Treaty, it condemned the republicans. Many of
the leading politicians in Irish life after the Treaty, therefore,
had at some stage of their careers come under the Church's
disapproval; they had been denied the sacraments and rejected

from the confessional. However devout their Catholicism might be, some were anti-clerical, and all shared the conviction that the Church's power to intervene in state matters must be limited.

For some years after the Treaty, the influence of the Church, considerable though it was, remained indirect. Attempts at direct political intervention by the hierarchy were rare, and often unsuccessful. De Valera resisted clerical pressure to take the Franco side during the Spanish civil war; he was prepared to back Sanctions against Catholic Holy; and later his Government rejected a design to convert Ireland into a Corporative State, on the Portuguese model, in line with Catholic social teaching. In the Constitution of 1937, too, he refrained from establishing Catholicism as the state religion. It recognized the special position of the Catholic Church 'as the guardian of the Faith professed by the great majority of citizens' but it also recognised the other religious denominations existing in Ireland at the time, and guaranteed freedom of conscience and the free profession and practice of religion, 'subject to public order and morality'. The Constitution reflected de Valera's own view, and his Government's, that relations between Church and State should be cordial, but detached.

The inter-party Government which came into power in 1948 had different ideas; the closer relationship between its members and the hierarchy finally precipitated a political crisis, when the Government obeyed a secret request by the hierarchy to withdraw a Health Bill that some of the bishops considered to be contrary to Catholic social teaching. The Minister of Health resigned, publishing the relevant correspondence in the newspapers; and immediately an embittered controversy arose concerning the boundary between Church and State; a dispute which was to create uneasiness about the future of democratic institutions in Ireland.

The Government's argument was that as the population of the country was over 90 per cent Catholic, and devout Catholic at that, the State must accept the hierarchy's ruling on points of Catholic teaching. The opposite viewpoint was related with a wealth of detail by the American writer Paul Blanshard in *The Irish and Catholic Power*, published in 1953, in which he asserted that Ireland had become a 'society where cultural freedom and to a certain extent genuine political freedom have been sacrificed to clerical dictatorship.' Blanshard had to concede that the record of Irish Governments in preserving the rights of the religious minorities, Protestants and Jews, had been good; cases of active discrimination or oppression, rare. This was the more surprising in that Catholics had a long list of scores to pay off from the past. But he argued that the Church had achieved such control over education that it must eventually achieve the power (as it already had the inclination) to extend its control over every branch of activity in Ireland. By the time he was writing, events appeared to confirm his prediction: individual bishops were beginning to talk in tendentious political terms, and to demand, and sometimes enforce, local regulations which would earlier had been considered matters for the state.

Up to this time the Protestants in the South had every reason to consider themselves fortunate. As the relics of the Ascendancy, they might have suffered from discriminatory legislative action or, worse, from under-cover persecution; certainly they felt that the safeguards in the Treaty were so inadequate as to be tantamount to a betrayal. In the event they suffered from few disabilities. As one of them wrote in 1953, in a Catholic periodical, the Protestant 'does not feel that he lives in a state of subjection. At most he feels that the unconscious pressure of an overwhelming majority is sometimes oppressive; a child can be crushed to death in the most good-humoured crowd. But in general he lives in a condition that he can recognise as liberty'. This liberty he owed mainly to those Protestants of the past who had broken away from the Ascendancy and become the leaders of nationalist movements, Grattan, Tone, Lord Edward Fitzgerald, the Emmets, Davis, Mitchel, Smith O'Brien, Butt, and Parnell: and although the Protestant influence in the nationalist movement had perceptibly dwindled by 1921, there were still influential Protestants in it: Childers Robert Barton, and Ernest Blythe. So long as the nationalist current flowed strong—so long as men like Tone, Davis, and Parnell remained national heroes—it would have been difficult to discriminate against Protestants on religious grounds; and in fact de Valera went beyond the call of equity in his care and consideration for the dwindling Protestant minority. Their schools were given special transport facilities, and Protestant representation was more than maintained in the Judiciary. The first President of Ireland under de Valera's 1937 Constitution was a Protestant, Douglas Hyde, the founder of the Gaelic League.

If the Protestants of the South had been able to divest themselves of their Ascendancy traditions, and throw themselves into the construction of the new Ireland with, say, Thomas Davis as their patron, they might have played as decisive a part in the years after the Treaty as in the years before. But with few exceptions, they dropped out of public life. Although they maintained a strong position in business, owing to their continuing ownership of many of the largest firms, such influence as they exercised in politics was mainly that which powerful business interests can employ indirectly; not that which independent minds exert within political parties. By 1950 they were represented by a handful of deputies in parliament; nor were there any signs of a resurgence among the younger generation. Most Protestants consoled themselves in a social enclave which preserved little contact with Irish affairs; and when on occasion their minority rights appeared to be challenged, they had few effective spokesmen.

Once only was their case stated in ringing terms: by Yeats, in the Senate, in 1925. Yeats was objecting to the introduction of a law forbidding divorce, which he considered to discriminate against the Protestant minority, of which he said, he was proud to consider himself a typical member. 'We against whom you have done this thing,' he went on, 'are not petty people. We are one of the great stocks of

Europe. We are the people of Burke; we are the people of Grattan; we are the people of Swift, the people of Emmet, the people of Parnell. We have created most of the modern literature of this country. We have created the best of its political intelligence. Yet I do not altogether regret what has happened. I shall be able to find out—if not I, my children will be able to find out—whether we have lost our stamina or not. . . . If we have not lost our stamina your victory will be brief, and your defeat final, and when it comes this nation may be transformed.' Yeats lived long enough to realise that whether or not the stamina was there, the minority was not putting it to any effective use.

At the same time, they were in danger of losing the protection they owed to the nationalist tradition. For two reasons, successive Governments were anxious to show themselves rather more than merely tolerant of the Protestants. One was gratitude: for the fact that Ireland had self-Government at all could be attributed to the lives and deaths of the Tones, Emmets, Davises, and Parnells. The other was more practical: in order that the world might be convinced of the absurdity of the Orange slogan, Home Rule is Rome Rule, it was necessary to be able to produce evidence that Home Rule need *not* be Rome Rule, even when over 90 per cent of the people were Catholics. But as nationalism died its natural slow death, so did the memory of the Protestant patriots; and as it became more and more evident that Partition would not be ended in the forseeable future, the need to keep up appearances grew less. Though this fact hardly entered into de Valera's calculations, the inter-party Government grew impatient with the formalities—for example, in connection with the annual grant to Trinity College. De Valera had kept it in step with the grants to University College; the inter-party Government, arguing that T.C.D. was not in the truest sense a national educational establishment, were not inclined to increase it *pari passu* with the grant to U.C.D.

In any case the future of the minority was of less significance than the future of democratic institutions, still solidly based, but subjected to growing verbal assaults. The growing tension between Church and State was largely, as Blanshard recognised, the product of the Irish educational system. Because English educational policy had achieved precisely the opposite of its intentions in Ireland, by 1921 schools were almost completely in the hands of the Churches. National Schools had as their manager the local parish priest (or rector, in the case of Protestants), a system that had one marked disadvantage; it was impossible to criticise a school without by implication criticising the priest; where he was too busy, or inefficient, or uninterested, the school suffered, and little could be done about it. And because the provision of secondary education was in the hands of the teaching orders, no state secondary schools were started.

At university level there was greater flexibility: but this was an accident of history. After Peel's university scheme had fallen through, a Catholic University had been founded in 1854 with Dr., later Cardinal, Newman as its first Rector. Unable to surmount the difficulties which beset an English Catholic in Ireland, he resigned, a disappointed man, three years later. For many years the university scraped along, not very effectively, but keeping higher education alive for those Catholics who could not or would not go to Trinity College; until in 1908 it was incorporated into the National University —a federal university embracing the colleges of Cork and Galway, and, in effect, Newman College in Dublin. The setting up of the Free State enabled this National University to expand and develop until its academic status was secure. It was not, strictly speaking, a Catholic university, because it did not come under the direct control of the Church. Catholics were permitted to enter as students without asking episcopal permission, whereas that permission had to be obtained if they wished to go to Trinity—annually the Archbishop of Dublin publicly announced that 'any Catholic who deliberately disobeys this law is guilty of a mortal sin'. But there was growing pressure within the Catholic Church to remove the National University from secular hands, thereby completing the Church's control over education.

Whatever the future might hold, it could not be said that Church and State had settled down—as, after the departure of the English, it had been expected that they would—into a stable, mutually satisfactory relationship. They had appeared to do so, when de Valera's constitution of 1937 had been welcomed by Vatican spokesmen as a balanced estimate of how much should be rendered unto Caesar. Fifteen years later the Constitution was being assailed by ultramontane Catholics in Ireland as un-Catholic; and the hierarchy, although outwardly accepting it, was putting a different interpretation on its provisions than de Valera had intended. All the combustible materials for a conflict between Church and State were in readiness; and more than once, in the early 1950's, they were nearly set alight.

At the same time as the Church was extending its hold over institutions, it was running the risk of losing its hold over the people, not so much by its actions as by its changing social status. After the Treaty it continued to grow in prestige and wealth. As late as the 1930's, to be a Catholic in a few districts was still to be socially unacceptable, unless protected by long-standing family ties or wealth; and the priest's standards of living usually reflected the standards of the bulk of his parishioners. But as Catholics in large numbers began to break down social barriers, becoming members of and eventually predominating in clubs and committees, the priest tended to rise with them. Whereas earlier he had been perforce satisfied with grubby furnished rooms or a ramshackle old house, the greater wealth of his parish enabled him to take better accommodation. His parishioners were pleased that he should be able to do so; they had long been humiliated by the knowledge that the Protestant rector with his tiny flock should have a large, opulent-looking rectory (as they never entered it, they were not to know that the rector frequently lived in it in greater discomfort than the priest in his lodgings). By the middle of the century the priest had

attained to a standard of living not only strikingly different
from that which he had enjoyed half a century before but also
considerably better than that of the clergy in most continental
countries. It began to come as a shock to Irish pilgrims on
their way to Lourdes to contrast the obvious poverty of the
French priest with the comparative prosperity of his Irish
counterpart.

Such was the hold of the Church on the people, however,
that this contrast usually tended to arouse animosity only
against the French nation, for its failure to appreciate and
provide for its clergy. And this hold was certainly not based
on fear. It was love and respect for the cloth, verging often
on servility, that led to the 'Yes-Father-No-Father' pattern
of conversation, the embarrassing deference so familiar to the
traveller in Ireland. Yet the possibility remained that this
affection might not last, if priests were pushed by it into a
social and political station in which they were detached from
their flocks. It had been strongly urged in the early part of
the century that the priest who was manager of this and chairman of that, as well as the bosom friend of the local gombeen
men (who would see to it that he was) might be in danger of
not only losing touch with his flock, but of alienating himself
from some of them, when local problems arose in which he
found himself, by virtue of his bureaucratic position, compelled to take sides. It was difficult to know how to avoid
this; some bishops did their best to prevent priests from
losing the common touch by imposing sumptuary laws, for
fear of growing anti-clericalism.

Yet in general, anti-clericalism was slow to develop. It was
often detectable locally, in parishes, say, where the priest
held obstinately to unpopular views; and on a national scale
it manifested itself in half-affectionate ribaldry at the expense
of certain bishops who were over-fond of the sound of their
own voices, or too inclined to arrogate infallibility to themselves on social and political concerns as well as in matters
of faith and morals. But on a serious scale anti-clericalism
was mainly the plaything of the Catholic intellectual, who

tended to transfer his resentment at growing clerical intervention into lay affairs by damning individual priests for, say,
dining and wining in expensive Dublin restaurants—a transference which he would justify by predicting that in a few
years time the growing wealth and power of the Church
would end by provoking the anti-clerical reaction that the
country had so long been spared; and that its ridiculous
puritanism could only end by driving all sensible people away
from the countryside to the towns and thence, in all probability, to Britain, to escape clerical control.

The attitude of the Church towards public morality certainly tended to retard Irish cultural development. In the
years immediately following the Treaty there seemed no
reason why the revival of Irish letters should not continue
apace. In the theatre a greater dramatist even than his Abbey
forerunners arose in Sean O'Casey; and with actors like
Barry Fitzgerald, F. J. McCormick and Sara Allgood the
Abbey tradition appeared to be in safe hands. In literature
Yeats fulfilled his genius, resisting the quiet temptations of
fame at life's end:

> 'Grant me an old man's frenzy
> Myself must I remake
> Till I am Timon and Lear
> Or that William Blake
> Who beat upon the wall
> Till Truth obeyed his call.

In exile, James Joyce had written the book that—with the
exception of *A la Recherche du Temps Perdu*—was to prove the
most influential novel of the first half of the century: *Ulysses*.
Of the older generation of writers, 'A.E.' Padraii Colum and
Seumas O'Sullivan were still writing. In the Theatre, as well as
Sean O'Casey, were Lennox Robinson, T. C. Murray, Denis
Johnston and Paul Vincent Carroll; in poetry Austin Clarke,
F. R. Higgins, Patrick Kavanagh; in fiction, Frank O'Connor
and Sean O'Faolain. The future looked full of promise.

In the Thirties this promise, which ought to have matured into achievement, began to disintegrate. Yeats went proudly on until his death; but many of his successors lapsed into alcoholic garrulity, or introverted resentment, or hackwork; at best some of them produced competent work, but nothing —apart from Kavanagh's *The Great Hunger*—that had the touch of greatness in it. In the theatre, O'Casey quarrelled with the Abbey and went to England, there to write a succession of plays lit with verbal felicity, but chilled by *saeva indignatio*; and one by one the promising young men either produced new plays of no great import, or deserted the Theatre. The Abbey, shedding all its great actors except McCormick, decayed into a provincial repertory theatre, churning out revivals of the Anglo-Irish classics interspersed with tired-looking new plays constructed around well-worn themes; and although Dublin remained relatively more alive, theatrically speaking, than London, it failed to evolve along fresh lines, or to maintain its newly-found traditions.

The worst sufferer was literature. Out of Joyce might have emerged a new approach to the novel in Ireland; but *Ulysses* was considered so patently obscene that the Censorship Board did not even feel it necessary to put it on their list of prohibited books. One by one the new Irish writers found themselves victims of the Board's displeasure; and one by one they either emigrated, or began to write almost exclusively for the English or American market—articles or stories in which their Irishness, if it appeared at all, was of the glib export variety that would appeal to readers in London or New York—or Hollywood. It was almost impossible for an unknown writer to have a book published in Ireland. The home market was so limited that Irish publishers would not venture on any but established authors; and established authors quickly found how much more profitable it was not only to write for the English and American markets but to take their books direct to English and American publishers. As a result, hopes of the further development of a distinctively Irish literature in English were dashed. Literature in the Irish language showed even less resilience. 'Modern Gaelic', an Irish critic wrote in *The Times Educational Supplement* in 1955, 'is the medieval past murmuring in its sleep.' He pointed out that the picture must not be painted too black; press and the radio in Ireland had maintained and improved their cultural standards. But for creative work the atmosphere after 1939 became unsuitable; and the cultural reawakening of which Pearse and MacDonagh had dreamed was shown to be no more than a dream.

The Censorship of Publications Board, estabilshed by the Cosgrave Government, was not the sole or even the chief cause of this decline; but it reflected an attitude of mind that in the long run was inimical to the growth and even to the understanding of literature. The Board was set up to examine and if necessary prohibit the sale of books which were in their general tendency indecent or obscene. Its members immediately interpreted their instructions as permitting them to ban books on the strength of individual passages containing indelicate words or references; with the result that the list of authors whose works were banned contained most of the distinguished British and American literary figures, and many other writers of world fame. The 'F's alone include Scott Fitzgerald, William Faulkner, C. S. Forester, Anatole France, and Sigmund Freud: the 'M's, Compton Mackenzie, Salvador de Madariaga, Thomas Mann, Somerset Maugham, Alberto Moravia, Charles Morgan and even a translation of the eighteenth-century Irish poet, Brian Merriman, by Frank O'Connor. On one occasion the Board even banned the report of an English Royal Commission on Population, because of its references to birth control.

The activities of the Board provoked a constant stream of complaints from Irish writers; the only concession the Government permitted was the establishment of an Appeal Board, making the machinery more cumbersome and expensive, but allowing a few books which had been banned to be unbanned. But the Appeal Board never came within measurable distance of undoing the damage done to Irish reading, as well as Irish writing, by the Board; damage all the more serious in that it provided an opportunity for hostility and ridicule outside Ireland, and in the North. Naturally it was not widely appreciated that the censorship was confined to obscenity (and subjects related to it, in the Church's opinion, like birth control): that political censorship did not exist. Nor was a Northerner likely to realise that the censorship was often ineffectual; copies of banned books were brought into the country by travellers, and circulated extensively among the novel-reading public. The mere institution of the Board, coupled with a few examples of its activities, was enough to provide the evidence Northerners needed to justify the suspicions that had kept them from joining the South in Home Rule.

The most grievous disappointment for the nationalists after the Treaty was the continued existence of Partition. Lloyd George had managed to persuade the Irish delegates that the Six-County statelet already established was only a makeshift; a Border Commission would be established to re-draw the boundaries in conformity with ethnographical facts. The Irish delegates could at this point console themselves with the belief that when revision of the Border was undertaken, it would be found that the Protestant and Unionist corner of Ireland was too small to constitute a viable economic and political unit; the English Government would therefore (it was presumed) instruct the Northerners to overcome their prejudices and join in a united Ireland under Dominion Home Rule. When the Boundary Commission was established, however, it decided that its function was merely to make minor changes, for local administrative convenience; that no transfer of towns or districts with nationalist majorities from North to South was contemplated.

The Irish member of the Commission, Eoin MacNeill, resigned when this information leaked out, leaving the Cosgrave Government in a very delicate position. To denounce the Commission's findings would be tantamount to denounc-

ing the Treaty, thereby throwing away everything the Cosgravites had fought for in the civil war, and admitting that the
republicans had been right after all. Not to denounce the
Commission would leave the Government again open to the
old accusation of treachery to the all-Ireland ideal. The fact
that both Griffith and Collins, who had heard Lloyd George's
promises about the Boundary Commission in person, were
dead, made the Government's position still more difficult.
In 1925 it decided to give way, conceding the existence of
the Six Counties as a separative administrative entity: Partition
received the Free State's written sanction.

The republicans at once denounced the agreement; but
following their defeat in the civil war they could not prevent
it. By the time de Valera entered office in 1932, Northern
Ireland was too firmly established for there to be any hope
of securing a revision of the Boundary agreement except by
force, which the South was in no position to apply so long as
an English garrison protected Northern Ireland. De Valera
argued, and continued to reiterate for many years, that he
would have felt morally entitled to use force to secure the
unity of the country; but the force available was not strong
enough, and throughout his sixteen years as Premier the
North suffered from little worse than insults hurled across the
Border.

When he went out of office in 1948, de Valera decided to
use his enforced leisure to make the anti-Partition cause
known to the world; he travelled with this intention in
Europe, Asia and even the Antipodes. At home, Costello
countered with a whipped-up anti-Partition campaign throughout Ireland. But by now Northern Ireland was still more
solidly established; the trends that the Northern Unionist
had watched in the South had only served to confirm him in
his conviction that he had been wise to stay in the United
Kingdom.

The South, in fact, while maintaining its passionate desire
to remove the Border at the earliest opportunity, had been
steadily building up a way of life inimical to any prospect of

unity. Some inkling of this had already reached the Irish people; they paid little attention to the Costello Government's campaign, beyond subscribing money at church door collections, and it soon fizzled out. De Valera's voyages were no more successful; he won some embarrassing eulogies from Irish exiles and specious promises from some enemies of Britain, but no support of any real value.

An attempt to make Partition a live issue at the Council of Europe in 1950 proved equally fruitless; in fact it rebounded, by creating the impression there that the Irish were suffering from persecution mania. This was doubly unfortunate, in that it seemed possible at one time that Ireland might play a worthy part in international gatherings. It had so happened that immediately after de Valera had come into office for the first time, Ireland's turn came round to hold the Presidency of the League of Nations. In September 1932 he delivered a presidential address which in its forcefulness and integrity suggested that a statesman had arisen who might rally the small nations in defence of their rights; and over Abyssinia and Spain, de Valera adhered firmly to the League, risking unpopularity at home by so doing. But the war took Ireland out of the European stream, leaving her, like Spain and Portugal, on one side; and when the United Nations Organisation was formed, her application to become a member was vetoed by the Russians. Nor did either de Valera or Costello feel that they could bring the country into the North Atlantic Treaty. It bound members to forego designs on each other's territory; and Ireland had firm designs on her missing Six Counties. Her only international forum, therefore, was in bodies with no executive power like the Council of Europe; and although her delegates were able to play their part in debates and in committee, they quickly found that any attempt to lobby at Strasbourg for a united Ireland was considered inappropriate, and almost improper; like selling insurance policies in a club. After the war, in fact, Ireland ceased to have any perceptible influence on the tide of European opinion.

All hope, therefore, of securing an all-Ireland government

peacably dwindled. Two possible solutions remained. One was the use of force. The failure of the I.R.A. bomb campaign in the late Thirties only convinced extremist republicans that a different type of campaign was needed; by 1955 a policy of raiding for arms had been adopted with the long-term aim of building up strength for use at some later date. The I.R.A. remained a proscribed organisation; and in 1955 its renewed activity alarmed the Government sufficiently for it to ban all references to the I.R.A. in the press. For by this time responsible opinion in the country was moving in an opposite direction. For some years previously individuals in the South, notably Professor George O'Brien and Ernest Blythe (who had been Finance Minister in the Cosgrave Government) had urged that the only way to bring in the North was by welcome, not by abuse. The failure of the anti-Partition campaign induced Blythe, himself an Ulster Protestant, to intensify his efforts, and in the 1950's Governments began swinging round to his view. There had already been some arrangements between the Northern and Southern administrations over matters of mutual concern; previously considered as a disagreeable necessity, co-operation on these projects began to be welcomed. Liam Cosgrave, son of the first Irish Premier and Minister for External Affairs in the Costello cabinet, began to take a new line on the North, his speeches displaying a conciliatory attitude that would have led to his expulsion from the party had he made them, say, ten years earlier.

When the I.R.A. threat grew serious, after armed raids on camps in Northern Ireland and in England, both Costello and de Valera came out strongly against the use of force. In November 1955, Costello said in the Dail that although he still considered the Partition of Ireland to be a grievous wrong, for which there could be no remedy except the removal of the parent cause, he stood by declarations he had made earlier that no solution to the problem could be found through force; force could only involve the country in civil war, and even if the Northern Unionists' resistance were overcome,

'Partition would still remain in the form of a deep division of feeling, a bitterness and resentment that would poison our national life for generations.' The pronouncement was significant, not as marking any change of policy—for as de Valera had said a few days before, force had never been seriously contemplated even by the republicans in the 1920's as a weapon against Partition—but as a sign of the growing realisation in the South that there was no solution to Partition except time; and that for time to act as healer, the South must renounce the use of force, not merely because it had become impracticable, but because violence would inevitably create more bitterness than it could remove.

At the same time, however, that this was gradually coming to be recognised in the South, the chances of any rekindling of a feeling for unity in the North were declining—and they had at no time after 1921 been very great. Not that the Northern Protestants had wanted Partition. Their opposition to the Home Rule campaign had sprung out of a desire to keep the whole of Ireland within the United Kingdom; only when it became clear that some degree of Home Rule was inevitable, were they prepared to accept the necessity for a divided Ireland. Even then, they had little desire for Home Rule for themselves. The establishment of the Northern Ireland Parliament at Stormont was imposed on them by what at the time was thought to be political necessity. It was assumed at Westminster that for many purposes Ireland would continue to be a unit; even those politicians who made no such assumption still felt it expedient to speak in terms of Ireland's ultimate unity. A system by which North and South both had legislatures it was thought, would enable some supranational body, representing both, to grow out of them.

The administrative structure of Northern Ireland, in fact, was a political accident. That it should turn out in certain respects to be defective was hardly surprising. The Boundary was drawn in such a way as to inhibit the development in the North of a party system on English or even on Southern Irish lines. Ulster had formerly comprised nine counties, of which four contained substantial Protestant-Unionist majorities—Antrim, Armagh, Derry, and Down; two were evenly balanced, with small Catholic-Nationalist majorities— Fermanagh and Tyrone; and three had substantial Catholic-Nationalist majorities—Cavan, Donegal, and Monaghan. Had the whole of Ulster been taken into Northern Ireland, the Protestant-Unionist majority would hardly have been big enough to provide a stable Government. On the other hand, it was felt that to restrict Northern Ireland to those areas where the Unionist majority existed might have been hard to justify on account of its small size. The decision was taken to form a six-country unit, leaving Cavan, Donegal and Monaghan to the South.

The Six-County Northern Ireland consisted of rather less than a million Protestants, and rather less than half a million Catholics. Though there were individual exceptions, this meant in effect that two-thirds of the population owed allegiance to the Crown, and one-third regarded themselves as wrongfully cut off from their native Ireland. In the circumstances, no flexible party system could develop. The fact that there were elections, both for Westminster and for the local parliament at Stormont, gave an impression of democratic activity; but the voter was not recording his preference between two parties, each of them anxious to form an administration: he was indicating whether he wished to see the State of Northern Ireland maintained or overthrown. Occasionally efforts were made to instill a party atmosphere. Various splinters from the Unionist Party tried to impress on the electorate that it was possible to vote against the official Unionist line and still be a good Unionist; and Labour parties courted Nationalist as well as Unionist votes. But these efforts had negligible results. The Unionist party, led successively by Lord Craigavon, by J. M. Andrews, and by Sir Basil Brooke (later Lord Brookeborough) easily maintained its dominance; and elections continued to resolve themselves into the straight question, for or against the maintenance of the Union with Great Britain.

A second defect was the difficulty of relating what happened at Stormont to what was happening at Westminster. The Unionists were by temperament and tradition Conservative; and their members who were elected to the House of Commons—to which Northern Ireland continued to send representatives, as part of the United Kingdom—normally voted with the Conservatives. When the Labour Party was in office at Westminster this naturally led to difficulties. Particularly in the period immediately following the second world war, Labour passed Acts which were opposed by the Northern Ireland Unionists, as Conservatives; but as soon as any such Act was on the Statute Book in Great Britain, the Northern Ireland Unionist Government felt compelled to introduce it at Stormont, and to use the same Labour arguments in its favour that they had just been denouncing or ridiculing at Westminster. For to preserve the administrative unity of the United Kingdom, the Stormont Government felt it necessary to proceed step by step with Westminster, except where Northern Ireland's political circumstances were considered to make this procedure unwise. In general, Stormont followed British legislative changes so closely that it laid itself open to the charge of being no more than a debating society, without real executive power; a rubber stamp.

As a result, the deliberations at Stormont never aroused much interest or enthusiasm in Northern Ireland. Yet Stormont probably performed a more important function than people there realised. The Northerner thinks of himself as an Irishman; he may be a loyalist, a vocal and demonstrative one, but he often does not much care for the English (who are more popular in the South, strangely enough, than they are in the North). Had Northern Ireland no means of ventilating its points of view and its grievances, other than a dozen members at Westminster, tensions might easily have arisen and led to serious dissatisfaction. As it was, Stormont not only acted as a safety valve; it also provided Northerners with at least some opportunity to ratify or not to ratify British legislation, as they thought fit. Even if ratification was usually a foregone conclusion, owing to the step-by-step convention, there remained at least the feeling of being in charge of their own destinies.

Whatever its defects, too, the system worked. It was helped at the start by the fact that the Nationalists of the North were on balance Home Rulers, rather than republicans. Although there was often ugly sectarian strife in Belfast, and although the outrages and burnings of 'the Troubles' extended to the North, the Nationalist Party for the most part contented itself with negative hostility to Partition, expressed through the ballot box. Northern republicans could constitute a danger to the Union, as the early stages of the bomb campaign in Britain before the second world war showed; but Northern Ireland, for all the clashes between Orangemen and Nationalists, remained surprisingly quiescent after 1925, when the Boundary Commission confirmed the six-county unit. During the war, for example, the presence of hundreds of military camps around Northern Ireland provided unlimited opportunities for sabotage; yet sabotage was uncommon. Partly, of course, this was due to the fact that the republicans had timed their efforts in Britain too soon, so that most of them had been rounded up and imprisoned or interned; but it remains a matter for conjecture why the wartime opportunities were not put to better use. When in the 1950's republican activity increased, the wonder was that it had not done so earlier.

Control of the Nationalists was achieved with the help of two instruments: a Special Powers Act, and 'gerrymandering'. In its early stages the Northern Ireland Government had not been given control over either the armed forces or the constabulary. But this was the period of 'the Troubles', when its security needs were greatest. Accordingly an Act was passed in 1922 which, as one member put it, could have been boiled down to a single sentence: 'the Home Secretary shall have power to do what he likes, or let somebody else do what he likes for him.' Under the Act the Home Secretary was empowered to make emergency regulations, dealing with

such things as cur fews, firearms, drilling, uniforms and meetings. The Act was widely criticised on the grounds that it
abrogated the rule of law, and defended on the grounds that
where there is in existence a body of men determined to
abrogate the rule of law themselves, it is necessary to fight
them with their own weapons. In 1933, when it had become
obvious that the political situation had congealed into virtual
permanency, the Act was accordingly made permanent;
the regulations, however, varied according to need. Its provisions were enforced with the help of a force known as the
'B Specials', a supplement to the constabulary, whose existence was often to be used as evidence by the South that
Northern Ireland was a police state.

From the South, too, would regularly come allegations
that the Northern electoral constituencies were 'gerry-
mandered'—arranged in such a way that the Nationalist
minority won less than its fair share of seats. In a sense, the
existence of single-member constituencies on the English
pattern itself operates against minorities, as the Liberal Party
found; and there was little evidence in the elections to Westminster that gerrymandering meant anything worse than this.
But in local elections the Unionists consolidated their position by refusing to go step-by-step, for once, with the British
in adopting univeral suffrage; rateable valuation remained the
basis of the Northern Ireland franchise, and some of the local
constituency boundaries were obviously drawn with the
intention of ensuring a Unionist majority—that of Derry,
for example. In elections for Stormont, too, plural voting
was permitted; the business and university vote remained.
The advantage to the Unionist party of these expedients to
preserve its supremacy were to some extent offset by the
harmful publicity arising from them; they were the basis of
a detailed exposure of Northern Ireland's 'democracy' by
the National Council for Civil Liberties—at that time considered a responsible body, genuinely concerned with civil
liberties; its communist element had not taken control.

These—to English minds—undemocratic ways did not,

however, lead to any strong feeling in Britain that the future of Partition ought to be reconsidered, before the second world war firmly established Northern Ireland's position. Without the Northern Ireland naval and air bases the Battle of the Atlantic, narrowly won, might have been narrowly lost: and that in itself was enough to swing British opinion in Northern Ireland's favour, making it certain that no progress could be made towards re-unifying Ireland at Westminster. By this time, too, North and South had been taking such different political and social paths that Partition had become a vested interest on both sides of the Border. Few Ulstermen, certainly not Carson or Craigavon, had considered Partition a final settlement in 1920: a quarter of a century later it had become so firmly rooted that, even in the highly improbable event of a union of hearts and minds between North and South, a political and eocnomic union had become almost an impossibility.

One of the most effective arguments in favour of preserving national unity before 1921 had been that Northern Ireland was the factory—Southern Ireland the farm; the two should be complementary. By 1950 this was no longer true. South of the Border industries had been laboriously built up which would be damaged, if not destroyed, the moment the customs barrier with the North was removed. Northern agriculture, too, had continued to flourish in its own right: in some respects, notably in marketing, it developed much more promisingly than in the South. And although industry in the North hardly flourished as expectation had promised—the unemployment level remained high even in the post-1945 era, when there was virtually full employment in Britain—it became increasingly integrated into the British, and became a rival, rather than an ally, of the Southern, economy. Any move which might have had the effect of depriving it of English markets, particularly in linen, and ship and aircraft construction, would have been considered hazardous. In any case, step-by-step legislation had introduced into the North welfare legislation which left the South ever further behind in education, health and social services. No move to end Partition could have been made without anxious thought, even by the Northern Nationalists, of the effect it would have on their and their children's material welfare.

A certain amount of effort had admittedly been made to draw closer the economic ties between North and South, especially where they were of mutual benefit to both. In connection with the Foyle Fisheries, in the development of hydro-electric power from the Erne basin, and in the taking-over by both Governments of the Great Northern Railway system, agreement was found possible: in the case of the Erne waters, by unilateral action with a common purpose; in the other two, by joint action. But these agreements went little further than arrangements made in many other parts of the world by Government with Government. They could hardly be held to foreshadow any impending change in the relationship between North and South. A more binding tie, probably, was the continued existence of social, cultural and sporting activities based on a united Ireland. Associations formed for a wide variety of purposes continued to operate as if no Border existed, and rugby football teams representing Ireland, for example, were picked from North and South. Even here, though, the links were tenuous. Disputes broke out in may such organisations, leading to splits along political lines; and by the 1950s the number of all-Ireland organisations had been greatly reduced.

By the 1950s, in fact, Partition was firmly established. Its only real weakness lay in the existence of the fringe of Catholic Nationalists around the perimeter. Morally, the retention of this minority was indefensible, for precisely the same arguments could be used to justify the retention of the Northern Protestants in a united Ireland; and the fact that the Nationalist minority was held in Northern Ireland against its will, by force—in the sense that had there been no troops or constabulary, the Border would simply have disintegrated—was a further excuse for counter-violence. By 1956 it began to look as if this violence might not long be delayed. The chief

fear was that some separatist organisation might decide that
another 1916-type rising would be appropriate, no matter
how small its chances of success. While this possibility remained, the stability of Northern Ireland could never be
assured. But apart from the risk of such a rising, the probability was that Northern Ireland as an administrative entity,
in the absence of any catastrophic economic slump, would
continue to grow away from the South.

In the middle of the twentieth century the Irish were still
almost as much the prisoners of their history as they had been
at the start of it. The same difficulties beset them, though in
rather different forms: the relationship between Church and
State; the rescue and preservation of their valued cultural
heritage; the division between North and South; and the
economic weaknesses arising out of inability to make best use
of the natural advantages of the soil. All these difficulties
were also, directly or indirectly, Britain's concern. The
existence in Britain of hundreds of thousands of Irish men and
women, not considered aliens in spite of the fact that the
country of their birth had declared itself an independent
republic, meant that Irish shocks, religious or political,
would tend to have repercussions in England. The existence
in Britain as well as in Ireland of a few fanatics, regarding
themselves as the accredited soldiers of a power—the all-
Ireland republic of the future—and therefore entitled to
assume a state of war, alone meant that the future must
remain uncertain. Strategically, Ireland was still important;
the greater the military emergency, the more would depend
on her. Economically, the link between Irish and British
currency, and their mutural commercial interests, would
involve a continuance of close ties between the two countries
whether they relished it or not. Even if some great economic
metamorphosis took place—the discovery, perhaps, of stocks
of some rare mineral essential to the development of atomic
energy—all the effects of history could not be expected to
disappear. The small farmers would remain intransigent in

their self-sufficiency; the I.R.A. would remain devoted in their quest for the republican Holy Grail (and as misguided in their sense of direction); the West Briton would remain riding or backing horses (or breeding them: the bloodstock industry continued to flourish); and Irish Catholicism would remain characteristically puritannical and pietistic, to alarm liberals and infuriate English Catholics. The Irish problem was not settled in 1921, nor in 1937, nor in 1949. It will not be settled in the foreseeable future; and the reason is: history.

BIBLIOGRAPHY

❧

Edmund Curtis's *A History of Ireland* (London, 1936) is the standard general work; it is hard going for English readers, because his main interest was in the mediaeval period—he also wrote a *History of Mediaeval Ireland* (London, 1938)—and his treatment of modern times is more cursory. The general history, too, takes the reader up only to the Treaty of 1921. A more digestible introduction is *A Short History of Ireland* by J. C. Beckett (London, 1952), which is admirably balanced and workmanlike, carrying the story on to the middle of the century. It should be read in conjunction with such works as James Carty's three-volume illustrated history *Ireland* (Dublin, 1948-51), where the scene is unfolded through the medium of contemporary accounts, commentaries, and pictures; Sean O'Faolain's *The Irish* (London, 1947) which the author calls an attempt at a psychological study; and the works of Constantia Maxwell: *Dublin Under the Georges* (London, 1936); *Country and Town in Ireland Under the Georges* (revised edition Dundalk, 1949); and *The Stranger in Ireland* (London, 1954). There is also a useful series of booklets initiated by the Cultural Relations Committee in Dublin, covering a wide variety of subjects; with the aim, when the series is complete, of providing a broad informed survey of Irish life and culture.

Lecky's *History of Ireland in the XVIIIth Century* needs no recommendation: it is one of the great histories in the language. He also wrote some biographical studies, *Leaders of Public Opinion in Ireland* (new edition London, 1912). On the whole, the biographical side has been strangely neglected, though O'Faolain's are good and readable: *The Great O'Neill* (London, 1942); *King of the Beggars*, a life of Daniel O'Connell (London, 1938) and *De Valera* (London, 1939). Another biography of de Valera, by M. J. MacManus (Dublin, 1944), is more detailed, but less balanced. MacManus's *Irish Cavalcade 1550-1850* (London, 1939) contains some entertaining extracts from contemporary sources; so does *Irish Public Opinion, 1750-1800* by R. B. McDowell (London, 1944), a valuable study of the period. McDowell's *Public Opinion and Government Policy in Ireland* (London, 1952), is rather harder going.

There are two good introductions to the story of Northern Ireland: *Ulster since 1800*, a collection of talks broadcast by the B.B.C. (London, 1954) and *Ulster under Home Rule*, edited by Thomas Wilson (Oxford, 1955), which together form a balanced survey. Most other works on Northern Ireland are avowedly or unconsciously propagandist—as, indeed, are most of the 'histories' published in the Republic.

Easily the most readable, though long and detailed, work on Irish nationalism is P. S. O'Hegarty's *A History of Ireland under the Union, 1801-1922* (London, 1952); but the author's lively prejudices run through it. It needs to be set off by a look at, say, *Ireland from '98 to '98*, by William O'Connor Morris (London, 1898), which gives what might be called a moderate-Unionist viewpoint, and *Ireland*, by J. Chartres Molony (London, 1936)—it is hard to define his prejudices, but they make stimulating reading. *Irish Nationalism and British Democracy*, by E. Strauss (London, 1951) gives a Marxist interpretation—and also investigates Anglo-Irish relations, a subject that has previously been inadequately studied. For the period leading up to and immediately following the Treaty of 1921, Dorothy Macardle's *The Irish Republic* (London, 1938) is the most detailed work, but it is firmly biassed on the Republican side—as can be seen by a comparison with the relevant chapters from P. S. O'Hegarty, equally biassed on the pro-Treaty side. Frank Pakenham gives an excellent account of the Treaty negotiations themselves in *Peace by Ordeal* (London, 1935). Terence de Vere White's *The Road of Excess* (Dublin, 1946), on Isaac Butt, and *Kevin O'Higgins* (London, 1948) are interesting biographical studies.

On the land and the people of Ireland, Constantia Maxwell's books, already mentioned, are useful. George O'Brien's economic histories were pioneer works in their field; though hard to obtain to-day, they are still the best guide to the period 1600-1850. They have been supplemented by such works as Edmund MacLysaght's *Irish Life in the 17th Century* (revised edition, Cork, 1950); K. H. Connell's *The Population of Ireland: 1750-1845* (Oxford, 1950) and Maurice James Craig's *Dublin 1660-1860* (London, 1952). An enormous number of books have been written by foreign travellers in Ireland, Giraldus Cambrensis, Edmund Spenser and Arthur Young, to name but three of them; hardly a year now passes without an addition to their number. The best introduction to the story of Irish agriculture is Joseph Johnston's *Irish Agriculture in Transition* (Oxford, 1951); for the important Land Acts period, M. J. Bonn and Horace Plunkett are useful sources.

T. W. Freeman's *Ireland, Its physical, historical, social and economic geography* (London, 1950) is the standard work in its field.

Researchers into the early cultural and religious history of Ireland are beset by complex textual and linguistic problems; consequently few reliable books have appeared on the subject. There is in one of the Cultural Relations Committee's booklets, *Saga and Myth in Ancient Ireland* (Dublin, 1956), by Gerard Murphy; and there is 'Studies in Irish History and Literature,' by James Carney. Daniel Corkery's *The Fortunes of the Irish Language* (Dublin, 1954), is the only such work in its field; the author earlier won renown for his *The Hidden Ireland* (Dublin, 1925), on Gaelic life in the eighteenth century. There is no satisfactory book of any sort on religion in Ireland, though there have been some studies of particular problems such as R. Dudley Edwards's *Church and State in Tudor Ireland*

(Dublin, 1935), and Denis Gwynn's *The Struggle for Catholic Emancipation* (London, 1928).

In lighter vein, there are plenty of books retelling the old legends; one of the most recent is *Legends of Ireland* by J. J. Campbell (London, 1955), pleasantly illustrated by Louis le Brocquy.

Early Irish architecture is now being brought to the general reader, as well as the specialist, by Harold G. Leask's *Irish Churches and Monastic Buildings*, of which the first volume has been produced (Dundalk, 1955). A comparable work on archaeology is much needed.

Perhaps not surprisingly, many of the authors who have tried to describe contemporary Ireland have had axes to grind. The symposium *The Vanishing Irish* (London, 1954, ed. John A. O'Brien), for example, was based on a fallacious theory. Yet it had some illuminating contributions. Paul Blanshard's *The Irish and Catholic Power* (London, 1955), though argued to a brief, also contained a great quantity of information. No good general survey exists; material for it await extraction from such sources as the Department of External Affairs *Bulletin*—a model of its kind; from many reasoned contributions to *Studies*, a Dublin Jesuit periodical; and from sundry articles in the press and in magazines during the post-Treaty period.

INDEX

❧